INVENTING
REALITY

*The Politics
of the Mass Media*

INVENTING REALITY

The Politics of the Mass Media

Michael Parenti

St. Martin's Press   *New York*

To Kathleen Lipscomb who works so devotedly to build a better reality while rejecting the invented one. And to the memory of Philip Meranto who did the same.

For information, write St. Martin's Press, Inc.
175 Fifth Avenue, New York, N.Y. 10010

cover design: Ben Santora

ISBN: 0-312-43473-1
ISBN: 0-312-43474-X (pbk.)

Library of Congress Cataloging-in-Publication Data

Parenti, Michael, 1933–
    Inventing reality.

    1. Mass media—Political aspects—United States.
2. Public opinion—United States. I. Title.
P95.82.U6P37 1986   070.1   85-61250
ISBN 0-312-43473-1

Contents

A Word to the Reader

For many people an issue does not exist until it appears in the news media. How we view issues, indeed, what we even define as an issue or event, what we see and hear, and what we do *not* see and hear are greatly determined by those who control the communications world. Be it labor unions, peace protesters, the Soviet Union, uprisings in Latin America, elections, crime, poverty, or defense spending, few of us know of things except as they are depicted in the news.

Even when we don't believe what the media say, we are still hearing or reading their viewpoints rather than some other. They are still setting the agenda, defining what it is we must believe or disbelieve, accept or reject. The media exert a subtle, persistent influence in defining the scope of respectable political discourse, channeling public attention in directions that are essentially supportive of the existing politico-economic system.

Be this as it may, growing numbers of people are becoming increasingly aware that the media are neither objective nor consistently accurate in their portrayal of things. There seems to be a growing understanding that we need to defend ourselves by monitoring and challenging the misinformation we are fed. In this book I will try to demonstrate *how* the news media distort important aspects of social and political life and *why*. The press's misrepresentations are not usually accidental, not merely the result of the complexity of actual events and the honest confusions of poorly prepared reporters. While those kinds of problems exist, another kind of distortion predominates, one not due to chance or to the idiosyncratic qualities of news production or newspeople. The major distortions are repeatable, systematic, and even systemic—the product not only of deliberate manipulation but of the ideological and economic conditions under which the media operate.

One book cannot cover all that might be said about the media. I will concentrate on national and international politico-economic class issues, saying relatively little about the racist and sexist biases in media content (beyond what is dealt with in the first chapter). I also do not deal with the entertainment media and the many hidden ideological and political biases found therein. That subject awaits a later volume. In the pages ahead we will explore the way the press distorts and suppresses the news about major domestic and foreign events and policies, the hidden and not so hidden ideological values, the mechanisms of information control, the role of newspeople, publishers, advertisers, and government, the way patterns of ownership influence information output, and the instances of dissent and deviancy in the major media.

Rather than attempt a comprehensive canvassing of the news complete with statistical breakdowns and content analyses, I trace media performance along several basic themes, providing representative samples of how the press treats or mistreats a subject. A more systematic and comprehensive undertaking would have had the virtue of thoroughness and maybe increased precision of a sort, but it would have made for a very huge and dull volume. In any case, numerous systematic studies are cited and summarized in the chapters that follow.

This book concentrates on the more influential and prestigious news media, specifically the three major networks: the Columbia Broadcasting System (CBS), the National Broadcasting Company (NBC), and the American Broadcasting Company (ABC), along with the *New York Times* and *Washington Post* (and their respective news services). These two newspapers, the *Post* and the *Times*, not only feed information to the public but to other news media as well. Occasional attention is also given herein to the newsweeklies, *Time* and *Newsweek,* and the *Wall Street Journal,* the *Los Angeles Times,* and lesser publications and broadcast media. Taken together these various outlets compose what I alternately describe as the "major media," the "establishment press," the "mainstream media," the "business-owned press," the "U.S. press," the "national media," or just the "press" and the "news media." Throughout this book I use the terms *news media* and *press* synonymously to mean the printed and broadcast news organizations. It so happens that *press* is singular and *media* plural, but I mean the same by both. The term *press* however does not include the entertainment sector of the media.

The above-mentioned news organizations represent the better quality part of the establishment press, being more informative and less distorted than most of the other (more conservative) media. If this book has a bias in selection, then, it is in the direction of understatement.

If the media so preempt the communication universe, then how can we evaluate them? And who is to say whether our criticisms are to be trusted? In attempting to expose the distortions and biases of the press, do we not unavoidably introduce biases of our own? And if objectivity is unattainable, are we not then left in the grip of a subjectivism in which one person's impressions are about as reliable (or unreliable) as another's? To be sure, there is always the danger that a dissenting viewpoint of the kind presented in this book will introduce distortions of its own. The reader should watch for these. But this new "danger" is probably not as great as the one posed by the press itself, because readers approach the dissenting viewpoint after having been conditioned throughout their lives to the sentiments and images of the dominant society. The heterodox arguments can more easily be recognized as such and are open to conscious challenge. Far more insidious are the notions and opinions that so fit into the dominant political culture's field of established images that they appear not as arguments and biased manipulations but as "the nature of things."

When exposed to a view that challenges the prevailing message, the reader is not then simply burdened with additional distortions. A dissident view provides us with an occasion to test the prevailing beliefs, to contrast and compare and open ourselves to information and questions that the mainstream media and the dominant belief system in general have ignored or suppressed. Through this clash of viewpoints we have a better chance of moving toward a closer approximation of the truth.

In addition, we have the test of experience itself. Common sense and everyday life oblige us to make judgments and act as if some images and information are closer to the truth than others. Misrepresentations can be eliminated by a process of feedback, as when subsequent events fail to fulfill the original images. For instance, after decades of mass media alarms about Red Menace threats that subsequently never materialized, we can raise some critical questions about the objectivity and reliability of the press regarding the issue of anticommunism and the cold war. (As indeed I do; see chapters 6, 7, and 8.)

There is also the internal evidence found in the press itself. We can detect inconsistencies in the press by drawing from other reports in the same mainstream press. We can note how information that supports the official view is given top play while developments that seem not to fit are relegated to the back pages. Also, like any liar the press is filled with contradictions. Seldom holding itself accountable for what it says, it can blithely produce information and opinions that conflict with previously held ones, without a word of explanation for the shift. We can also learn to question what the establishment press tells us by noting the absence of supporting evidence, the failure to amplify and explain. We can ask: Why are the assertions that appear again and again in the news not measured against observable actualities? We can thereby become more aware when and how the news media are inviting us to believe something without establishing any reason for the belief.

Much of the evidence herein has been gathered from extensive and detailed studies produced by academic scholars, journalists, and other independent investigators. Also helpful has been the information provided in such dissenting publications as the *Nation,* the *Progressive, Political Affairs, In These Times,* the *Guardian,* the *Daily World,* and *Mother Jones*—publications that have proved right more often than not on a wide range of issues that the major media regularly misrepresent.

Some readers will complain of this book's "one-sidedness." But if it is true that "we need to hear all sides and not just one," then all the more reason why the criticisms and information usually suppressed or downplayed by the American press deserve the attention accorded them in the pages to follow. In any case, it can be observed that people who never complain about the one-sidedness of their mainstream political education are the first to complain of the one-sidedness of any challenge to it. Far from seeking a diversity of views, they defend themselves from the first exposure to such diversity, preferring to leave their conventional political opinions unchallenged.

A former member of the Federal Communications Commission, Nicholas Johnson, once urged people to "talk back" to their television sets. We can talk back to all the media a lot better and demand a lot more only when we know how we are being manipulated and why we are being lied to. This book is an attempt at understanding how and why the media are the way they are so that we might better defend ourselves not only by talking back in the privacy of our living rooms but by organizing and struggling to become the active agents of our own lives and the creators of our own reality.

ACKNOWLEDGMENTS

No author works in a vacuum. This critique builds on work that came before it. I want to express my gratitude to persons who played no active role in the preparation of this manuscript but whose efforts provided a valuable foundation and inspiration for my own, specifically George Seldes, James Aronson, Noam Chomsky, Herbert Gans,

Robert Cirino, Todd Gitlin, Alexander Cockburn, Peter Drier, Andrew Kopkind, Edward Herman, Frank Brodhead, William Dorman, David Paletz, Robert Entman, and last but certainly not least, Herbert Schiller. For research and editorial assistance rendered, my thanks to John Ambrosio, Norman Bauman, Laura Brown, Janet Coffman, Richard Hofrichter, Dwight Hunter, David Leech, and most of all Kathleen Lipscomb. Philip Green of Smith College, Paul Blanchard of Eastern Kentucky University, David Moore of the University of New Hampshire, and Allan Johnson of the University of Connecticut at Hartford also provided valuable critiques. An expression of appreciation is owed to W. H. Ferry and Carol Ferry, Amey Garber, and Clara Hendel and the late Samuel Hendel for the financial support they extended to the project while I was at the Institute for Policy Studies. Finally, my thanks to the people at St. Martin's Press, especially my editor Peter Dougherty, Sarah Rosenthal, David Kaufman, Judy Rundel, Marcia Cohen, Denise Quirk, and the many others whose skills and labor at the editorial, production, printing, and sales end were so crucial in making *Inventing Reality* a reality.

Philip Meranto, the political scientist and activist and a close and special friend of mine, was an important source of support and inspiration to my work and my life. His untimely death remains a cause of real grief to me and to many others. Even if he did not live to see its completion, he was—in his own way—especially crucial to the creation of this book.

1

From Cronkite's Complaint to Orwell's Oversight

The mass media in the United States are privately-owned, profit-making corporations—like so many other institutions in our capitalist society. To understand how the media function, we need to understand a few things about the capitalist system itself. Most of the land, labor, natural resources, and technology of this and other nations are controlled by a few giant corporations and banks for the purpose of making profits for their owners. This process of capital accumulation, the essence of the capitalist system, in turn, exerts a strong influence over our political and social institutions. The news media seldom talk about this (and we shall see why), but it is time we did.

CAPITALISM AND CULTURE

The capitalist class, that tiny portion of the population that lives securely and affluently principally off the labor of others, has a commanding say in how and for whom the wealth of the nation is produced. The imperatives of the private market determine the kinds of jobs that are (or are not) available; the wages we earn; the prices, rents, and mortgages we pay; the quality of the goods and services we get; and even the quality of the air we breathe, the food we eat, and the water we drink.[1]

Capitalism's purpose is not to create jobs; in fact, capitalists are constantly devising ways of eliminating jobs in order to cut labor costs. Nor is its purpose to build communities, for capitalists will build or destroy communities as investment opportunities dictate. Nor is capitalism dedicated to protecting the family or traditional life, for no system in human history has been more relentless in battering down ancient practices and destroying both rural and urban home-grown cultures. Nor is capitalism intent upon protecting the environment on behalf of generations yet to come; for corporations will treat

1

the environment like a septic tank in order to cut production costs and maximize profits without regard for future generations or for the generation enduring it all today. Nor can we say that capitalists are committed to economic efficiency as such, since they regularly pass on their hidden diseconomies to the public in the form of overproduction, overpricing, pollution, unemployment, population dislocation, harmful products, and personal injury. And as the military budget shows, they actively court waste and duplication if it brings fatter contracts and bigger profits.

Capitalism has no loyalty to anything but its own process of capital accumulation, no loyalty to anything but itself. Nor could it be otherwise if one wished to survive as a capitalist; for the first law of the market is to make a profit off other people's labor or go out of business. Private profitability rather than social need is the determining condition of capital investment.Throughout history, the accumulation of wealth has brought with it a growth in organizations designed for the protection of wealth, starting with the bands of armed men whom Engels correctly defined as the essence of the early state. Marx and Engels understood that the state has several functions: It carries out tasks that cannot be performed privately, and it tends to the common defense of the people. But a major purpose of the state in class society is to protect those who own the wealth of a nation from those who labor.[2]

It may come as a surprise to discover that throughout most of the seventeenth, eighteenth, and early nineteenth centuries, leading bourgeois philosophers and economists understood and openly stated, as did John Locke in 1690 that "government was created for the protection of property," and Adam Smith in 1776 that civil authority "is in reality instituted for the defense of the rich against the poor, or of those who have some property against those who have none at all." As class differences become more pronounced, Smith observed, so does the need for a state: "The acquisition of valuable and extensive property . . . necessarily requires the establishment of civil government."[3] And as the scope of capitalism widens, so does the state—from principality to confederation to nation to an international network of counterinsurgency client states—in order to make the world safe for capital accumulation.

Even within a political system like ours which allows for mass electoral participation, the rich are able to exercise an extraordinary influence over the leaders of government. In fact, they usually *are* the leaders, directly occupying the top legislative, judicial, and executive positions, including governorships, cabinet posts and the presidency itself. In addition, the immense sums of money at their disposal allow them to dominate both political campaigns and the policymaking process with lavish contributions and well-paid lobbyists.

Even more important, business *as a system,* as a way of organizing property, capital, and labor, is a pervasive social force and not just another of many interests in the political arena. It occupies a strategic position within the economic system: in a sense, it *is* the economic system. So on most major politico-economic issues, business gets its way with government because there exists no alternative way of organizing the economy within the existing capitalist structure. Because business controls the very economy of the nation, government perforce enters into a unique and intimate relationship with it. The health of the *capitalist* economy is treated by policymakers as a necessary condition for the health of the nation. The goals of big business (rapid growth, high profits, and secure markets at home and abroad) become the goals of government, and the "national interest" becomes identified with the dominant domestic and overseas capitalist interests. In order to keep the peace, business may occasionally accept reforms and regulations it does not like, but government cannot ignore business's own reason for being, that is, the accumulation of capital. In a capitalist system, public policies cannot persistently violate the central imperative of capital accumulation. Sooner or later, business as a system must be met on its own terms or be replaced by another system.

Today, knowledge of the relationship between wealth, class, and state is suppressed like a dirty secret; or it is dismissed by officials, opinion makers, and news pundits as just so much Marxist ideological mouthing. The accepted posture is to minimize or deny the linkages between capitalist economic power and a supposedly democratic state, between private wealth and public authority. But in truth the power of money prevails over the needs of the people in more ways than are usually acknowledged; and the existing state can no more be neutral toward, and independent of, those who control the economy than can the other institutions of society.

But what has all this to do with the press? The press is one of the "other institutions" I just alluded to and one of the most important in maintaining the hegemony of the corporate class and the capitalist system itself. During the nineteenth century, as industry drew a growing proportion of the population into its sphere of work and consumption, business leaders became more concerned with seeing that cultural life coincided with the demands of industrial production and that the public's political sentiments were supportive of the existing social order. Not only would industrialists administer the work discipline of the machine, they would try to teach people proper attitudes and loyalties. They would extend their influence over people from the factory to the political halls to the community itself.[4]

Anarchists, socialists, syndicalists, and other purveyors of radical ideas were mercilessly hounded out of the factories, schools, professions, and communities of America. Pinkertons, Klansmen, and vigilantes—often in the pay of the bosses along with police, militia, and the army were regularly employed to crush labor opposition and political dissidence.[5] But as Napoleon once said, you can do anything with bayonets except sit on them. A class that relies solely on the state's bayonets to maintain its rule is never secure. So along with suppression, the business class enlisted to its cause such other institutions as the church, the charities, the law, the schools, and the popular press. To secure their hegemony as captains of industry, businessmen, as Stuart Ewen wrote, "aspired to become captains of consciousness."[6]

Today corporate leaders and their well-paid deputies dominate the boards and top posts of society's educational, communicational, artistic, entertainment, legal, and scientific institutions. These institutions are ruled very much like business firms themselves, by boards of directors (or trustees or regents, as they might be called) drawn mostly from the business class or those in the pay of that class. Numbering between ten and twenty-five persons, these boards have final say over the institution's system of rewards and punishments, its budget and personnel, its investments, and its purposes. They exercise power either by occupying the top executive positions or by hiring and firing those who do. Their power to change the institution's management if it does not perform as they desire is what gives them control over policy.

The boards exercise power not by popular demand or consensus but by *state* charter. Incorporated by the state, they can call upon the courts and the police to enforce their decisions against the competing claims of staff, clients, or other constituents. These boards are non-elected, self-selected, self-perpetuating, ruling coteries of affluent persons who are answerable to no one but themselves. They are checked by no internal electoral system, no opposition parties, no obligation to report to the rank and file or win support from any of the people whose lives they affect with their decisions. Yet institutions so ruled—including the nation's news organizations—are said to be the mainstay of "democratic pluralism."

In a word, the cultural order is not independent of the business system. Nor are cultural institutions independent of each other, being owned outright or directly controlled by the more active members of the business class in what amounts to a system of interlocking and often interchanging directorates. We know of more than one business leader who not only presides over a bank or corporation but has served as a cabinet member in Washington, is a regent of a large university, a trustee of a civic art center, and a board member of a church or foundation or major newspaper or television network—or all of the above.

Those persons who believe the United States is a pluralistic society resist the notion of a business-dominated culture. They see cultural institutions as standing outside the political arena, distinctly separate from business and politics. They make much about keeping the media, arts, sciences, foundations, schools, colleges, professions, and churches free of the taint of political ideologies so that these institutions might not be deprived of their neutrality and autonomy. Since the pluralists believe that big business is just one of many interests in the political arena and one that does not dominate the state, they cannot imagine that it dominates civil society and cultural life.

But if history teaches us anything it is that the power of the propertied class never stands alone. It wraps itself in the flag and claims a devotion to God, country, and the public good. Behind the state is a whole supporting network of doctrines, values, myths, and institutions that are not normally thought of as political but which serve a political purpose. The state, as Gramsci noted, is "only the outer ditch behind which there [stands] a powerful system of fortresses and earthworks."[7] These supportive institutions help create the ideology that transforms a ruling class interest into a "general interest," justifying existing class relations as the only natural and workable ones, the preferred and optimal, although not perfect, societal arrangements. So the capitalist class is the ruling class, controlling society's cultural institutions and ideational production as well as its labor, land, and natural resources.

Not entirely, however. The corporate-financial class of America is very powerful but not omnipotent. It makes mistakes, suffers internal divisions over tactics and policies, and must constantly deal with the resistance of workers, consumers, taxpayers, voters, and other protesters. The ruling class rules, but not always in the way it might want. It sometimes must make concessions to resistant publics or at least maintain an appearance of so doing. To best secure and legitimate its rule, it must minimize the appearance and use of its undemocratic, coercive power.

This hypocrisy is not merely "the tribute that vice pays to virtue." In fact, vice never pays tribute to virtue, but it does to power—to the democratic power of the people, who with demonstrations, protests, boycotts, strikes, sit-ins, civil disobedience, and even civil disorders have struggled against regressive laws, oppressive work conditions, excessive taxes, and for an expansion of democratic rights and material benefits. The power of these democratic forces limits the ability of the moneyed interests to reduce all persons and things to grist for the profit mill.

To maintain the system that is so good to them, the rich and powerful devote much attention to persuasion and propaganda. Control over the communication field and the flow of mass information, helps secure the legitimacy of the owning class's politico-economic power. We don't have a free and independent press in the United States but one that is tied by purchase and persuasion to wealthy elites and their government counterparts.

Of course, not everyone sees it that way. Many people who hear about "a controlled press" think only of something that exists in other lands. If anything, the more conservative among them advocate greater restrictions on the U.S. media, in imitation of the censorship they say they are fighting when they say they are fighting Communism. Others who complain about the U.S. news media's shortcomings believe "our" press, for all its faults, is a free and independent one, certainly freer than in most other countries.

In this book I choose to investigate the U.S. news media not by comparing them to the media of Great Britain, the Soviet Union, China, France, Paraguay, Nazi Germany, or wherever, but by measuring them against their own assertions about being independent, objective, neutral, informative, balanced, and truthful. I will argue and try to demonstrate that in regard to the most crucial questions of political and economic life, the media do not, and cannot, live up to their claims; and I will try to explain how and why they fail to do so.

The structures of control within the U.S. media are different from the institutionalized formal censorship we might expect of a government-controlled press; they are less visible and more subtle, not monolithic yet hierarchical, transmitted to the many by those who work for the few, essentially undemocratic and narrow in perspective, tied to the rich and powerful but not totally immune to the pressures of an agitated public, propagandistic yet sometimes providing hard information that is intentionally or unintentionally revealing.

CRONKITE AND OTHER CRITICS

The U.S. news media operate under an established ideology that claims they have no established ideology, no racial, gender, or class bias. Supposedly committed to no persuasion, they just report things as they see them. Now and then we hear murmurs to the contrary. For instance, for nearly two decades, every evening in the week, the dean of America's newscasters, Walter Cronkite, would end his CBS television news show with the statement: "And that's the way it is." On the eve of his retirement in 1980, Cronkite admitted that isn't the way it is: "My lips have been kind of buttoned for almost twenty years . . . . CBS News doesn't really believe in commentary," he charged.[8]

It was a remarkable admission. The man who had been given honorary degrees by leading universities and who had been voted in one opinion poll the nation's most trusted public figure was saying that he had spent almost two decades under the censorship of network bosses. To be sure, it was a comfortable sort of repression. Cronkite's last ten-year contract with CBS went for $20 million, a sum that has been known to ease the pain of buttoned lips. But finally Walter Cronkite had his moment of truth. Yet he only *complained*, and never *explained*: Why was he so restricted by those who exercised such power over him?

That we *think* the American press is a free and independent institution may only be a measure of our successful habituation to a subtler, more familiar form of supression. The worst forms of tyranny—or certainly the most successful ones—are not those we rail against but those that so insinuate themselves into the imagery of our consciousness and the fabric of our lives as not to be perceived as tyranny.

This is not to say the press has escaped all criticism; indeed, more frequently than ever, the media are under attack from various quarters. First, there are the salvos from political and religious ultra-rightists. An example of the Christian right assault might be the televised sermon by fundamentalist preacher Jimmy Lee Swaggart, from San Antonio, Texas, on November 4, 1984. Swaggart assailed the media as "godless" and infected by "secular humanism"—which he said was a code word for atheism. He said 40 percent of journalists are for socialism. Because of the media's undermining effects "we will rot from within without the Soviet Union having to fire a shot," he exclaimed. Having "forgotten the bible," the media have difficulty "recognizing what Communism really is." "We cooperated with the Soviets for a half-century," and all we got was "subterfuge, lying, darkness, and death." The Communists in Nicaragua "are slashing red paint on the doors of Christians" and "then they'll go into every church and home and take out the people and preachers who then disappear." But our "leftist bureaucrats" and "weak-kneed sisters in Congress" block any move against Communism. The media corrode family values, weaken our moral fiber and invite interior decay and the eventual victory of the Communists, the preacher concluded.

Swaggart's diatribe is mostly fantasy. However, we can see that from his ideological perspective, the media indeed do appear as atheistic, liberal, and soft on communism. I will try to show that while the media do not carry out the kind of fire-and-brimstone crusade against "the evils of Communism" desired by the radical right, they are dedicated to anticommunism in a more effective and quite thorough fashion.

Not too far from the far right stands the conservative corporate community, which attacks the media for "failing to show business's side of things" and for running occasional reports about corporate pollution, wasteful defense contracts, corporate crime, and the crimes of conservative political leaders (for example, Watergate). Business would prefer that the news media avoid any mention of the large profits that big business makes (especially embarrassing during hard times) and stories about unemployment, and the struggles of minorities, women, and the poor, and reports on those who protest armaments, nuclear power, and corporate mistreatment of the environment. All of this—along with TV dramas like "Dynasty" and "Dallas," which occasionally portray individual tycoons as ruthless cutthroats—convinces corporate conservatives that the media are a liberal tool bent on portraying business in the worst possible light.

These rightist attacks help the media maintain an appearance of neutrality and objectivity. The charge made by leftist critics that the media are complicit with the dominant powers seems to be refuted when these same powerful interests attack the media's supposedly antibusiness bias. The truth is that while the press may not be totally uncritical nor totally adulatory toward the big business community, it is not an autonomous adversary, independent of the corporate class. In fact, the media underplay most of the more damaging information and commentary about corporate doings. What is reported is but the tip of the iceberg. But even this is more than business cares to endure and is seen as an attack on the entire business system. Corporate conservatives would prefer a press dedicated to an exclusively laudatory, unblemished picture of American business, complete with regular upbeat reports on the nation's economic health and business's role in creating an ever-expanding prosperity.

Not all the criticism is from political, religious, and corporate conservatives. Centrists and liberals, including some journalists, have criticized the press for failing to do its job of informing the American public about the crucial issues. Criticism from those on the political center focuses less on content than on the lack of it. They complain that the news is superficial and trivial, that it focuses on personalities rather than issues, on surface happenings rather than substantive matters, that it is more interested in entertaining than informing us.

I agree with such observations and in the pages ahead will offer supporting examples. But that kind of criticism remains more of a complaint than an analysis. When the centrist and liberal critics get around to trying to explain why stories are so poorly reported they are likely to blame the journalists. The *Columbia Journalism Review* and other such publications run articles telling how stories are mishandled because reporters are misled by their sources, not well informed, too dependent on officialdom, or given to indulging their "personal predilections and prejudices."[9]

These kinds of criticisms are often true, but they place too much blame on the weakest, lowliest link in the news manufacturing chain: the reporter. The critics say nothing about the editors who cut and rewrite the reporters' copy and who control their jobs; and they say nothing about the people who hire, fire, pay, and promote the editors and who exercise ultimate control over them. The centrist-liberal critique fails to note that while the journalist's product may be gravely wanting in certain qualities, including objectivity and balance, it remains acceptable to the journalist's superiors. It is the kind of copy they deem suitable for their readers. And as will be seen, the reporter who produces more penetrating stories—especially ones that reveal too much about the exploitative, undemocratic nature of capitalist society at home and abroad—will run into difficulties with superiors. By fingering the journalist as the main or only culprit, liberal critics are implicitly treating reporters as free agents when in fact they are not. The "working press" works for someone other than itself.

Sometimes media critics will fault not the journalists or anyone else involved in manufacturing the news but the structure of the media themselves. By its very nature, we are told, television emphasizes the visual over the ideational. Action events, national leaders, and political candidates have visual appeal; issues and policy analysis do not. Hence there is bound to be more surface than substance in the news.[10] The problem also is said to exist—to a lesser extent—with the print media, which have limited space and time to frame vastly complex events on a daily basis. So, it is said, the media latch on to simple images and explanations in order to reduce their subject matter to easily manageable components.

There is no denying that stereotyping and reductionism are the common tools of shallow thinking, but why must such shallowness be treated as inevitable? That the media so frequently resort to slick surface treatment does not mean such treatment is the *only* way the media can function. Rather than being a criticism, this "blaming the nautre of the media" is a disguised defense. It gets everyone off the hook and treats television, or whatever medium, like a disembodied technological force all its own. However, it is not television as such that chooses to cling to surface events but the people who run it. With the right script and right intentions, visual media can offer engrossingly informative and penetrating presentations on vital subjects, as demonstrated by the many fine independently produced documentaries the major networks deign not to carry.

In contrast to the above views, I argue that the news media do not fail to do their job, rather they perform their function all too well. Their objective is not to produce an alert, critical, and informed citizenry but the kind of people who will vote for Richard Nixon, Jimmy Carter, or Ronald Reagan. Their aim is to create the kind of opinion climate that makes such choices seem plausible, an opinion universe dominated by corporate and govermental elites, almost all of whom share the same ideological perspective about political and economic reality. True, these elites do not always appreciate how well they are served by a press that would be less credible and less effective if it were *exclusively* and more blatantly a propaganda arm of business and government, but this does not mean the press is free and independent.

The basic distortions in the media are not innocent errors, for they are not random; rather they move in the same overall direction again and again, favoring management over labor, corporatism over anticorporatism, the affluent over the poor, private enterprise over socialism, Whites over Blacks, males over females, officialdom over protesters, conventional politics over dissidence, anticommunism and arms-race militarism over disarmament, national chauvinism over internationalism, U.S. dominance of the Third World over revolutionary change. The press does many things and serves many functions, but its major role, its irreducible responsibility is to continually recreate a view of reality supportive of existing social and economic class power. That is what I will try to demonstrate in this book.

CLASS, RACE, AND GENDER

One indication of how the press serves the privileged and the powerful is found in how it treats the underprivileged and the powerless. The news media are largely an affluent White male domain. Blacks, Latinos, Asians, women, and the poor are accorded brief mention on special occasions. The poor are most likely to receive coverage during Thanksgiving and Christmas time when some indigents are administered turkey dinners, the message being that there is comfort, food, and shelter even for the more unfortunate among us. With the Reagan cutbacks in human services and the recession of 1982 and

1983, the poor, especially the "new poor" became an object of media interest for brief intermittent spans. By 1984, with hunger and homelessness as bad as ever, the media hit upon a new theme: "economic recovery." Although the number of Americans living in poverty had increased from twenty-five million to thirty-five million between 1981 and 1985, the media tended to lose interest in the poor.[11]

Women account for only about 10 percent of persons in the news, usually appearing as celebrities or the wives of celebrities, or unusual "firsts": the first woman astronaut, the first woman on the Supreme Court, the first woman vice-presidential candidate for a major party. But the more general battle for economic, social, and sexual equality and for material survival and betterment that women are waging on many fronts is ignored or slighted.

So with Blacks and other minorities whose struggles for jobs, decent housing, safe neighborhoods, viable political organizations, and adequate medical care, and whose cultural contributions to—and attempts to win fair play in—sports, art, literature, entertainment, music, religion, labor, and education have received little notice from the White media.[12] The Black candidate who attracts millions of votes in presidential primaries while taking a progressive stance on issues is likely to win unsympathetic or slighting press treatment as did Jesse Jackson in 1984.

Women, Blacks, and other minorities are also drastically underrepresented as employees in the communication industry. According to former *Boston Globe* editor Thomas Winship, the majority of the 1,700 daily newspapers in the United States have never employed a single Black, Latino, or Asian-American journalist. Barely 5 percent of all employed professional journalists are people of color and most of these work for the handful of minority-owned publications and radio stations.[13] Likewise, women account for only 6.5 percent of all reporters.[14] (In these kinds of statistics Black, Chicano, Asian, and other minority women are usually counted twice: as women and as minorities.)

The *class* dimensions of the women's struggle and the Black struggle, and indeed, the systemic class dimensions of poverty itself are judged to be simply not a fit subject for the mainstream news media. Equality is seen as a matter of individual achievement that has no collective material base. Class, as an exploitative relationship between owners and employees, and as a determinant of wealth and power, is a subject the news media dare not touch. However, class as a designation of occupation, income, and life style wins occasional recognition with such references as "middle class," "low income," "upper middle," "professional class," "white collar," and "blue collar."

Consider how class biases operate in how crimes are reported and

in what is even defined as a crime. Press coverage focuses public
attention on crime in the streets with scarcely a mention of "crime in
the suites," downplaying such corporate crimes as briberies, embezzle-
ments, kickbacks, monopolistic restraints of trade, illegal uses of public funds by private interests, occupational safety violations, unsafe
consumer goods, and environmental poisonings—which are, or should
be, crimes, and which can cost the public dearly in money and lives.[15]
Every year more than 14,000 workers in the United States are killed
on the job; another 100,000 die prematurely and 400,000 become
seriously ill from work-related diseases. Many, if not most, of these
deaths and injuries occur because greater consideration is given by
management to profits and production than to occupational safety
and environmental standards. Yet these crimes are rarely defined and
reported as crimes by the news media.

How the press defines and reports on crime, then, is largely determined by the class and racial background of the victim and victimizer.
Affluent victims are more likely to receive press attention than poor
ones, leaving the false impression that most victims of crime are from
upper- and middle-class backgrounds. And low-income lawbreakers,
especially Blacks, Latinos, and other minorities, are more likely to be
publicized as criminals than the corporate leaders whose crimes may
be even more serious and of wider scope and repercussion than the
street criminal's.[16]

While the press reports occasional abuses in the economic system, it
treats corporate capitalism as fostering individual initiative and inven-
tiveness, and as being providential rather than exploitative. The contradictions of capitalism, for instance, between the need to keep wages
down in order to maximize profits and the need to keep wages up in order
to maintain demand, are seldom if ever dwelt upon in the media. The
waste, duplication, stagnation, unemployment, inflation, and anarchy of
production that comes with an unplanned economy, and the failure of a
market economy to respond to social need rather than private greed, are
seldom linked to anything in the nature of capitalism. Recessions are
treated as natural, albeit unfortunate, events, somewhat akin to earth-
quakes or droughts, caused by something innocent called "hard times."
Inflation and pollution are supposedly caused by everyone, since we all
spend and consume. One television reporter put it this way: "Inflation is
the culprit and in inflation everyone is guilty."[17] In the news media, slums
are caused by people who live in them and not by real estate speculators,
fast-buck developers, tax-evading investors, and rent-gouging landlords.
Poverty is a problem of the poor, who need to be taught better values and
a more middle-class life style.

While the poor are always with us, for the media it is the middle class to which America belongs. The middle class is implicitly virtuous because it is seen as the repository of stability and order. Thus on CBS Evening News, anchorperson Dan Rather referred to the "$17,000 to $41,000 range" as "the great middle class, the glue that holds society together."[18] The press does not link poverty, instability, and disorder to the injustices and irrationalities of the capitalist system.

IMAGE POLITICS

The press sees the established governmental leadership as essential to the maintenance of social order; and it gives more credence to public officials, corporate representatives, church leaders, and university officers than it does to protesters, taxpayers, consumers, workers, parishioners, and students.[19]

The foremost leader in the United States is the president, "who is viewed as the ultimate protector of order."[20] A systematic examination of twenty-five years of presidential news in the *New York Times* and *Time* magazine, as well as ten years of CBS broadcasts, reveals a "consistent pattern of favorable coverage of the President," with sympathetic stories outnumbering critical ones by two to one.[21] More often than not, a president's viewpoint, especially if it has no liberal slant, is transmitted by the press with no opposing set of facts. Thus when President Reagan claimed credit for the 1982 extension of the Voting Rights Act and for appointing more minority members and females to administrative posts and waging a more vigorous enforcement of civil rights than previous administrations, the press faithfully reported his claims without pointing out that in fact he had threatened to veto the Voting Rights Act (and only signed it because it passed both houses by veto-proof majorities) and had actually cut back on minority and female appointments and on civil rights enforcement.[22] And in the 1984 campaign when President Reagan asserted he would "never" attack Social Security, most of the major media gave top play to his statement without noting that in previous years he had repeatedly attacked Social Security, equating it and other entitlement programs with welfare—which he hated.

The 1984 presidential election campaign revealed the media's conservative bias to those who cared to look. According to a survey by *Editor and Publisher* magazine, 387 daily newspapers in the United States endorsed the right-wing Republican Ronald Reagan for president, while 63 supported the Democrat Walter Mondale.[23] And this kind of conservative editorial bias carries over to news coverage, as media critic Ben Bagdikian found looking at earlier studies:

Is it possible that newspapers might endorse Republicans, print conservative columnists, editorialize in favor of conservative issues, but still counterbalance this with pro-liberal bias in their news columns? In the mid-sixties I looked at the current published studies of political bias in the news. There were 84 systematic studies that found significant bias. There was a very high correlation between editorial policy and news bias. Of the 84 studies of bias, 74 found pro-Republican bias in the news in papers with pro-Republican editorial policies. There were seven instances of pro-Democratic bias in papers with pro-Democratic editorials. Only in three of the 84 cases was news bias the opposite of editorial position. So where political bias in the news is found, it is overwhelmingly pro-Republican and pro-conservative. . . . There is much talk of a "liberal conspiracy" in the press; but the real question is how liberal electoral politics survives at all with the overwhelming opposition of the conservative press.[24]

A George Washington University study of television network evening news during the 1984 presidential campaign found that five out of six stories on Walter Mondale presented him in a negative manner focusing on minor mishaps and the candidate's presumed lack of appeal, rather than on the issues he was raising.[25]

The conservative biases of the supposedly liberal media have a feedback effect on political life. As John Kenneth Galbraith noted, political conservatism benefits from:

... the deep desire of politicians, Democrats in particular, for respectability—their need to show that they are individuals of sound confidence-inspiring judgment. And what is the test of respectability? It is, broadly whether speech and action are consistent with the comfort and well-being of the people of property and position. A radical is anyone who causes discomfort or otherwise offends such interests. Thus, in our politics, we test even liberals by their conservatism.[26]

Candidates learn that if they take a stand on controversial issues, the press is less likely to get their position across to the public than to concentrate on the controversy arising from the position taken. Suddenly their judgment and suitability will be called into question. So rather than the press using its coverage to fit the campaign, candidates trim their campaigns in anticipation of coverage. In the act of reporting on political life, the media actively help shape it.

The media create conservative effects by slighting the issues and focusing on candidate image. Even when attention is given to issues, it is usually to conjecture on how the candidate used them to help his image and advance his electoral chances. Once considered an adjunct to political discussion, image now seems to be the whole point of the discussion. "It is not the issues we are asked to judge: it is the nuances of the presentation."[27]

The George Washington University study conducted by the media specialist Michael Robinson found no liberal bias in campaign coverage but rather a "hollowness," and a lack of content. The campaign was treated more as a horse race than a clash of programs and policies.[28] Who will run? Who will be nominated? Who's ahead? How will voters respond? Who will win? These preoccupations are supplemented with generous offerings of surface events and personality trivia. Commenting on the 1976 presidential contest Malcolm MacDougall observed, (with forgivable overstatement):

> I saw President Ford bump his head leaving an airplane. . . . I saw Carter playing softball in Plains, Georgia. I saw Carter kissing Amy, I saw Carter hugging Lillian. I saw Carter, in dungarees, walking hand in hand through the peanut farm with Rosalynn. I saw Carter going into church, coming out of church. . . . I saw Ford misstate the problems of Eastern Europe— and a week of people commenting about his misstatement. I saw Ford bump his head again. I saw Ford in Ohio say how glad he was to be back in Iowa. I saw marching bands and hecklers, and I learned about the size of crowds and the significance of the size of the crowds. . . .
> But in all the hours of high anxiety that I spent watching the network news, never did I hear what the candidates had to say about the campaign issues. That was not news.[29]

MacDougall's impressions are borne out by studies of the 1968, 1972, and 1976 campaigns, which found that newspapers devoted respectively 56 percent, 64 percent, and 61 percent of their presidential coverage to the personal attributes of candidates. Television gave even more emphasis to personality than the printed media. And in the 1976 campaign, by a ratio of more than four to one, both print and broadcast media stressed personality and campaign events over issue discussion.[30] The media, like the major political parties themselves, treat campaigns not as an opportunity to develop democratic accountability and debate issues, but solely as a competition for office. The focus is on the race itself with little thought raised about what the race is supposed to be about, what makes it so meaningful, and why should it be considered an exercise in democratic governance.

By focusing on "human interest" trivia, on contest rather than content, the media make it difficult for the public to give intelligent expression to political life and to mobilize around the issues. Thus the media have—intentionally or not—a conservative effect on public discourse. Given short shrift are the concerns of millions of people regarding nuclear arms escalation, Pentagon spending, tax reform, war in Central America, unemployment, and poverty. The democratic input, the great public debate about the state of the Union and its national policies, the heightening of political consciousness and information levels—all the things democratic electoral campaigns are supposed to foster—are crowded off the stage by image politics.

Not only during election campaigns but just about on every other occasion the news media prefer surface to substance, emphasizing the eye-catching visuals, the attention-catching "special angle" report, and the reassuring and comforting stories, while slighting the deeper, more important but politically more troublesome and more controversial themes. There is so much concentration on surface events that we often have trouble grasping the content of things, so much focus on action and personality that we fail to see the purposive goal of the action. For instance, during 1981, President Reagan dismantled major portions of forty years of domestic social legislation, initiated enormous tax cuts for rich individuals and corporations, dramatically escalated an already huge military spending program, and launched a series of cold-war confrontations against the Soviet Union—all policies of great import. However, the theme that predominated in most of the stories about those crucial actions was whether Reagan was "winning" or "losing" in his contests with Congress, the bureaucracy, labor, and foreign governments. Thus momentous political issues were reduced to catchy but trivial questions about Reagan's political "score card," his efficacy as a leader, and his personal popularity.[31]

MONOPOLY POLITICS

Such as it is, media electoral coverage is lavishly bestowed on the two major parties, while minor parties are totally ignored or allotted but a few minutes, if that, over the entire campaign. Thus the media help perpetuate the procapitalist, two-party monopoly.

In recent contests, presidential candidates of the Communist Party, the Citizens Party, the Socialist Workers Party, the Workers World Party, and others did all the things presidential candidates are supposed to do. They met thousands of voters on street corners, spoke on college campuses and at voter forums, issued position papers and press releases, traveled around the country, and probably spoke directly to more people than did the major candidates. But on election day, most voters had never heard of them.[32] Deprived of mass media coverage, a third party cannot reach the voting masses. Most people remain unaware not only of its candidates but of its programs, issues, and critiques of status quo politics.

Simon Gerson, who managed the 1980 Communist Party campaign for Gus Hall and Angela Davis, complained of "the consistent spiking of news about them."[33] Other third-party candidates testify to a similar experience.[34] As a nationally known ecologist, author Barry Commoner was a frequent guest on national television shows—until the day he was nominated presidential candidate for the Citizen's Party and became virtually a nonperson.[35]

While the local media are sometimes accessible to third-party candidates—especially radio talk shows—it is only when they happen to be visiting the area. Unlike the Democrats and Republicans who remain a constant focus for local as well as national media, third-party candidates receive no recurring coverage.[36] Once they leave town, they leave the local media's vision. Being momentary rather than constant, the local exposure they receive is of limited impact.

Despite being censored out of campaigns by the mainstream media, third-party candidates do manage to garnish a considerable number of votes, taken together a total of between one and two million in each presidential election. But the people who vote for them are rendered as invisible as the candidates themselves. During election-night coverage of presidential and congressional elections, minor-party candidates go unmentioned and their votes unreported. As Peter Camejo, the 1976 presidential candidate of the Socialist Workers Party, commented: "Before the election, Democrats and Republicans and the media waged a campaign to convince the American people that a vote for a third party would not count. To convince them further, they simply didn't count the votes for most third-party candidates on election night."[37]

Media exposure confers legitimacy on one's candidacy. By giving elaborate national coverage only to Republicans and Democrats, news organizations are letting us know that these are the only ones worth considering. Candidates who are not taken seriously by the media swiftly discover that they are not taken seriously by many voters. Even when they make face-to-face contact with live audiences and with voters on street corners, they still lack legitimacy as candidates for national office, being more a curiosity than a serious choice. People may like what third-party candidates say, because often they are the only ones saying anything, but they usually won't vote for someone who doesn't have a chance. Since third-party candidates are not in the news, they are considered to be not really in the race; and since they are not in the race, this justifies treating them as if they are not news.

The argument made against giving national coverage to minor-party candidates is just that—they are minor; they do not represent the main concerns of the electorate; they are unknowns and of no significance to the national campaign. But as Aaron Orange of the Socialist Labor Party stated before a Senate subcommittee: "How can a candidate attract the following. . .that would convince the broadcasters that he is a 'significant' candidate? Isn't it a fact that in our present society one can become a 'significant' candidate only as a result of repeated exposure on the airwaves?"[38]

Were the media to give them national exposure, third-party candidates might very well win millions of votes, qualify for federal funds, and become serious contenders—as indeed happened when John Anderson ran as an independent in 1980. And even if failing to win the presidency, with major media exposure the candidate would very likely have a real impact on the issues and the climate of political opinion—as John Anderson did not have because he raised no serious politico-economic challenges to the major candidates but ran on an "I-can-do-it-better" platform, thereby making himself safe for big contributors and major media exposure. Candidates from the more radical parties, however, pose serious challenges to corporate power and to the government policies that bolster such power—which is enough reason to censor them.

Whether a candidate is a prominent or an unknown personage is less important in determining media treatment than his or her politics. John Anderson was an obscure congressman who did miserably in the 1980 Republican presidential primaries; yet, given his mainstream politics and safe credentials, he was treated like a major candidate when he later ran as an independent. Dozens of Democratic and Republican contenders, such as Reuben Askew, Wilbur Mills, Patsy Mink, John Ashbrook, Sam Yorty, Paul McCloskey, and Shirley Chisholm "were brought from relative obscurity to the public's attention by the media. Few had any chance of winning their party's nomination and none did," yet they were treated as real candidates.[39] In contrast, persons like Barry Commoner, Angela Davis, Gus Hall, and Benjamin Spock (the People's Party presidential candidate of 1972), were nationally known figures. Before Dr. Spock began his campaign, millions of Americans were already familiar with his name, having read his books on baby care and many knew of him as a dedicated peace activist.[40] Yet because of media blackout, only a tiny fraction of the public ever knew of his candidacy and his views, despite almost a year of Spock's active campaigning.[41]

To ensure impartiality on the public airwaves, Section 315 of the Communications Act requires that stations give equal time to legally qualified candidates if air time is granted to any one candidate. In 1959 this "equal time doctrine" was amended so as not to apply to coverage of "bona-fide" news events, including on-the-spot interviews, documentaries, campaign appearances, and by the 1960s, debates between major candidates, if sponsored by organizations other than the media. In effect, the broadcast media can give almost any kind of coverage to major candidates without putting themselves under an obligation to other candidates. Meanwhile the print media are completely free to censor third-party candidates since they do not use the public airwaves and need no public license. To impose an obligation on them to give some space to differing views has been judged an interference with their "freedom of speech."

DO THE MEDIA MANAGE OUR MINDS?

Are the media independent of government influence? If not, what is the nature of that influence? Are the media dominated by particular class interests? If so, does this dominance carry over into news content? Does control of news content translate into propaganda? Does propaganda translate into indoctrination of the public mind? And does indoctrination translate into support for policies? These questions guide the present inquiry: let us run through them again, a little more slowly.

1. In the United States a free press is defined as one unhampered by repressive laws. As we shall find, government interference with the news is not the only or even the major problem. More often the danger is that the press goes along willingly with officialdom's view of things at home and abroad, frequently manifesting a disregard for accuracy equal to that of policymakers. To be sure, questions are sometimes raised and criticisms voiced, but most of these are confined to challenging the *efficacy* of a particular policy rather than its underlying interests especially if the interests are powerful ones.

2. The newspeople who participate in the many forums on freedom of the press usually concentrate on threats to the press from without, leaving untouched the question of coercion from within, specifically from media owners.[42] Are the media free from censorial interference by their owners? Does ownership translate into actual control over information, or does responsibility for the news still rest in the hands of journalists and editors who are free to report what they want—limited only by professional canons of objectivity? As we shall see, the working press, including newspaper editors and television news producers and even the top media executives are beholden to media owners and corporate advertisers. More specifically, the owners exercise control through the power to hire and fire, to promote and demote anyone they want and by

regularly intervening directly into the news production process
with verbal and written directives.

3. But does control over media content and personnel translate
into ruling class propaganda? Even if we allow that owners
ultimately determine what is or is not publicized, can it be
assumed that the end product serves their interests and gives
only their viewpoint? I will argue that, except for momentary
departures, a capitalist ideological perspective regarding events
at home and abroad rather consistently predominates. The
system of control works, although not with absolute perfec-
tion and is not devoid of items that might at times be discom-
forting to the rich and powerful.

4. A final concern: Does ruling class propaganda translate into
indoctrination of the public? It might be argued that even if
the news is cast in a capitalist ideological mold, the public
does not swallow it and has ways of withstanding the propaganda. The news may be manipulated by the press lords, but
are we manipulated by the news? It is this last question I want
to deal with here at some length. For if the press exercises only
an inconsequential influence over the public, then we are dealing with a tempest in a teapot and are being unduly alarmist
about "mind management."

Early studies of the media's impact on voting choices found that
people seemed surprisingly immune from media manipulation. Campaign propaganda usually reinforced the public's preferences rather
than altered them. People exposed themselves to media appeals in a
selective way, giving more credence and attention to messages that
bolstered their own views. Their opinions and information intake also
were influenced by peers, social groups, and community, so the individual did not stand without a buffer against the impact of the media.
The press, it was concluded, had only a "minimal effect."[43]

At first glance, these findings are reassuring: People seem fairly
self-directed in their responses to the media and do not allow themselves to be mindlessly directed. Democracy is safe. But troublesome
questions remain. If through "selective exposure" and "selective attention" we utilize the media mainly to reinforce our established predispositions, where do the predispositions themselves come from? We
can point to various socializing agencies: family, school, peer groups,
work place—and the media themselves. Certainly some of our inter-
nalized political predispositions come from the dominant political culture that the media have had a hand in shaping—and directly from
earlier exposure to the media themselves.

Our ability to discriminate is limited in part by how we have been conditioned by previous media exposures. The selectivity we exercise is not an autonomous antidote to propaganda but may feed right into it, choosing one or another variation of the same establishment offering. Opinions that depart too far from the mainstream are likely to be rejected out of hand. In such situations, our "selectivity" is designed to *avoid* information and views that contradict the dominant propaganda, a propaganda we long ago implicitly embraced as representative of "the nature of things." Thus, an implanted set of conditioned responses are now mistakenly identified as our self-generated political perceptions, and the public's selective ingestion of the media's conventional fare is wrongly treated as evidence of the "minimal effect" of news organizations.

In addition, more recent empirical evidence suggests that, contrary to the earlier "minimal effects" theory, the news media are able to direct our attention to certain issues and shape our opinions about them. One study found that "participants exposed to a steady stream of news about defense or about pollution came to believe that defense or pollution were more consequential problems."[44] Other studies found that fluctuations in public concern for problems like civil rights, Vietnam, crime, and inflation over the last two decades reflected variations in the attention paid to them by the major media.[45]

Theorists who maintain that the media have only a minimal effect on campaigns ought to try convincing those political candidates who believe they survive and perish because of media exposure or the lack of it. And as we saw earlier, the inability to buy media time or attract press coverage consigns third-party candidates to the dim periphery of American politics. The power to ignore political viewpoints other than the standard two-party offerings is more than minimal, it is monumental. Media exposure frequently may be the single most crucial mobilizer of votes, even if certainly not the only one.

If much of our informational and opinion intake is filtered through our previously established mental predilections, these predilections are often not part of our conscious discernment but of our unexamined perceptual conditioning—which brings us back to an earlier point: *Rather than being rational guardians against propaganda, our predispositional sets, having been shaped by prolonged exposure to earlier outputs of that same propaganda, may be active accomplices.*

Furthermore, there are many things about which we may not have a predetermined opinion. Lacking any competing information, we often unwarily embrace what we read or hear. In those instances, the media are not merely reinforcing previously held opinions, they are implanting new ones, although these implants themselves seldom fall upon *tabula rasa* brains and usually do not conflict too drastically with established biases. For example, millions of Americans who have an unfavorable view of the Sandinista government in Nicaragua came by that opinion through exposure to press reports rather than from direct contact with the Nicaraguan revolution. Here then is an original implant; people are prepared to hate and fear a foreign government on the basis of what they read in the papers or hear on television and radio. But this negative view is persuasive to them also because it is congruous with a long-standing and largely uncriticized anticommunist, cold-war propaganda that has shaped the climate of opinion for decades.

Thus the press can effectively direct our perceptions when we have no information to the contrary and when the message seems congruent with earlier notions about these events (which themselves may be in part media created). In this way the original implant is also a reinforcement of earlier perceptions. Seemingly distinct reports about diverse events have a hidden continuity and a cumulative impact that again support previous views. To see this process as one of "minimal effects" because it merely reinforces existing views and does not change them is to overlook the fact that it was never intended to change them and was indeed designed to reinforce the dominant orthodoxy.

As to whether the negative view of the Sandinistas translates into support for a U.S. government policy of aggression against Nicaragua is yet another question. For an entirely different set of reasons, such as fear of loss of American lives, fear of a larger war, opposition to the draft and to the higher taxes needed to pay for war, people may be reluctant to go along with U.S. intervention. Yet the negative image about Nicaragua propagated by government and press does leave policymakers with a lot of room to carry out aggressive measures short of direct intervention by U.S. troops. So even if the press does not elicit total public support for a particular policy, it is still not without a substantial influence in creating a *climate of opinion* that allows the government to get away with a lot, and it prevents a competing opinion about Nicaragua from occupying the high ground in the political arena. Even if those who are antagonistic toward Nicaragua constitute but a minority of the public, members of Congress and other politicians find it difficult, if not impossible, to say a positive word about the Sandinista revolution given the *publicly visible opinion* created by media and government around that issue and given the way that opinion hooks into decades of anticommunist propaganda.[46]

If the press cannot mold our every opinion, it can frame the perceptual reality around which our opinions take shape. Here may lie the most important effect of the news media: they set the issue agenda for the rest of us, choosing what to emphasize and what to ignore or suppress, in effect, organizing much of our political world for us. *The media may not always be able to tell us what to think, but they are strikingly successful in telling us what to think about.*[47]

Along with other social, cultural, and educational agencies, the media teach us tunnel vision, conditioning us to perceive the problems of society as isolated particulars, thereby stunting our critical vision. Larger causalities are reduced to immediately distinct events, while the linkages of wealth, power, and policy go unreported or are buried under a congestion of surface impressions and personalities. There is nothing too essential and revealing that cannot be ignored by the American press and nothing too trivial and superficial that cannot be accorded protracted play.

In sum, the media set the limits on public discourse and public understanding. They may not always mold opinion but they do not always have to. It is enough that they create opinion visibility, giving legitimacy to certain views and illegitimacy to others. The media do the same to substantive issues that they do to candidates, raising some from oblivion and conferring legitimacy upon them, while consigning others to limbo. This power to determine the issue agenda, the information flow, and the parameters of political debate so that it extends from ultra-right to no further than moderate center, is if not total, still totally awesome.

BEYOND ORWELL'S *1984*

The news media operate with far more finesse than did the heartless, lacerating instruments of control portrayed in George Orwell's *1984*.[48] The picture Orwell draws of a Spartan barracks society with a centrally controlled electronic surveillance system barking exercise commands at a hapless, demoralized Winston Smith in his home, leaves no doubt in Winston's mind and ours that he is being oppressed. Something quite different goes on with our news media. For instance, for twenty-five years the United States portrayed the shah of Iran just as the State Department and the big oil companies wanted: a benign ruler and modernizer of his nation, rather than as the autocrat and plunderer he was. Hailed as a staunch ally of the West, the shah was photographed with presidents and senators and regularly interviewed on American television. Personality profiles and features were run on him and his family, making him a familiar and perfectly likable public personage—with not a word about the thousands of men, women, and children, the students, workers and peasants this person-able fellow had tortured and murdered. Here was an Orwellian inversion of the truth if ever there was one, but most of us didn't know it. When the Iranian students took over the U.S. embassy in 1979 and took American hostages, one of the demands was that the U.S. media publicize the shah's atrocities. For a short time, the American public was treated to some of the truth, to testimony by persons who had suffered unspeakable oppression. We heard of parents and children tortured in front of each other, including one youngster displayed before the cameras, who had had his arms chopped off in the presence of his father. It left many people shocked, including members of Congress who, like the rest of us, had been taught by the media to think of the shah as an upright person worthy of millions of dollars in U.S. aid and CIA assistance.

The sinister commandant who tortures Winston in Orwell's *1984* lets us know he is an oppressor. The vision of the future is of a boot pressing down on a human face, he tells his victim. The ideological control exercised in the United States today is far more insidious. Power is always more secure when cooptive, covert, and manipulative than when nakedly brutish. The support elicited through the control of minds is more durable than the support extracted at the point of a bayonet. The essentially undemocratic nature of the mainstream media, like the other business-dominated institutions of society, must be hidden behind a neutralistic, voluntaristic, pluralistic facade. "For manipulation to be most effective, evidence of its presence should be nonexistent. . . . It is essential, therefore, that people who are manipulated believe in the neutrality of their key social institutions," writes Herbert Schiller.[49]

If Big Brother comes to America, he will not be a fearsome, foreboding figure with a heart-chilling, omnipresent glare as in *1984*. He will come with a smile on his face, a quip on his lips, a wave to the crowd, and a press that (a) dutifully reports the suppressive measures he is taking to save the nation from internal chaos and foreign threat; and (b) gingerly questions whether he will be able to succeed.

Notes

1. Documentation and further discussion of these points may be found in my *Democracy for the Few*, 4th ed. (New York: St. Martin's Press, 1983).
2. Portions of this discussion are from an earlier essay of mine: "Monopoly Culture," *Political Affairs*, March 1985.
3. John Locke, *Treatise on Civil Government* (New York: Appleton-Century-

Crofts, 1937); also Adam Smith, *An Inquiry into the Nature and Causes of the Wealth of Nations* (Chicago: Encyclopedia Britannica, 1952), pp. 309, 311.

4. Stuart Ewen, *Captains of Consciousness* (New York: McGraw-Hill, 1976), pp. 13–19.

5. William Preston, Jr., *Aliens and Dissenters* (Cambridge, Mass.: Harvard University Press, 1963), p. 24.

6. Ewen, *Captains of Consciousness*, p. 19.

7. Antonio Gramsci, *Selections from the Prison Notebooks*, Quinton Hoare and Geoffrey Nowell-Smith, eds. (New York: International Publishers, 1971), p. 226.

8. Marguerite Michaels, "Walter Wants the News to Say a Lot More," *Parade*, March 23, 1980, p.4.

9. The quotation is from Walter Laqueur, "Foreign News Coverage: From Bad to Worse," *Washington Journalism Review*, June 1983, p. 34. Laqueur's article is a typical example of blaming the reporters, as is Barry Commoner's "Talking to a Mule," *Columbia Journalism Review*, January/February 1981.

10. This point is made by almost everyone who writes on the media. For an example see Doris Garber, *Mass Media and American Politics* (Washington, D.C.: Congressional Quarterly Press, 1980).

11. Kevin Kelley in the *Guardian*, December 26, 1984.

12. Consider just one of these areas: How do our reporters treat racism in sports? Hardly at all. See Richard Lapchick, *Broken Promises: Racism in American Sports* (New York: St. Martin's Press, 1984).

13. Kevin Kelley, "In Black and White—But Mostly White" *Guardian*, December 12, 1984.

14. "Women in the Wasteland Fight Back." Unpublished report by the National Organization of Women, Washington, D.C., 1974.

15. See the discussion on the media and crime in Robert Elias, *The Politics of Victimization* (New York: Oxford University Press, 1985).

16. *Ibid.*; and the studies cited therein.

17. Garner Ted Armstrong, Channel 9 News, Ithaca, N.Y., February 11, 1976.

18. CBS Evening News, September 10, 1984.

19. See chapter 5 for a detailed discussion of how the media report on workers and protestors.

20. Herbert Gans, "The Message Behind the News," *Columbia Journalism Review*, January/February 1979, p. 45.

21. Michael Grossman and Martha Kumar, *Portraying the President* (Baltimore: Johns Hopkins University Press, 1981).

22. The above facts and figures are from James Nathan Miller, "Ronald Reagan and the Techniques of Deception," *Atlantic Monthly*, February 1984, pp. 62–68.

23. *Editor & Publisher*, November 3, 1984.

24 Ben Bagdikian, *The Effete Conspiracy* (New York: Harper & Row, 1974) pp. 146, 148.

25. Judy Bachrach reporting in *Washington Weekly*, November 12, 1984.

26. John Kenneth Galbraith quoted in a speech by Ed Asner, president of the Screen Actors Guild, San Francisco, June 21, 1984.

27. John Corry, "How TV Dilutes Political Debates," *New York Times*, October 21, 1984. Although Corry says nothing about it, the same is true to a lesser degree of the printed media.

28. *Public Opinion*, June/July 1980.

29. Malcolm MacDougall, "The Barkers of Snake Oil Politics," *Politics Today*, January/February 1980, p. 35.

30. Garber, *Mass Media and American Politics*, pp. 169–180: and the discussion

in Jimmie Rex McClellan, *The Two-Party Monopoly* (Ph.D. dissertation, Institute for Policy Studies, Washington, D.C., 1984), p. 190.

31. W. Lance Bennett, *News, The Politics of Illusion* (New York: Longman, 1983), pp. 9–10.

32. McClellan, *Two-Party Monopoly;* also Frank Smallwood, *The Other Candidates: Third Parties in Presidential Elections* (Hanover, N.H.: University Press of New England, 1983), p. 108.

33. Simon W. Gerson, correspondence in the *Columbia Journalism Review,* March/April 1981.

34. Smallwood, *The Other Candidates.*

35. Commoner, "Talking to a Mule," p. 31.

36. McClellan, *Two-Party Monopoly,* p. 188.

37. Quoted in McClellan, *Two-Party Monopoly,* pp. 184–85; see also Smallwood, *The Other Candidates.*

38. U.S. Congress, Senate Committee on Commerce, *Hearings Before the Subcommittee on Communications,* March 1973, quoted and cited in McClellan, *Two-Party Monopoly,* pp. 188–89.

39. McClellan, *Two-Party Monopoly,* p. 209.

40. Ronald Van Doren, *Charting the Candidates '72* (New York: Pinnacle, 1972), p. 206.

41. Spock had five brief appearances on national television, each a few minutes or so, only one of which was prime time; see McClellan, *Two-Party Monopoly,* pp. 209–210.

42. For instance, the round-table discussion in *Harper's,* January 1985, p. 37*ff.*

43. P. Lazarsfeld, B. Berelson, and H. Gaudet, *The People's Choice.* (New York: Columbia University Press, 1948); C. I. Hovel et al., *Experiments on Mass Communication* (Princeton, N.J.: Princeton University Press, 1949).

44. S. Iyengar, M. Peters, and D. Kinder, "Experimental Demonstrations of the 'Not-So-Minimal' Consequences of Television News Programs," *American Political Science Review,* 76, December 1982, p. 852.

45. G. R. Funkhouser, "The Issues of the Sixties," *Public Opinion Quarterly,* 37, pp. 62–75; Michael MacKuen and Steven Coombs, *More than News* (Beverly Hills, Calif.: Sage Publications, 1981); also the essay by MacKuen therein.

46. See chapters 7,8, and 9 for treatment of media anticommunism.

47. The point was first made by B. Cohen, *The Press and Foreign Policy* (Princeton, N.J., Princeton University Press, 1963), p. 16; a similar point is made in Maxwell McCombs and Donald Shaw, *The Emergence of American Political Issues: the Agenda-Setting Function of the Press (St. Paul, Minn.: West, 1977), p. 5.*

48. Noam Chomsky, "1984: Orwell's and Ours," forthcoming in *The Thoreau Quarterly,* vol. 16.

49. Herbert Schiller, *The Mind Managers* (Boston: Beacon Press, 1973), p. 11.

2

"Freedom of the Press Belongs to the Man Who Owns One"

In the United States, we have been taught, wealth and power are widely distributed among a broad middle class. But as noted earlier, most American institutions, be they hospitals, museums, universities, businesses, banks, scientific laboratories, or mass media, are not owned and controlled by the middle class but by a relatively small number of corporate rich. When trying to understand the content and purposes of the media, this pattern of ownership takes on special significance.

THE MONEYED MEDIA

Freedom of the press, A. J. Liebling once said, is for those who own the presses. Who specifically owns the mass media in the United States? Ten business and financial corporations control the three major television and radio networks (NBC, CBS, ABC), 34 subsidiary television stations, 201 cable TV systems, 62 radio stations, 20 record companies, 59 magazines including *Time* and *Newsweek*, 58 newspapers including the *New York Times*, the *Washington Post*, the *Wall Street Journal*, and the *Los Angeles Times*, 41 book publishers, and various motion picture companies like Columbia Pictures and Twentieth-Century Fox. Three-quarters of the major stockholders of ABC, CBS, and NBC are banks, such as Chase Manhattan, Morgan Guaranty Trust, Citibank, and Bank of America.[1]

The overall pattern is one of increasing concentration of ownership and earnings. According to a 1982 *Los Angeles Times* survey, independent daily newspapers are being gobbled up by the chains at the rate of fifty or sixty a year. Ten newspaper chains earn over half of all newspaper revenues in this country. Five media conglomerates share 95 percent of the records and tapes market, with Warners and CBS alone controlling 65 percent of the market. Eight Hollywood studios account for 89 percent of U.S. feature film rentals. Three television networks earn over two-thirds of total U.S. television revenues. Seven paperback publishers dominate the mass market for books.[2]

Of the existing "independent" television and radio stations, 80 percent are network affiliates. Practically the only shows these "independents" produce are the local evening newscasts, the rest of their time being devoted to network programs. Most of the remaining stations are affiliated with the Public Broadcasting System (PBS), which receives almost all its money from the federal government and from corporate donors and their foundations, with a smaller share from listener subscriptions.

In the newspaper world the giant chains buy up not only independent papers but also other chains. Most of the large circulation dailies are owned by chains like Newhouse, Knight-Ridder, and Gannett. In its 1978 annual report, Gannett described itself as "a nationwide newspaper company with 78 dailies in 30 states." Less than 4 percent of American cities have competing newspapers under separate ownership; and in cities where there is a "choice," the newspapers offer little variety in editorial policy, being mostly conservative. Most of the "independents" rely on the wire services and big circulation papers for syndicated columnists and for national and international coverage. Like television stations, they are independent more in name than content.

As with any business, the mass media's first obligation is to make money for their owners.[3] And they do that very well. Although declining in numbers, newspapers continue to be a major profit-making business in the United States, employing over 432,000 people. Through mergers, packaged news service, union busting, and staff cutting, the larger conglomerates show handsome profits. The annual advertising revenues of newspapers in the United States ($15.6 billion in 1980) continue to top that of television and radio combined.[4] The press can hardly be critical of high corporation profits when it enjoys a rate of return on investments equal to or higher than that enjoyed by most oil companies.

The same pattern of high profits holds for television. In 1980, the three networks netted an all-time high of $8.8 billion from advertising revenues.[5] Corporations underwrite almost all prime-time shows—both on public and commercial television.

Like other businesses, the media corporations are diversified and multinational, controlling film, television, and radio outlets throughout Latin America, Asia, and the Middle East—as well as Europe and

North America.[6] In recent years, independent publishing houses have been bought up by the giant corporations who place a great emphasis on mass-market books and profits; thus, Simon & Schuster is owned by Gulf & Western, and Putnam by MCA. Other big corporations like Litton, IBM, Raytheon, Xerox, and major oil companies are acquiring media properties. "Is it beyond belief that most of the books in the racks a few years hence may be chosen for you, like television programs, by Mobil, Exxon, and the rest?"[7]

Many newspapers, magazines, networks, and movie studios are themselves giant corporations or subsidiaries of corporate conglomerates. Consider *Time* magazine—whose editors according to one ex-*Time* reporter, "have never been shy about its incestuous relations with the captains of industry."[8] *Time,* along with *Fortune, Sports Illustrated, Money, Life,* and *Discover* is owned by Time Inc., a colossal multinational corporation with revenues of $2.5 billion. Time Inc. also owns Time-Life Books; Little, Brown and Co.; the Book-of-the-Month Club; and large interests in publishing firms in Germany, France, Mexico and Japan. In addition, Time Inc. owns Temple Industries, making it one of the biggest landowners in the United States. It also owns a marketing data company, a television station in Michigan, Inland Container Corporation, Home Box Office, American Television and Communications Corporation, and Pioneer Press, which publishes suburban Chicago newspapers.

WHO'S AT THE TOP?

The networks, newspapers, magazines, and movie companies are run like all other corporations in the United States, by boards of directors composed mostly of persons drawn from the moneyed stratum of society. Representatives of the more powerful New York banks sit on the boards of major networks and control network fiduciary and debt-financing functions.

Many directors of radio, television, newspaper, and publishing companies are also partners or directors of banks, insurance companies, big law firms, universities, and foundations. Overall, the directors of media corporations "are linked with powerful business organizations, not with public interest groups; with management, not labor; with well-established think tanks and charities, not their grassroots counterparts."[9] Thus the Ford Motor Company—already exercising a palpable influence on American society with an annual business of $43 billion—has directors on the corporate boards of the *New York Times,* the *Washington Post,* and the *Los Angeles Times.*[10]

At the local level the pattern is the same. "Almost any newspaper is part of the establishment of any city," observes *Los Angeles Times* reporter William Trombley. (The same could be said of most local radio and television stations.) "This means the paper has natural sympathies with business interests and other vested interests in the community. . . . Independence and integrity are weakened further when newspaper executives accept positions on boards of directors, whether corporate boards or groups as seemingly innocent as Boy Scouts."[11]

Most of the wealthy business directors who sit on the boards of media corporations are unknown to the public. Others, however, are famous media tycoons, such as the late Henry Luce, William Randolph Hearst, Jr., Walter Annenberg, and Rupert Murdoch. Consider the last mentioned: Rupert Murdoch, an Australian, owns newspapers in major cities throughout that country, including Australia's only national daily, along with television stations, publishing houses, record companies, and a major airline. In Great Britain, Murdoch owns the *London Times;* and the *London Sunday Times;* two sex and scandal sheets with combined circulation of over 8 million; a string of special interest magazines; provincial newspapers; and paper manufacturing, printing, and newsprint transport firms. In the United States, the inexorable Murdoch has gained control of the *New York Post, New York Magazine* (including *Cue*), the *Village Voice*, the *Chicago Sun-Times*, and two dailies and some seventeen suburban weeklies in Texas.[12] By 1985 he was in the process of buying Metromedia's seven television stations in New York, Boston, and other major cities, giving him access to 21 percent of the U.S. viewing audience. According to its 1981 annual report, News Corporation Ltd., the parent corporation of Murdoch's empire, earned over $1 billion. Murdoch's own after-tax profits were $51.6 million.

Like Annenberg, Luce, and other media owners, Murdoch is a political conservative. His newspapers in Australia, Great Britain, and the United States, with one or two exceptions, back right-wing political candidates like Margaret Thatcher and Ronald Reagan and advocate strong probusiness, antilabor, antiwelfare state, and anticommunist views.

MANY VOICES, ONE CHORUS

While having an abundance of numbers and giving an appearance of diversity, the mass media actually are highly centralized outlets that proffer a remarkably homogenized fare. News services for dailies throughout the entire nation are provided by the Associated Press,

United Press International (which may soon merge with AP or go under), the *New York Times* and *Los Angeles Times-Washington Post* wire services, and several foreign wire services like Reuters. The ideological viewpoint of these news conduits are pretty much the same, "marked by a prefabricated standardization of news which is constricting and frightening."[13] A growing portion of newspaper space is given over to "soft" rather than "hard" news, to trivialized features and gossip items, to "celebrities in the limelight," to crime, scandal, and sensationalism. Television, radio, and newspaper coverage of national and local affairs is usually scant, superficial, and oriented toward "events" and "personalities," consisting of a few short "headline" stories and a number of conservative or simply banal commentaries and editorials.[14]

The same right-wing commentators, such as Evans and Novack, George Will, William Buckley, and James Kilpatrick, along with an occasional centrist or liberal like Joseph Kraft or Tom Wicker appear in papers coast to coast the same day. Many dailies in the smaller cities publish canned editorials and political cartoons supplied by the "syndicated word factories."

> Pouring into the editorial offices every day from the syndicates are pictures, news features, women's features, drawings, maps, cartoons, sports columns, political commentary, advice to the lovelorn (modernized for a swinging generation), horoscopes, farm advice, stamp and coin columns, dressmaking guides, household hints, book reviews, and film and theater criticism.[15]

Whichever newspaper one reads or television station one views, in whatever part of the United States, one is struck by the indistinguishable and immediately familiar quality of the news and views presented and of the people presenting them. One confronts a precooked, controlled, centralized, national news industry that is in sharp contrast to the "pluralistic diversity" of opinion that is said to prevail in the United States.

To think that information and viewpoints circulate in "a free market of ideas" is to conjure up a misleading metaphor. A "market" suggests a place of plenitude, with the consumer moving from stall to stall as at any bazaar, sampling and picking from an array of wares. But the existing media market of ideas is more like the larger economic market of which it is a part: oligopolistic, standardized, and most accessible to those who possess vast amounts of capital, or who hold views that are pleasing to the possessors of capital.

To be sure, in this controlled market there is a vast array of publications—for motorcycle owners, dog owners, and homeowners, for brides and singles, for fishing, hunting, and dating, for camping and gardening, for weight watching and weightlifting, for karate and judo, for sailing, swimming, and jogging, for auto mechanics, auto racing, horse racing, and horse raising, for music fans, movie fans, television fans, soap opera devotees, and computer fanatics, for just about every conceivable diversion and taste. Relatively few of these have anything to do with meaningful political and social affairs. Most are devoted to mass media distractions and mass market consumerism. The diversity of publications, both serious and trivial, should not be mistaken for a plurality of ideas and ideologies, nor a wealth of political information. As one group of scholars noted after an extensive study: "Protection against government is now not enough to guarantee that a [person] who has something to say shall have a chance to say it. The owners and managers of the press determine which person, which facts, which version of the facts, and which ideas shall reach the public."[16]

IS IT ALL ECONOMICS?

More than a century ago Karl Marx observed that those who control the material means of production also control the mental means of production. So in every epoch the ruling ideas are the ideas of the ruling class. Indeed, it seems so today. Viewpoints supported by money have no trouble gaining mass exposure and sympathetic media treatment, while those offensive to moneyed interests languish either for want of the costly sums needed to reach a vast public or because of the prohibitions exercised by media owners and management. In a word, the mass media are a class-dominated media—bound by the parameters of ownership in a capitalist society.

The media play a twofold role. While seen as something apart from business, they actually *are* a big business. But like the "nonprofit" churches, universities, law schools, professional associations, arts and political parties, the media also are an institution geared for ideological control. Their role is to reproduce the conditions of social and class stability, to carry out the monopoly management of image and information, *but in such a way as to engineer an appearance of class neutrality and an appearance of independence from the corporate class that owns them.*

Some persons would deny that oligopolistic ownership fosters a uniformity of ideas. They argue that even if the media do show a concentration of ownership, this does not explain everything about their content, for mass communication is influenced by an array of social, cultural, and psychological forces. For instance, the professional values of journalists ensure a good deal of independence in the media. To focus exclusively on the economic factor is to lapse into a simplistic materialist reductionism. Economic power is not everything, the argument goes.

No one says economic power is everything, but it is quite a lot. And having taken note of the other factors, need we then hastily dismiss the material (and ideological) class interests that result from capitalist ownership and control, as do more orthodox writers who prefer to blame the media's "shortcomings" on inept reporters, an ignorant public, and cultural biases? Social experience is no less economic because it is also cultural and psychological. Life does not come in neatly divided and mutually exclusive subject areas as do academic departments. The "cultural" is not something to be counterposed as distinct from, and competitive with, the economic. How could there not be a linkage between cultural and economic interests? How could there be a viable society in which the two were chronically apart and opposed to each other?

Most things are simultaneously cultural and economic. An automobile, a television advertisement, a board of trustees, a cosmetic kit, and a tool kit are all cultural *and* economic. The technology, commodities, services, institutions, and systems of ownership and command have both a cultural and economic dimension, and for that matter a psychological one as well. Indeed, it would be hard to imagine any of the dimensions existing in a context devoid of the others. This does not mean they operate with perfect coordination, but it is time we stopped thinking about them as being mutually exclusive and conceptually competitive.

Economic power does not automatically translate into cultural hegemony, but it makes such hegemony much more likely. Those who own the media must make conscious efforts in selecting the right managers and editors, and setting down proper guidelines and permissible boundaries—so that they might exercise maximum control with a minimum of direct and naked intervention. More on this in the next chapter.

Notes

1. Benjamin Compaine, ed., *Who Owns the Media? Concentration of Ownership in the Mass Communication Industry* (New York: Harmony Books, 1979); Peter Dreier and Steve Weinberg, "Interlocking Directorates," *Columbia Journalism Review*, November/December 1979, pp. 51–68. Christopher Sterling and Timothy Haight, *The*

Mass Media (New York: Praeger, 1978); *In These Times,* December 16–22, 1981; Peter Brosnan, "Who Owns the Networks?" *Nation,* November 25, 1978, pp. 561, 577–79. For an earlier study see George Seldes, *Lords of the Press,* 2nd ed., (New York: Messner, 1938).

2. Compaine, *Who Owns the Media?;* Sterling and Haight, *The Mass Media; Alternative Media,* Spring 1981.

3. Deidre Carmody, "More Newspapers Change Hands, With the Role of Chains Increasing," *New York Times,* February 15, 1977. Carmody notes that the primary concern of the big-chain buyers is profits.

4. *Washington Post,* September 8, 1981.

5. *Washington Post,* August 10, 1981.

6. Herbert Schiller, *Mass Communication and American Empire* (New York: Augustus Kelley, 1969); and Herbert Schiller, *Communication and Cultural Domination* (New York: Pantheon, 1978).

7. Leonard Lewin, "Publishing Goes Multinational," *Nation,* May 13, 1978; *New York Times,* May 18, 1977; Compaine, *Who Owns the Media?*

8. John Tirman, "Doing Time," *Progressive,* August 1981, p. 48.

9. Dreier and Weinberg, "Interlocking Directorates," p. 51; Compaine, *Who Owns the Media?;* also the Editors, "Dollar Journalism," *Nation,* November 11, 1978, p. 493.

10. Dreier and Weinberg, "Interlocking Directorates," p.52.

11. *Ibid.,* p. 68; also Edward Hayes, "The Mass Media and Metropolitan Politics: The Functioning of a Controlled Press," (unpublished manuscript, Athens, Ohio, 1974).

12. Thomas Hayes, "Murdoch's Publishing Empire," *New York Times,* February 9, 1981.

13. James Aronson, *The Press and the Cold War* (Boston: Beacon Press, 1973), p. 19.

14. For a critique of local news shows see Ron Powers, *The Newscasters* (New York: St. Martin's Press, 1977).

15. Aronson, *The Press and the Cold War,* p. 19.

16. Report by the Commission on Freedom of the Press, quoted in Robert Cirino, *Don't Blame the People* (New York: Vintage, 1972), p. 47.

3

Who Controls the News? The Myths of Independence and Objectivity

Does ownership of the media transfer into control over information? Or are journalists free to write what they want? Reporters themselves offer contradictory testimony on this question; some say they are independent agents while others complain of control and censorship.

CONDITIONAL AUTONOMY AND SELF-CENSORSHIP

Mainstream journalists are accorded a certain degree of independence if they demonstrate their ability to produce copy that is not only competently crafted but also free of any politically discordant tones. Indeed, competence itself is measured in part by one's ability to report things from an ideologically acceptable perspective, defined as "balanced" and "objective." In a word, journalists are granted autonomy by demonstrating that they will not use it beyond acceptable limits. They are independent agents in a conditional way, free to report what they like as long as their superiors like what they report.

Journalists (like social scientists and others) rarely doubt their own objectivity even as they faithfully echo the established political vocabularies and the prevailing politico-economic orthodoxy. Since they do not cross any forbidden lines, they are not reined in. So they are likely to have no awareness they are on an ideological leash. This is why some journalists insist they are free agents. Only when they stray off the beaten path is the pressure from above likely to be felt.

If every reporter had to be policed continually by superiors when producing the news, the system could not maintain its democratic appearance. As it turns out, there is no necessity for editors and owners to exercise constant control; intermittent control will do.

There is no need for ubiquitous supervision, just occasional intervention. The *anticipation* that superiors might disapprove of this or that story is usually enough to discourage a reporter from writing it, or an editor from assigning it. Many of the limitations placed on reporting come not from direct censorship but from self-censorship, from journalists who design their stories so as to anticipate complaints from superiors. This anticipatory avoidance makes direct intervention by owners a less frequent necessity and leaves the journalist with a greater feeling of autonomy than might be justified by the actual power relationship.

"Some intervention by owners is direct and blunt," observes veteran journalist Ben Bagdikian. "But most of the screening is subtle, some not even occurring at a conscious level, as when subordinates learn by habit to conform to owners' ideas."[1] Likewise, Gans notes that self-censorship "can also be unconscious, in which case journalists may not be aware they are responding to pressure."[2] Gans mentions one reporter who considered arguing with an editor for deleting an uncomplimentary fact about the CIA "but inasmuch as too much disagreement with superiors types people as 'cranks,' she decided to save her scarce political capital for an issue about which she felt more strongly."[3]

Many people who learn to hold their fire eventually end up never finding occasion to do battle. After awhile anticipatory avoidance becomes a kind of second nature. Rather than seeing self-censorship as a more subtle form of censorship, journalists will describe themselves as "realistic," "pragmatic," or "playing it cool."[4] In their ability to live in a constant, if not always conscious, state of anticipatory response while maintaining an appearance of independence, newspeople are not much different from subordinates in other hierarchical organizations.

When determining what to treat as news, media organizations often take their cues from one another, moving in a kind of rough unison, a phenomenon that has been called "pack journalism." The pack may run in one direction or it may suddenly stampede in another. But it is not entirely free to roam as it chooses, for past images influence present ones, and if a media opinion already exists about what is important and true, it usually will shape subsequent reporting on the topic.

If an opinion prevails for any great length of time without benefit of critical examination or hard evidence, it is usually because of a durable ideological underpinning. Opinion inertia is easier to sustain if it is rolling with, rather than against, the ideological tilt of the land. By definition, opinion inertia favors the existing framework of institution, power, and persuasion and generally operates with conservative effect.

And pack journalism itself is usually a conformist journalism. But where does the conformity come from? Journalists are exposed to the same communities, schools, universities, graduate schools, popular culture—and media—that socialize other Americans into the dominant belief system. They react to much the same news that inundates their audiences. They seldom look to the radical press for a different viewpoint or for information that has gone unreported in the mainstream media. The establishment biases they inject into the news reinforce their preconceived view of the world. *With cyclical effect, they find confirmation for the images they report in the images they have already created.*

This is not to imply that everything they write and say will automatically please their superiors. There is always the danger that a reporter or editor might report something that does not rest well with those at the top. On such occasions owners will rein in editors and editors will curb reporters. The radical writer James Aronson relates how as a young reporter for the *New York Post* in the 1940s, he was asked by his news editor if he was disappointed in not receiving an assistant editorship that ought to have been his.

> I was about to say, "Yes, but . . . " when he spoke in the Victorian manner of his mellow mood, "You were not advanced, my young friend, because your political views are at variance with those held by the managers of this enterprise and therefore not acceptable to them." . . . He was telling me, of course, that there was still time to change my views if I had any thought about getting to the top. But I think we both knew what my answer had to be.[5]

Thinking back to when he worked as a reporter for the *New York Times* in 1947, Aronson again recalls:

> My political and social philosophy had made it increasingly difficult to write "objective" stories for a newspaper committed to United States policy, which was relentlessly developing the Cold War. A censorship so subtle that is was invisible affected everyone on the staff. The "approach" (it was never a vulgar "line") was made clear in casual conversations, in the editing of copy for "clarity," and in the deletion of any forthright interpretation as "emotionalism." Work became a conflict with conscience, although there was never an open challenge to conscience.[6]

Reflecting on his experiences with the *Post* and the *Times,* Aronson concluded: "The surest way to isolation was the espousal of unpopular radical views."[7] Another former journalist relates his experiences with a *Time* magazine news bureau:

> At one time or another those of us out in the field would be sent a suggestion, really a directive from the central office, maybe originating

from [Henry] Luce himself, to cover a story or play up some angle. . . . If I protested and said that the suggestion didn't make sense, or was loaded, or presumed something that just was not true, they would say, "Oh, of course, sure, use your own judgment." There was a big show of not forcing [anyone] to obey a direct order. But after I balked a few more times, I found myself ignored and then reassigned."[8]

The consequence of this kind of control is that "coverage is limited and certain questions never get asked," according to Len Ackland, a *Chicago Tribune* writer. Reporters think twice before delving into sensitive areas. "They worry about the editing. They worry about being removed from choice beats, or being fired."[9] Or they end up resigning as did Malcolm Browne who said he left the television industry in 1966 because he was unable to communicate the deeper aspects of the Vietnam War to the American public. When dealing with the economic and political problems relating to the war, he often found that "the producer switches you off and cuts the footage that he deems most illustrative of what you're talking about."[10]

In 1949, correspondent Aslan Humbaraci resigned from the *New York Times* because his journalistic efforts in Turkey met with systematic hostility from Turkish officials and from the U.S. embassy and U.S. military mission in that country. Worst of all, he complained, his reporting in the *Times* itself, "when it was not completely suppressed, was cut, rewritten, buried somewhere in the back pages or distorted, if it did not happen to fit in with State Department policy." In his letter of resignation to the *Times,* Humbaraci wrote:

> The suppression of civil liberties [in Turkey], the brutal treatment of peasants by a ruthless gendarmerie, the police terror in the towns, the revolt of the peasants in remote Anatolian villages, the arrest and imprisonment and torturing of political prisoners, the persecution of intellectuals, the scandalous abuse by officials, and the offical support extended to the extreme right wing have found no place in the columns of the *New York Times.* Further, I cannot remember any anti-Russian news from any sources in Turkey that has not been published in the *Times*—especially news depicting Russia as Turkey's enemy and the menace to Turkey's existence.[11]

Humbaraci wrote that letter in 1949. The *Times's* reporting on Turkey has not changed significantly since then.

James O'Shea, former business editor of the *Des Moines Register,* argues that the media's pattern of business ownership and interlocking directorates are "going to affect the reporter, I don't care who he is; or it will affect his editors. You're more cautious. That's not the way it should be, but that's what happens. A lot of reporters and editors will tell you that it has no effect on them, but I don't believe it."[12] Finally, Chris Welles, a former journalist and now director of a program on business journalism at Columbia University, comments: "I daresay anyone who has been in the business for more than a few months can cite plenty of examples of editorial compromises due to pressure, real and imagined, from publishers, owners, and advertisers."[13]

WHO REPORTS?

The image of the news reporter propagated by the Hollywood films of an earlier era is of a tough-talking, two-fisted, regular guy, more at home in a bar than a country club, scornful of bluebloods and stuffed shirts. With a fedora shoved back on his head and sleeves rolled up, he gives his typewriter a furious two-finger pounding, pausing only to snap his suspenders and gulp coffee from a cardboard container, showing himself every inch the courageous investigator, ready to "blow this town wide open" with revelations that rock City Hall and other venal powers.

Turning from Hollywood fantasy to reality, we find that most journalists were raised in upper-middle-class homes. Only one in five come from blue-collar or low-status white-collar families. Almost all have college degrees and a majority have attended graduate school. Despite journalism's reputation as a low-paid profession, most newspeople have family incomes that put them in the top 10 percent bracket. Network correspondents, senior editors, and producers make considerably more, usually well into the high six-figure range. As of 1983, evening news anchorpersons and commentators like Dan Rather, Tom Brokaw, and Barbara Walters reportedly earned between $1 million and $2 million a year.[14]

As in other fields, so in the world of journalism: "knowing and pleasing the right people, and coming from a prestigious background do not hurt in the competition for promotions."[15] Syndicated columnists like Stewart and Joseph Alsop, William Buckley, and George Will often start out with personal wealth or diplomas from elite schools or important political friends and business connections—or all of the above. The apprenticeship they serve in the lower ranks is usually a brief one, if any. Jonathan Schell's meteoric rise from college graduate to a leading New Yorker writer was helped by his Harvard background, a father who was a successful Manhattan lawyer, and a family friend, William Shawn, editor of the New Yorker.[16] Benjamin Bradlee's family connections with multimillionaire Eugene Meyer helped him get a reporter's job on the *Washington Post,* owned by Meyer. And while still a young reporter, Bradlee was invited into his publisher's social circle, not a usual practice, but Bradlee came from "aristocratic northeastern stock," a family of bankers. Bradlee later became Washington bureau chief of *Newsweek* (owned by the Grahams) and was then picked by Katharine Graham (Eugene Meyer's daughter) to be managing editor of the *Post.*[17]

Most newspeople lack contact with working-class people, have a low opinion of labor unions, and know very little about people outside their own social class.[18] A 1982 survey found that, by large majorities, journalists oppose state ownership of major corporations and believe private enterprise is a fair system, and deregulation of business a good thing for the country. Most newspeople, however, also are liberal in their choice of presidential candidates and in their belief that government should assist the poor and guarantee employment for all. Forty-six percent agree that American economic exploitation has contributed to Third World poverty, and 50 percent think that the main purpose of U.S. foreign policy has been to protect American business interests—views that rarely, if ever, find their way into their news reports and commentaries. Newspeople also tend to be liberal in their personal opinions regarding abortion, gay rights, environmental protection, and other "cultural" issues.[19]

In regard to economic and class issues, however, most journalists are educated into a world view that supports rather than opposes the existing corporate system. Most journalism schools offer politically conventional curricula. Under the name of "objectivity" and "professionalism," a journalist student can easily go through an entire program without ever raising critical questions about how and why the capitalist economic system functions and malfunctions as it does. Corporations and foundations have endowed journalism schools with courses and programs designed to make newspeople "more understanding" of the business viewpoint. For most journalists, who have only a feeble grasp of economics, such programs influence their perceptions.

Numerous conservative think tanks like the American Enterprise Institute and the Hoover Institute send pamphlets, "expert" reports, and other publications to newspeople across the nation, alerting them to the harmful effects of government regulations, corporate taxes, and labor unions, and making a case for bigger defense spending, a stronger national security state, and a more militant foreign policy. Even if this flood of material does not win the hearts and minds of all journalists, it is read by many and regularly referred to in their stories and news analyses. As the sociologist Peter Drier notes, the massive and unrelenting inundation of business propaganda is likely to affect the consciousness of the working press—especially in the absence of an alternative view of equal currency.[20]

Prestigious awards and prizes, funded by big corporations, are given every year for excellence in business reporting. For instance, the University of Missouri School of Journalism awards a prize for energy reporting that is subsidized by the National Gas Association. And the Media Awards for Economic Understanding, which in one year received 1400 entries from journalists, is supported by Chambion International Corporation.[21] The Bagehot Fellowship, "an intensive program of study at Columbia University for journalists interested in improving their understanding of economics, business and finance," has featured such guest speakers as Paul Volcker, head of the Federal Reserve System; Donald Regan, formerly secretary of the Treasury and subsequently chief of staff to President Reagan; financier Felix Rohatyn; and David Rockefeller.[22] Since editors are inclined to judge and promote reporters according to the number of awards they win, there is no shortage of eager journalistic applicants. These corporate-backed awards and training programs help "to shape the kinds of stories journalists pursue and the kinds of standards that editors recognize."[23]

Business corporations offer other more familiar enticements, such as dinners, parties, gifts, and free trips to luxury hotels for "conferences" that boost the wonders of this or that industry. Peter Drier notes that newspeople claim they are free to write whatever they please about these junkets, but few ever produce critical reports. Most newspaper sections, such as food, auto, real estate, travel, fashion, sports, and business, offer little more than puffery and promotional copy, with stories initiated by business, written by sympathetic reporters, and rewarded with advertising revenue, observes Drier.[24]

Persons of almost any political persuasion can get jobs at the lower entry ranks of journalism (unless they have gained some notoriety as radicals or have other credentials that markedly indicate political deviancy.) The process of selection becomes more ideologically exacting the higher one goes up the communication hierarchy. Above the ordinary reporters stand the more prominent and influential columnists and commentators who are drawn from that portion of the spectrum ranging from arch-conservative to mildly liberal. "From the ideological point of view," observes Noam Chomsky, "the mass media are almost 100 percent 'state capitalist'. . . . Here in the United States there is an astonishing degree of ideological uniformity for such a complex country. Not a single socialist voice in the mass media, not even a timid one; perhaps there are some marginal exceptions, but I cannot think of any, offhand."[25]

A CHAIN OF COMMAND: EDITORS, PRODUCERS, AND OWNERS

Actual responsibility for daily (or weekly) news production rests not with reporters but with the managing newspaper editors and the radio and television producers. Without having to answer to reporters, they can cut, rewrite, or kill any story they choose, subject only to "the advice, consent and final review" of their executive superiors.[26] The top news executives meet on a weekly or sometimes daily basis with editors and producers in order to keep tabs on story selection. News and corporate executives "have virtually unlimited power and can suggest, select, and veto stories whenever they choose. But because they have other duties and because they are expected to abide by the corporate division of labor . . . they do not exercise their power on a day-to-day basis."[27] Nor do they need to since editors and producers are likely to do what their supervisors want anyway. As one editor told Gans, "it is not what [the executive] will do or will veto, but what we expect that he will do or veto; that's his influence."[28] Daily censorship is made unnecessary by the anticipatory responses of self-censorship. "There are hundreds of dailies," concludes Bagdikian, "in which editorials on certain subjects are as predictable as a catechism, whose news departments are designed to overreact or underreact to certain kinds of news, notably financial and political, not because of incompetence or sensationalism but because of the impulse to create a picture closer to the dreams of the ownership."[29]

Journalists are subjected to on-the-job ideological conditioning conducted informally through hints and casual inferences that masquerade as "professional" advice. Thus they might be admonished not to get too "emotionally involved" and not to lose their "objectivity," when they are producing copy that is disturbing to persons of wealth and power. Veteran newspeople "have remarkably finely tuned antennae for finding out the limits" to which they can go, remarked one former reporter.[30] "Some intervention by owners is direct and blunt," writes Bagdikian. "But most of the screening is subtle, some not even occurring at a conscious level, as when subordinates learn by habit to conform to owners' ideas."[31]

When *Washington Post* editorial writer Roger Wilkins once asked Meg Greenfield, then deputy editor of the *Post* editorial page, about a particularly controversial subject, she said, "I don't know much. I'm like you. I've never been a 'cause' person." Wilkins, a dedicated progressive and the only Black editorial writer on the staff, pondered her comment:

That was either a serious misreading of me or Meg was gently instructing me in the preferred approach to the work at hand. Other things she mentioned at other times confirmed the latter suspicion. Higher passions were tolerable foibles in minor associates, but not appropriate for more serious members of our [editorial] staff, the principal shapers of the *Post's* opinion. . . . We would judge each day's events as they were presented to us in a rational case-by-case basis in a framework of intellectualism that favored the credibility and stability of our institutions.[32]

Wilkins eventually left the *Post,* but Greenfield was promoted to editorial page editor.

If, with all the hints, journalists still sometimes report things in a way they should not, direct interposition from organization superiors or sometimes advertisers becomes necessary. In the final analysis, the news is not what reporters report but what editors and owners decide to print. Going back some years, a former employee of *Time* remembers how Whittaker Chambers, foreign news editor of that magazine in the summer of 1944, repeatedly suppressed dispatches from *Time's* overseas correspondents. Chambers tailored the news "to make it conform to his own right-wing view of world affairs." "So many of John Hersey's stories from Moscow were suppressed that he stopped sending news and confined his cables to accounts of Shostakovich's newest symphony and other cultural events. Reporting from China, Theodore H. White saw his criticisms of Chiang Kai-shek's autocratic regime replaced with encomiums of Chiang as a defender of democratic principles."[33] *Time's* researchers protested the distortions but Chambers prevailed, for he was producing stories his publisher, Henry Luce, liked.

More recently, U.S. reporters in Nicaragua voiced their frustration at being unable to get any stories printed that rubbed too hard against the prevailing view of a repressive, aggressive Sandinista government.[34] In time, as the example of John Hersey in Moscow shows, reporters give up and censor themselves.

Editors, too, must answer to top executives and owners. To maintain an appearance of their own editorial integrity, they sometimes speak in their master's voice. Former managing editor of the *New York Times* Turner Catledge notes how he used to pass publisher Arthur Hays Sulzberger's numerous criticisms to reporters and editors as if they were his own so that his staff would not feel "the publisher was constantly looking over their shoulders. In truth, however, he was."[35]

The top news executives are themselves subject to the judgments of the ruling corporate directors and owners who exercise final monetary and corporate power and, when necessary, final judgment over the way the news is handled and over who is hired or fired at any of the levels below them. Except for a few liberal publishers, the upper echelons are monopolized by persons of mainstream conservative and right-wing persuasion. As one writer observes:

> Through the decision-making echelons of the three great bureaucracies of broadcasting—from the level of network president upward—there is not a person who I would judge is a liberal in the sense that, say, Senators McGovern, Fulbright, and Javits are considered to be, although there were several who identified with the Western conservatism of Ronald Reagan. The ruling powers at the networks are decidedly Establishment in their politics and in general closer to the right of the political center than to the left.[36]

"In the real world of the newsroom and board room," asserts Bagdikian, "the news is fiddled with by management, either crudely through direct intervention or more subtly by picking editors who know what is expected of them."[37] Otis Chandler, publisher of the *Los Angeles Times,* readily admits there exists an ideological selection process: "I'm the chief executive. I set policy and I'm not going to surround myself with people who disagree with me. In general areas of conservatism vs. liberalism, I surround myself with people who generally see the way I do. . . . I consider myself middle-of-the-road and I feel most of my editors are centrists."[38]

Infused with notions of professional "integrity," some editors will deny they are the objects of corporate ideological control. Faced with an organizational chart that concentrates power in the hands of publisher Arthur Ochs Sulzberger, *Times* editors still insisted that power was widely diffused and that they had a good deal of influence in imposing their own professional standards of objectivity on the publisher. One editor claimed that if Sulzberger ran the paper from the top down, "I don't think there's anyone on the present staff who would be staying." "If the publisher told the managing editor every day what to run on page one, I can't think of Abe Rosenthal staying very long under those conditions." he maintained.[39]

What this editor was overlooking was that Sulzberger would not hire nor keep anyone he might have to censor every day. Managing editor Abe Rosenthal, the man who complained about the *Times's* "left liberal" and "advocacy" tendencies in the later 1960s, regularly killed copy in order to "pull the paper back to center" (his own words). Rosenthal's idea of "center" included a more friendly and positive view of corporate business, big defense spending, and U.S. counterinsurgency and anticommunist efforts in various parts of the world. This "center" was a place on the political spectrum not far from where the White House, the State Department, the Pentagon, and the giant corporations stood. There was no likelihood of Rosenthal being overridden every day by Sulzberger since he was doing very much what the publisher wanted. So the managing editor performed "independently" of his publisher, that is, without daily interference, because such interference was not necessary. But we must not mistake this kind of conditional autonomy for actual autonomy; there is no reason to believe that Rosenthal could have opposed Sulzberger even if he had ever wanted to.

Ironically enough, the editor who offered this dubious example of how professional integrity operates at the *Times* was himself subsequently transferred to a less responsible post as part of a major shakeup designed to remove people who were guilty of "anti-business bias" and "advocacy."[40] He did not resign in a fit of professional integrity.

Owners often make a show of not interfering in an editor's independence, but "the suggestions of powerful superiors are, in fact, thinly veiled orders, requiring circumlocutions in which commands are phrased as requests."[41] Sometimes suggestions made by owners can be brushed aside by editors, but not too often. And if the owner insists, then the editor obeys. Gans writes: "Older journalists at *Time* told me that Henry Luce used to flood them with story suggestions, many of which were ignored; but those he deemed most important and urgent were not."[42]

If an editor proves recalcitrant, the owner's velvet glove comes off. In the early 1950s Joseph Pulitzer, publisher of the *St. Louis Post-Dispatch*, decided that his liberal editors were being too critical of the anticommunist escapades of Senator Joseph McCarthy. Eventually Pulitzer's urgent requests ("Please, please, please lay off the McCarthy hearings. . . .") were replaced by a direct and final command that silenced his editors: "I must ask that the words 'McCarthy' or 'McCarthyism' or any oblique reference to either shall not appear on the editorial page without my specific approval in the issues of December 7, 8, 9, 10, 11, and 12."[43]

H. B. DuPont and his associates, owners of the Wilmington, Delaware, *Morning News* and *Evening Journal,* issued these memoranda to their editors:

· On an editorial praising President Kennedy's Supreme Court appointments: "Why should we devote space to one who is an enemy of private enterprise and the capitalistic system?
· When [one DuPont executive] objected to running a letter to the editor signed by sixty-four University of Delaware students favoring integration, the editors asked if they should close the column to all letters from students. His answer was, "Yes."

DOING TIME AT *TIME*

Reporters and researchers gather information and compile "files"; writers read the files and construct highly-stylized prose; senior editors edit and frequently rewrite the writers' version; "top" editors edit the senior editors' copy. . . . Even the corporate brass will get in on the act now and then. . . .

By fragmenting the functions of journalism, *Time* fragments responsibility for content—and vastly enlarges the capacity for editorial control.

"The bias in any *Time* story," says one *Time* writer, "begins with the query. From the moment it is sent out, the shape of the story has been established." . . . "There is a certain amount of freedom we have," observes a veteran of the Washington bureau, "but that really works two ways. You can soothe your conscience by throwing in a few opinions of your own at the end of your file, but you know that these will usually be discarded." The chief of correspondents, he adds, is careful about whom he hires and where a reporter is assigned. Effective dissent is checked at any of several junctions in the system, and frustration in the bureaus is an oft-heard refrain. Says one reporter, "It's really a masturbatory job.". . .

Stuart Schoffman, who was a *Time* writer for four years, now describes that role as one of "an apparatchik in the service of the corporation's ideas. It is only in retrospect that I realized I was mouthing opinions not my own."

John Tirman, "Doing Time," Progressive, *August 1981, p. 51.*

· On an editorial noting that French Socialists had outmaneuvered French Communists: "Should the *News-Journal* take the position of favoring actions of any Socialist Party? I believe it is a grave error for a DuPont to follow the philosophy of the ultra-liberal whose objectives are destruction of capitalistic systems."[44]

C. Peter Jorgensen, publisher of Century Newspapers Inc., advised all editors of his three Boston-area weeklies that he did

not intend to pay for paper and ink, or staff time and effort, to print news or opinion pieces which in any way might be construed to lend support, comfort, assistance, or aid to political candidates who are opposed by Republican candidates in the November election. You are specifically instructed to submit any and all political stories which mention any candidate in any race and any photographs, letters, editorials, cutlines, or any other kind of written material whatsoever relative to the election or elected officials and their record, to the publisher prior to publication. . . . If this is unclear in any way, resolve every question in your mind with a decision NOT to print.[45]

No state censor could have been more explicit and more thorough. When publishers ram their dictates down their editors' throats, the editors learn to swallow; but occasionally one of them quits. The publisher of News-Herald Newspapers, Inc., which puts out newspapers in five economically depressed communities in Michigan, wrote a memo provoking editor John Cusumano to resign. It read: "From now on plant closings, business failures and layoffs will not appear on the front page of any of our newspapers. It will be our policy to aggressively support, promote, and report business organizations within our circulation area and/or those business organizations who support us with their advertising."[46]

It is a rare event when a journalistic defender of capitalism stops pretending he or she is an independent agent and explicitly admits that a class power relationship exists in the media. In 1983 a conservative coulumnist for the *Washington Post,* James Kilpatrick, did just that in regard to a controversy at Howard University. It seems that after giving prominent coverage to a sex discrimination case involving the university, the editor of the Howard student newspaper, Janice McKnight, was expelled, because of discrepancies in her admission application of four years before. McKnight charged that the action constituted a violation of freedom of the press. Entering the fray in one of his columns, Kilpatrick allowed that McKnight "was fired because of her editorial insistence" and then asserted that "Howard's president clearly had the power to remove her as editor." Warming to his subject, Kilpatrick continued:

> Where did McKnight get the right and power to publish whatever she damn well pleases? The answer is, nowhere. The Hilltop is not her paper; she has invested not a dime in its costs of publication. Like every other student editor, she is here today and gone tomorrow. . . . I was for 17 years editor of a major newspaper, but I never had the slightest misapprehension of any "free press rights." If my publisher, in his gentle way, said that we ought to think a while before running one of my fire-eating editorials, that was it; the piece didn't run. It was his paper, not mine. . . . If student journalists want unabridged freedom of the press, their course of action is clear: let them buy their press and move off campus. Until that happens, let them grow up to what life in the real world is all about."[47]

Here Kilpatrick admits, indeed, proclaims, that contrary to the established mythology, he was never editor of a free and independent press. His publisher exercised prior censorship over his editorials. All of which is just fine because freedom of the press, for Kilpatrick, is not a political right but a prerogative of property and wealth. He is correct when he concludes that's "what life in the real world is all about." It is just not often mainstream newspeople so forthrightly announce such truths about the real world.

There is, then, nothing mysterious about who controls the ideological direction and political content of the news. As with any profit-making corporation, the chain of command runs from the top down, with final authority in the hands of those who own or who represent the ownership interests of the company. As Gans writes, "News organizations are not democratic; in fact, they are described as militaristic by some journalists. . . ."[48] The links that bind reporter to editor to news executive to corporate executive to board members to banker are not just work relationships but class power relationships.

HE WHO PAYS THE PIPER

Along with the ideological and informational constraints imposed by media executives and owners, the working press must reckon with the pressures exerted by corporate advertisers. Consider the *New York Times's* coverage of the auto safety issue. During 1973 and 1974 when the automobile industry was pressuring Congress to repeal the seatbelt and air-bag regulations that might have saved between 5,000 and 10,000 lives a year, the *Times* ran stories that were, as one *Times* staff person admitted, "more or less put together by the advertisers."[49] *Times* publisher Arthur Ochs Sulzberger openly admitted that he urged his editors to present the industry position in coverage of safety and auto pollution because, he said, it "would affect the advertising." The auto industry was a major newspaper advertiser, responsible for about 18 percent of ad revenues in 1973 and 1974.[50]

The notion that the media are manipulated by those with money is dismissed by media apologists as a "conspiracy theory" or "devil theory," but there is nothing conspiratorial about it. Being the people who pay the bills, advertisers openly regard their influence over media content as something of a "right." Media executives like Frank Stanton, CBS president, readily say as much, "Since we are advertiser-supported we must take into account the general objective and desires of advertisers as a whole."[51]

When deciding on which media to spend their billions, corporate advertisers are directed in part by ideological preferences. Deprived of advertisers, progressive publications like *Mother Jones,* the *Nation,* and the *Progressive* are always facing insolvency, never able to launch the kind of massive mailing and mainstream campaigns that might build up their circulations. Needless to say, it is the corporate system's journalist defenders and apologists, not its critics, who attract the moneyed advertisers.

On the power of advertisers, Todd Gitlin writes:

> The knowledge of who pays the bills can't be dispelled, even though it doesn't always rise to consciousness. Network executives internalize the desires of advertisers. CBS's Herman Keld . . . didn't qualify his answer when I asked him whether ad agencies—and affiliates—are taken into account in programming decisions. "I would say they are always taken into account. Always taken into account. . . ."
>
> No single advertiser can wield veto power over a network. Yet without even troubling to think about it, network executives are likely to rule out any show that would probably offend a critical mass of advertisers.[52]

When ownership was more dispersed, the press was more of an autonomous force in society, it has been argued. The supposedly independent editor and crusading publisher of an earlier era have been replaced by the big corporate executive.[53] To be sure, the concentration of ownership is an aggravating factor in the accumulation of corporate power, but the business class also does quite well under decentralized media ownership. The locally owned media are vulnerable to the pressures of advertisers and other business interests. *More important than the degree of owner concentration is the class nature of the ownership.* Les Brown's observations about local television station owners holds for local radio and newspaper owners as well: "Many of the stations are owned by persons of hard right-wing bias who are pillars of the local power structure and who believe their public service obligations to be met by promoting love for the flag. They would have networks concentrate on spreading patriotism and rallying the country to the war effort, and they would keep the air waves free from the voices of dissent."[54]

The power of advertisers over the local "independent" press is touched on by veteran reporter Art Shields who tells of his experience working for a paper in an Ohio mill town almost seventy years ago:

> Ed was advertising manager as well as editor. He cautioned me to report nothing the merchants and brewers didn't like. "We can't live without their good will," he said. "Be especially careful when you write about the brewery," Ed went on. "It's our best advertiser. . . ."
>
> I ran into another roadblock when I told Ed I expected to get good stories from my friends in the big U.S. Steel plant, where I had been working. But the editor didn't share my enthusiasm. "Better check with management before you write what workers tell you," he said. "The steel mill runs this town."[55]

More recently a reporter for the *Willamette Week,* an "above-ground alternative paper" in Portland, Oregon, asked her editor why the paper needed a business department, and he responded, "Because business is where the power is and we have to rub their backs." She noted that the supposedly liberal weekly regularly avoided any criticism of business practices. "Numerous articles containing mildly critical information on business" were rewritten because the editor wanted only "positive" pieces.[56] Similarly, in a study of how absentee mine owners dominated an impoverished Appalachian valley, John Gaventa found that the media in the area never questioned the power and policies of the coal company. The issues that involved the interests of the corporation and significantly affected the exploited and impoverished citizenry simply did not receive any press exposure.[57] After a review of the many county weeklies published in the United States, Calvin Trillin concluded that very few "ever print anything that might cause discomfort to anyone with any economic power."[58]

Along with a desire to protect a particular product or industry, advertisers on both the national and local levels will withdraw financial support in order to stamp out political heterodoxy. Gans finds that national advertisers usually do not cancel ads in the news media because the reporting reflects unfavorably on their own products as such, but because they dislike the "liberal biases" which they think are creeping into the news.[59]

THE MYTH OF OBJECTIVITY

Corporate power permeates the entire social fabric of our society. Along with owning the media, the corporate business class, as already noted, controls much of the rest of America too, including its financial, legal, educational, medical, cultural, and recreational institutions.[60] Thus the dominant capitalist interests not only structure the way the media report reality, they structure much of reality itself. The ideological character of the news, then, is partly a reflection of the journalist's "routine reliance on raw materials which are already ideological."[61] Opinions that support existing arrangements of economic and political power are more easily treated as facts, while facts that are troublesome to the prevailing distribution of class power are likely to be dismissed as opinionated. And those who censor dissenting views see themselves as protectors of objectivity and keepers of heterodoxy when, in fact, they are the guardians of ideological conformity.

Erstwhile journalist Bernard Sanders, later to become the Socialist mayor of Burlington, Vermont, offers this account of how orthodoxy masquerades as objectivity:

> I did a documentary film about [the American Socialist] Eugene Debs. It depicted his role in the labor movement and his opposition to big business in this country. Every TV station I brought it to rejected the film on the grounds that it wasn't objective; it didn't show both sides. I gathered they wanted a plug for capitalism. Can you imagine if I had done a film celebrating the accomplishments of John D. Rockefeller or Henry Ford—those stations would never have insisted on hearing the socialist side. They would never have complained about a lack of objectivity.[62]

Relying heavily on institutional authorities for much of their information, newspeople are disinclined to be too critical of established sources. One sociologist studied a sample of 2,850 stories from the *New York Times* and *Washington Post* and found that 78 percent were based largely on statements by public officials. In *Time* and *Newsweek*, 20 percent of the column inches were given to the president alone.[63] Studies of television coverage of foreign affairs find a general neglect of the views of foreign governments (except for an occasional crisis) and a general absence of views that do not coincide with the ones propagated by U.S. foreign policy elites and the U.S. government.[64] Much of what is reported as "news" is little more than the uncritical transmission of official opinions to an unsuspecting public.

As already noted, journalists may or may not endorse or even recognize the value parameters within which they work. No matter how they happen to see themselves, the fact remains that they do not and usually cannot investigate the questions that rub against the ideological limits of their employers. These include why wealth and power are so unequally distributed in the United States and between developed and exploited nations; why corporations have so much power and citizens so little; why capitalism is in a chronic state of crisis and instability; why unemployment, inflation, and poverty persist; and why the United States is involved militarily in Central America and is hostile toward any nation that moves in a noncapitalistic direction.[65]

Objectivity means reporting U.S. overseas involvements from the perspective of the multinational corporations, the Pentagon, the White House, and the State Department, and rarely questioning the legitimacy of military intervention (although allowing critical remarks about its effectiveness). Objectivity has meant saying almost nothing about the tenacious influence exercised by giant corporations over Congress and the White House. "Objectivity," writes Jack Newfield, "is believing people with power and printing their press releases. Objectivity is not shouting 'liar' in a crowded country."[66]

Objectivity means that reporters should avoid becoming politically active, and should keep their distance from their subject, while
commentators, editors, and owners socialize, dine, and vacation with
the political, military, and corporate leaders whose views and policies
they are supposed to be objective about.[67] During the 1980 elections,
George Will was an active member of Ronald Reagan's campaign
team and helped Reagan prepare for his debates with President Carter.
Without informing his audience of this, Will, the objective commentator for ABC News and columnist for *Newsweek* and the *Washington
Post*, than praised Reagan's masterful performance in the debates.
Despite the conflict of interest and the fraud that might have been
involved, Will suffered no sanctions from his employers who, on other
days, guard the journalistic citadel of objectivity from the taint of
political involvement.

Objectivity means that while reporters should avoid conflicts of
interest, hundreds of publishers and media corporate directors can
also be directors of other powerful corporations, banks, universities,
foundations, and think tanks. Objectivity means not reporting anything about how these corporate interlocking directorates represent a
conflict of interest that might interfere with the directors' judgments
regarding news selection and selection of editors, managers, and
reporters.[68]

The journalist Britt Hume urged that newspeople "shouldn't try
to be objective, they should try to be honest." Instead of passing along
the approved versions of things, they should attempt to find out if the
officeholder or corporate representative or whoever is telling the truth.
"What [reporters] pass off as objectivity," Hume concludes, "is just a
mindless kind of neutrality."[69]

Reflecting on the 1972 presidential campaign, former *New York
Times* correspondent, David Halberstam, notes that "objectivity,"
which was "the basic rule of journalistic theology," prevented the
press from uncovering important deceptions:

> So objectivity was prized and if objectivity in no way conformed to
> reality, then all the worse for reality. The editors were objective and they
> prided themselves very much on that. It did not bother them that almost
> everything else they did each day was subjective. Which 12 stories they
> put on the front page was a subjective decision. Which stories went on
> the inside page. Which stories were written and did not go into the paper.
> Which stories were never even assigned. . . .
>   So, in truth, despite all the fine talk of objectivity, the only thing that
> mildly approached objectivity was the form in which the reporter wrote
> the news, a technical style which required the journalist to appear to be
> much dumber and more innocent than in fact he was. So he wrote in a

bland, uncritical way which gave greater credence to the utterances of public officials, no matter how mindless these utterances. . . .
Thus the press voluntarily surrendered a vast amount of its real independence; it treated the words and actions of the government of the United States with a credence that those words and actions did not necessarily merit.[70]

By confining his attack to the media's treatment of the government, Halberstam himself may be acting "much dumber and more innocent" than he is, for he makes no mention of how the objectivity rule fails to give critical attention to the enormities of *business* power both in and out of government.

NOT ENOUGH TIME, SPACE, AND MONEY?

All sorts of vital issues go unmentioned in the electronic and printed news media. To try to cover all that is happening in the world would be impossible, it is argued, because it would be too expensive and there is not enough newsprint space and air time to give a more complete picture. Let's examine this argument.

1. The major newspapers, networks, newsweeklies, and wire services compose a vast news-gathering infrastructure with correspondents and stringers throughout much of the world (AP has a hundred reporters in Washington, D.C., alone). Despite these imposing resources, many important and revealing stories are broken by small publications with only a fraction of the material resources and staff available to the mass media. The startling news that the CIA was funding cultural, academic, and student organizations was first publicized by the now defunct *Ramparts* magazine. Ralph Nader's widely received work on automobile safety was ignored by the mainstream press and first began appearing in the *Nation,* a small low-budget magazine on the liberal left. Journalist Seymour Hersh sent his account of the My Lai massacre to an outfit almost nobody had ever heard of, Dispatch News Service— after none of the major wire services would pick it up.[71]
Stories about hunger in America, the chemical poisoning of our environment and our people, the illegal activities of the CIA at home and abroad, U.S. sponsored torture in Iran and Latin America, the dangers of nuclear power plants and other

such revelations were uncovered by radical publications long before they were finally picked up—if ever—by the mainstream press. Adam Hochschild, a columnist and erstwhile editor of *Mother Jones* observes that investigative reporters working for small progressive publications run into little or no competition from mainstream journalists when digging into many important and revealing stories:

> There are more than 1,000 correspondents in Washington, D.C., falling all over each other trying to "develop sources" in the White House. . . . The press competes all right, but over ridiculous things. Last year. . . some 12,000 newspeople covered each of the political conventions: events whose principal results—the nominations of Carter and Reagan—were known in advance.[72]

2. Another excuse given for inadequate and superficial coverage is that twenty-two minutes of televised evening news (with eight minutes for commercials) simply do not allow enough time for anything more than "snapshot-and-headline services." In truth, if one were to count the political daytime talk show, late night news shows, local and national evening news, and hourly news programs on commercial and public radio and television, there is almost round-the-clock news programming. But almost all of it is thin and repetitious in content. Although the network evening news has only a scant twenty-two minutes, it finds time for plenty of trivial or frivolous subjects that are clearly intended to entertain rather than inform. If the evening news were expanded to one hour, this would not guarantee more depth coverage. If anything, the evasive surface quality of television news would become more evident, and an hour of it more unsatisfying—as demonstrated by the local TV news shows that now offer hour programs. Time is not an iron-clad factor in determining how in-depth one might go. In five minutes one could make devastating revelations and connections on any number of issues, but how often would a network news team attempt to do so?

Similarly it is not true that our leading newspapers lack the newsprint space for more comprehensive coverage of the day's events. Radical newspapers of one-tenth the length delve into controversial issues with more depth and revelation than the bulkier commercial papers. As CBS correspondent Bill Moyers commented, "It is the capitalists who do not find it commercially rewarding to give the journalists the time to cover the world."[74]

To be sure, more comprehensive news coverage, although desired by the public, is not encouraged because it costs more. Ironically enough, as profits from news programs have grown, the willingness to invest in more substantive news content has diminished. With higher profits there come "the competitive pressures to be more popular and appealing. The result is an increasing emphasis on eye-catching graphics, slick packaging and alluring promotion of highly paid [newscast] stars."[73]

Critics have noted that news media have a penchant for stories that are simple and finite in scope so as to be easily grasped and sensational enough to attract as large an audience as possible. But there are many simple, finite, and quite sensational stories that are not touched. For instance, in October 1982 the media gave sensational coverage to the several deaths caused when someone slipped poison into Tylenol capsules that were later sold at drug stores. Yet these same media ignored the far greater number of deaths (ninety-seven abroad and twenty-seven in the United States) caused when Eli Lilly and Company marketed an "anti-arthritis pill" called Oraflex. The Food and Drug Administration allowed Oraflex to go on sale in April 1981 despite an FDA investigator's earlier report indicating that Lilly was withholding data on the dangerous side effects of the drug. Clearly here was a sensational story of mass murder and skulduggery, of possible corporate malfeasance and government collusion, yet the press did not bother with it. Why the difference in handling the two stories? The Tylenol killings seemed to have been the work of deranged persons; the corporate manufacturers (and advertisers) could not be blamed. Therefore, the story was not only simple and sensational, but safe, free of any criticism of the marketing ethics of drug advertisers and of big business in general—which was not the case with Oraflex.[75]

As observed in Chapter 1, some critics say the problem of coverage rests with the journalists themselves. In 1971, the then president of the American Society of Newspaper Editors, Newbold Noyes, remarked:

> It is obvious that we are lazy and superficial in much of our reporting. Often we do not even bother to challenge ourselves with the difficult question as to what really is going on. We rely, instead, on certain stereotypes as to what makes a news story. . . . Why is a speech, a press conference, a court decision, a Congressional hearing always news, while the real situations behind these surface things go un-noted? Why? Because it is easy that way, and because that is the way we have always done it.[76]

But is it really just a matter of laziness and inertia? Behind the superficiality of the news there stands a whole configuration of power

"OBJECTIVITY" BY OMISSION

The news is slanted not only in what it says but in what it leaves unsaid. Every year "Project Censored," a panel of media critics including such notables as Jessica Mitford, Ben Bagdikian, Noam Chomsky and Nicholas Johnson, picks ten stories that the media have kept from the public. Among the unreported stories in 1982 were: that the U.S. cast the only dissenting vote in the UN on a resolution endorsing a treaty to outlaw nuclear weapons; that some leading U.S. corporations did extensive business with Nazi Germany during World War II and had been sympathetic to that regime; that nearly all the chemical fertilizer used in recent years, amounting to $2 billion a year, was found to be worthless by researchers; that the reform legislation inspired by 20 years of civil rights struggle supposedly guaranteeing equal access to jobs, housing and education was largely dismantled by the Reagan administration without significant media coverage or public input; and that the nation's largest laboratories responsible for testing the toxicity and carcinogenic qualities of products, performed fraudulent tests on chemicals used in deodorant soaps, medications and pesticides. The "Project Censored" panel report was itself almost entirely ignored by the commercial press.

Based on David Armstrong, "Ten Stories the Media Didn't Tell," Guardian, June 1, 1983.

and interest that makes the lazy, conventional way of presenting things also the politically safer, less troublesome way. Noyes seems to hint at some realization of this when he adds; "I think the worst of our lazy and superficial performance today is that we of the press are allowing ourselves to be manipulated by various interests." But the question remains, *why* would the press allow itself to be manipulated by such interests?

Correspondents who report on Third World insurgencies and other such revolutionary turmoil by ensconcing themselves in a luxury hotel, waiting for handouts from the U.S. embassy, or from the military junta that is trying to destroy and discredit the insurgency may be guilty of laziness; but *they are also producing copy their editors and publishers find acceptable.* When one of them does otherwise, he or she may run into difficulties. When Herbert Matthews reported the Cuban revolution directly from the field, offering detailed accounts of the popular support the guerrillas enjoyed and the early accomplishments of the regime, he was removed from the story by the *New York*

Times. Matthews had unique access to the Cuban leadership. As he writes in his memoirs:

> I was in a position to get the *New York Times* information from the highest Cuban sources which nobody could duplicate.
> Here was the most important development in Latin American history since the wars of independence a century and a half ago. Here was one of the rare phenomena of modern history—a social revolution of the most drastic kind on which I, and I alone, could report from the inside, as it went along. It was a golden opportunity for the *New York Times.* But I was muzzled![77]

Matthews was silenced on the Cuban issue because his reports were not sufficiently in step with the anti-Castro, anticommunist tidal wave that was flooding the media. Far from being lazy, he showed himself to be the go-getter par excellence, and for that he got into difficulties with his employers. If reporters hold back and allow themselves to be manipulated by vested interests, it is because they have learned that such behavior has its rewards, and a more challenging kind of journalism has its punishments.

More than two decades later, another *New York Times* reporter learned the same lesson. In 1982, Ray Bonner wrote a series of reports about the Salvadoran military's massacre of almost 1,000 peasants near El Mozote. The articles put the lie to White House claims that El Salvador was making great strides in human rights. Ultra-rightist groups in the United States, led by Accuracy in the Media, launched a campaign to have Bonner removed; the *Wall Street Journal* denounced him as the *Times*'s "overly credulous reporter." The U.S. embassy in San Salvador cut Bonner off from embassy contacts. Under mounting pressure Bonner admitted he started "to pull back a little bit." Despite his attempt at self-censorship, the *Times* pulled him out of El Salvador. Bonner resigned soon after, noting that his experience had a chilling effect on "many other reporters" who told him "Boy, I don't want the same thing to happen to me. I'm going to be careful."[78]

MAINTAINING APPEARANCES

How is it that the idea of a free and independent press persists in the face of strong hierarchical corporate controls—even among many members of the working press who should know better? We can answer that question by summarizing some previous points.

First, there is ideological congruity between many members of the working press and media owners. When reporters and editors look at the world in much the same way as their bosses, censorship becomes an intermittent rather than constant affair, something whose existence can be more easily denied.

Second, *within* the existing ideological consensus there does exist a certain range of views on what to do about domestic and foreign policy issues—which do not challenge the fundamental pro-capitalist, antisocialist mythology yet give an appearance of diversity.

Third, there is much anticipatory self-censorship practiced by reporters, editors, and producers even while not admitted or consciously perceived by the practitioners themselves.

Fourth, the rewards and punishments designed to induce conformity also socialize people into the existing system. With one's career at stake, it is not too hard for the newsperson to start seeing things the same way superiors do. Sanctions not only force conformity, in time they change people's political perceptions so that the conformity becomes voluntary, so to speak.

Fifth, the more obvious and undeniable instances of coercion, bias, and censorship are seen as aberrations. Bauman notes that *New York Times* journalists who were critical of the newspaper's handling of a particular story insisted that it was an isolated problem.[79]

Sixth, reporters and editors who say they are guided (and protected) by professional integrity and journalistic standards of autonomy and objectivity have rarely, if ever, defined what they mean by these terms. "Professional integrity" remains largely unexplained and somewhat contradictory. For instance, an editor's claim to having final say on what his paper prints would seem to contradict a reporter's claim to independence in what he writes. Likewise, newspeople can cloak themselves in the mantle of objectivity only by ignoring the differences of perspective that make objectivity a highly debatable concept. In order to maintain a sense of self-respect and independence, many newspeople deny the realities of class power under which they manufacture the news. "The mass media are capitalist institutions," notes Chomsky. "The fact that these institutions reflect the ideology of dominant economic interests is hardly surprising."[80] What might be surprising is how some representatives of the established media institutions keep trying to deny that fact.

For reasons of their own, media corporate executives and owners also sometimes maintain that their editors and reporters enjoy independence. After censoring and then removing a liberal editor, H. B. DuPont denied that his newspapers served his personal political biases; he reaffirmed that they "operated independently with the objective of being a constructive influence in the community, in the state, and in the nation."[81] Thus do owners lend a democratic facade to an undemocratic relation in order to better secure and legitimate the power they wield. Furthermore, for many of the reasons already stated, they may actually believe that autonomy and objectivity are the operational rules. They have no reason to overrule compliant editors who are thereby seen as "independent." And they find it easy to believe that the dominant view—which is their view—is the objective one. Indeed, owners are even less immune to the self-serving myths of objectivity and autonomy than editors and reporters.

In order to operate effectively, the news media must have credibility; they must win a certain amount of trust from the public. To win that credibility they must give the appearance of objectivity as befitting a "free and independent press." Were owners to announce that their media were the instruments of their own political biases and their class power, they would reveal themselves as they are, and they would weaken the media's credibility and the media's class control functions. Therefore, they must take care not to exercise too blatant a control over the news. Needless to say, the frequent acts of news suppression they do perform are themselves rarely if ever reported as news.

Notes

1. Ben Bagdikian, *The Media Monopoly* (Boston: Beacon Press, 1983).
2. Herbert Gans, *Deciding What's News* (New York: Vintage, 1979), p. 251.
3. Gans, *Deciding What's News*, p. 196.
4. Observations by former *Washington Post* correspondent John Dinges; interview, January 18, 1982.
5. James Aronson, *The Press and the Cold War* (Boston: Beacon Press, 1970), pp. 3–4.
6. *Ibid.*, p. 6.
7. *Ibid.*, p. 3.
8. Interview, August 17, 1981. This respondent chose to remain anonymous.
9. Peter Drier and Steve Weinberg, "Interlocking Directorates," *Columbia Journalism Review*, November/December 1979, p. 68.
10. Malcolm Browne writing in *Variety* November 2, 1966; quoted in Aronson, *The Press and the Cold War*, p. 210.
11. Quoted in Aronson, *The Press and the Cold War*, p. 56.
12. Quoted in Drier and Weinberg, "Interlocking Directorates."
13. *Columbia Journalism Review*, May/June 1983, p. 56.
14. See the survey by S. Robert Lichter and Stanley Rothman in *Washington Post*, January 3, 1982; also *Parade*, March 20, 1983; and Gans *Deciding What's News*, p. 209.
15. Gans, *Deciding What's News*, p. 107.
16. Ben Bagdikian, "The Wrong Kind of Reader," *Progressive*, May 1973, p. 52.
17. Deborah Davis, *Katharine the Great, Katharine Graham and the Washington Post* (New York, Harcourt Brace Jovanovich, 1979) pp. 140–41.
18. Gans, *Deciding What's News*, p. 208.

19. Lichter and Rothman, *loc. cit.*

20. Peter Drier, "Business and the Media," unpublished monograph, 1983.

21. Ibid.; also "Contests Help to Improve Business/Finance Writing," *Editor and Publisher,* December 29, 1979.

22. See *Columbia Journalism Review,* January/February 1985, p. 13.

23. Drier, "Business and the Media."

24. Ibid.

25. Noam Chomsky, "Ideological Conformity in America," *Nation,* January 27, 1979, p. 77. On infrequent occasions, opinion pieces by writers of Socialist persuasion appear in publications like the *New York Times* and *Boston Globe,* but they rarely deal with questions of capitalism and socialism.

26. Gans, *Deciding What's News,* p. 94.

27. Ibid.

28. Ibid.

29. Ben Bagdikian, *The Effete Conspiracy* (New York: Harper & Row, 1972), p. 78; also Bagdikian's *The Media Monopoly* (Boston: Beacon Press, 1983).

30. Conversation with a former Associated Press correspondent, March 1, 1985, Washington, D.C.

31. Bagdikian, *The Media Monopoly.*

32. Roger Wilkins, *A Man's Life* (New York: Simon & Schuster, 1982), p. 329.

33. Dorothy Sterling, letter to the *New York Times,* March 11, 1984.

34. As reported to my associate Kathleen Lipscomb in Managua, January 2–3, 1985.

35. Turner Catledge, *My Life and the Times,* quoted in Todd Gitlin, *The Whole World Is Watching* (Berkeley: University of California Press, 1980), p. 39.

36. Les Brown, *Television, The Business Behind the Box* (New York: Harcourt Brace Jovanovich, 1971), pp. 219–220.

37. Bagdikian, *Effete Conspiracy,* p. 69.

38. Diana Tillinghast, "Inside the Los Angeles Times," unpublished monograph, 1980, quoted in David Paletz and Robert Entman, *Media Power Politics,* (New York: Free Press, 1971), p. 15.

39. Norman Bauman, "Newspapers: More or Less Put Together by the Advertisers?" unpublished monograph, 1977, p. 24.

40. Ibid.; also Chris Argyris, *Behind the Front Page* (San Francisco: Jossey-Bass, 1974).

41. Gans, *Deciding What's News,* p. 101.

42. Ibid., p. 342n.

43. Edwin Bayley, *Joe McCarthy and the Press* (New York: Pantheon, 1981), pp. 139–141.

44. Bagdikian, *Effete Conspiracy, p.* 76.

45. Quoted in *Columbia Journalism Review,* January/February 1985, p. 18.

46. *Workers World,* April 9, 1982.

47. *Washington Post,* February 18, 1983.

48. Gans, *Deciding What's News, p.* 85.

49. Bauman, "Newspapers: More or Less Put Together. . . ."

50. Ibid; Bauman interviewed *Times* editors for this information.

51. Eric Barnouw, *The Sponsor* (New York: Oxford University Press, 1978), p. 57.

52. Todd Gitlin, "When the Right Talks, TV Listens," *Nation,* October 15, 1983, p. 335.

53. Bagdikian makes this argument in *The Media Monopoly,* chapters 1 and 2.

54. Les Brown, *Television, The Business Behind the Box* (New York: Harcourt Brace Jovanovich, 1971), p. 214.
55. Art Shields, *My Shaping Years* (New York: International Publishers, 1982), p. 124.
56. Interview with Laurie Wimmer, November 9, 1982.
57. John Gaventa, *Power and Powerlessness* (Urbana: University of Illinois Press, 1981).
58. Calvin Trillin, "U.S. Journal: Kentucky," *New Yorker*, December 27, 1969, p. 33.
59. Gans, *Deciding What's News*, p. 254.
60. For a fuller discussion of this see my *Power and the Powerless* (New York: St. Martin's Press, 1978).
61. Mark Fishman, *Manufacturing the News* (Austin: University of Texas Press, 1980).
62. Interview with the author, October 4, 1979.
63. Leon Sigal, *Reporters and Officials* (Lexington, Mass: D. C. Heath, 1973).
64. Robert Entman and David Paletz, "The War in Southeast Asia: Tunnel Vision on Television," in William C. Adams, ed. *Television Coverage of International Affairs* (Norwood, N.J.: Ablex, 1982); and the other studies in that same volume; also Anita Mallinckrodt, "The Real Evening News," unpublished monograph, Washington, D.C., 1983.
65. Gans, *Deciding What's News*, p. 277.
66. Jack Newfield, "Honest Men, Good Writers," *Village Voice* May 18, 1972. For a study of the corporate influence in the American political system, see my *Democracy for the Few*, 4th ed. (New York: St. Martin's Press, 1983)
67. See the *Washington Post's* report on David Brinkley's birthday party, November 16, 1981.
68. Drier and Weinberg, "Interlocking Directorates," p. 51.
69. Quoted in Timothy Crouse, *The Boys on the Bus: Riding With the Campaign Press Corps*, (New York: Random House, 1973).
70. David Halberstam, quoted by Kevin Donovan in *Ithica New Times*, February 29, 1976, p. 6.
71. Adam Hochschild, "A Tale of Two Exposes," *Mother Jones*, September/October 1981, p. 10.
72. Ibid.
73. Tony Schwartz, "Why TV News Is Increasingly Being Packaged as Entertainment," *New York Times*, October 17, 1982.
74. Quoted in Sally Bedell, "Why TV News Can't Be a Complete View of the World," *New York Times*, August 8, 1982.
75. Moe Stavnezer, "The Killing Drug They Don't Like to Discuss," *Guardian*, December 22, 1982, p. 7. Oraflex was banned finally in August 1982.
76. Comments reported in Tristram Coffin, ed. *The Washington Spector*, September 1, 1980.
77. Herbert Matthews, *A World in Revolution*," (New York: Scribners, 1971) p. 338; also Matthews's *The Cuban Story* (New York: George Braziller, 1961) p. 281ff.
78. Joel Millman, "How the Press Distorts the News from Central America," *Progressive*, October 1984, p. 20.
79. Bauman, "Newspapers: More or Less Put Together. . . ." p. 24.
80. Chomsky, "Ideological Conformity in America," p. 78.
81. Bagdikian, *Effete Conspiracy*, p. 77.

4

The Big Sell

Much of our media experience is neither news nor entertainment. Some 60 to 80 percent of newspaper space and about 22 percent of television time (even more on radio) is devoted to advertising. The average viewer who watches four hours of television daily, sees at least 100 to 120 commercials a day, or 36,400 to 43,680 a year. Many of the images in our heads, the expressions in our conversation, the jingles and tunes we hum, and, of course, the products we find ourselves using, are from the world of the Big Sell. Advertising not only urges products upon us, we in part become one of its products. We are, if anything, consumers. And even if we have learned to turn away from the television set when commercials come on and pass over the eye-catching ads in our newspapers and magazines, we cannot hope to remain untouched by the persistent, ubiquitous bombardment.

Most of us think of advertising as the sideshow we must tolerate in order to experience the media's more substantial offerings. Advertising picks up most of the costs of newspapers and magazines and all the costs of radio and television. Thus it is thought of as a means to an end. But a moment's reflection should tell us it is the other way round: The media's content, the news and entertainment, the features and "specials," are really the *means,* the lures to get us exposed to the advertisements. ("Journalists," said one press representative, "are just people who write on the back of advertisements."[1]) The *end* is the advertising, the process of inducing people to spend as much money as possible on consumer products and services. Entertainment and news are merely instrumental to the goal of the advertiser. They are there to win audiences for the advertisers, to keep people tuned in and turned on. The objective is commercial gain, the sale of mass-produced goods to a mass market; only for that reason are advertisers willing to pay enormous sums for what passes as entertainment and news.

Mass advertising has not always been with us. It grew with mass media, or rather mass media grew with *it.* Mass advertising was a response to significant transformations in the productive system. The growth of modern technology and mass production brought changes in the lives of millions of Americans. The small community with its local economy and homebred recreational and cultural life gave way to an urbanized, industrial society of people who were obliged to turn more and more to a mass commodity market.[2]

The age of mass consumption came to the United States most visibly in the 1920s, interrupted by the Great Depression and World War II, then exploding upon us with accumulated vigor in the postwar era. With it came the advertising industry, called into being by the economic imperative of having to market vast quantities of consumer goods and services. Among the new products were those that enabled advertising itself to happen: the penny-press newspaper, the low-priced slick magazine, the radio, and finally the television set—all in their turn were to become both mass consumption items and prime conduits for mass consumption advertising. Today the family and local community are no longer the primary units for production, recreation, self-definition, or even personal loyalty. Self-images, role models, and emotional attachments are increasingly sought from those whose specialty is to produce and manipulate images and from the images themselves.

THE CONSUMER IDEOLOGY

The obvious purpose of ads and commercials is to sell goods and services, but advertisers do more than that. Over and above any particular product, they sell an entire way of life, a way of experiencing social reality that is compatible with the needs of a mass-production, mass-consumption, capitalist society. Media advertising is both a propagator and a product of a consumer ideology.

People have always had to consume in order to live, and in every class society, consumption styles have been a measure of one's status. But modern consumerism is a relatively recent development in which masses of people seek to accumulate things other than what they need and often other than what they can truly enjoy. Consumption is no longer just a means to life but a meaning for life. This is the essence of the consumer ideology. As propagated through mass advertising, the ideology standardizes tastes and legitimizes both the products of the system and the system itself, representing the commodity-ridden life as "the good life" and "the American Way." The consumer ideology, or consumerism, builds a mass psychology of "moreness" that knows no limit; hence the increase in material abundance ironically also can bring a heightened sense of scarcity and a sense of unfulfilled acquisition.

Advertisements often do not explicitly urge the consumer to buy a

WHAT THE COMMERCIALS DO NOT TELL US

Commercials do not announce [a product's price] nor accurately represent its size, weight and dimensions. On the contrary, such features are intentionally distorted by tricks of staging, such as special camera angles and lighting, and by tricks of wording, such as "family size" or "economy size."

Product descriptions are vague and ambiguous. Ingredients, for example, are rarely mentioned, certainly not by generic name. On the contrary, they are often deliberately disguised by invented terms: "pain-reliever," "antiwetness spray product," "cough suppressant," "sleep remedy," "germ-chaser," and so on. Food and candy are described as "chocolatey" or "peanuty," glossing over how much real chocolate or real peanuts are used, if any. Breakfast foods are described as "yummy," never as "sugary."

Who is it that produces products advertised on television often remains a mystery. Brand names are stressed, but not corporate ownerships or affiliations; it is a rare television watcher who knows that the company producing Twinkies and Wonderbread is owned by General Mills, that Creative Playthings is owned by CBS, Inc., that White Cloud and Charmin—toilet paper rivals on the air—are both made by companies which Procter and Gamble owns.

For what reason does General Mills, a food and agricultural conglomerate, sell toys, while ITT, an international conglomerate that once specialized in communications, sells food? Commercials do not tell.

Rose Goldsen, "The Great American Consciousness Machine," Journal of Social Reconstruction, 1, April–June 1980, pp. 98–99.

given product, rather they promise that the product will enhance a person's life, opening a whole range of desiderata including youthfulness, attractiveness, social grace, security, success, conviviality, sex, romance, and the admiration of others. Strictly speaking the advertisement does not *sell* the product as such. Rarely does the television commercial say "Buy Pepsi"; instead it urges us to "Join the Pepsi Generation."

Most consumers, if questioned on the matter, would agree that many commercials are exaggerated, unrealistic, and even untrue; but this skepticism does not immunize them from the advertisement hype. One can be critical of a particular commercial yet be swayed by it at some subliminal level, or by the overall impact of watching a thousand commercials a week. Thus millions of people bought high-priced designer jeans even if few actually believed the product would win them entry into that never-never world of slim-hipped glamorous people who joyfully wiggled their blue-denim posteriors into the TV camera, in an endless succession of commercials during the early 1980s.

The consumer ideology not only fabricates false needs, it panders in a false way to real ones. The desire for companionship, love, approval, and pleasure, the need to escape from drudgery and boredom, the search for security for oneself and one's family, such things are vital human concerns. The consumer ideology does something more pernicious than just activate our urge for conspicuous consumption; like so much else in the media and like other forms of false consciousness, consumerism plays on real human needs in deceptive and ultimately unfulfilling ways.

One of the goals of advertising is to turn the consumer's critical perception away from the product—and away from the system that produces it—and toward herself or himself.[3] Many commercials characterize people as loudmouthed imbeciles whose problems are solved when they encounter the right medication, cosmetic, cleanser, or gadget. In this way industry confines the social imagination and cultural experience of millions, teaching people to define their needs and life styles according to the dictates of the commodity market.

The reader of advertising copy and the viewer of commercials discover that they are not doing right for baby's needs or hubby's or wifey's desires; that they are failing in their careers because of poor appearance, sloppy dress, or bad breath; that they are not treating their complexion, hair, or nails properly; that they suffer unnecessary cold misery and headache pains; that they don't know how to make the tastiest coffee, pie, pudding, or chicken dinner; nor, if left to their own devices, would they be able to clean their floors, sinks, and toilets correctly or tend to their lawns, gardens, appliances, and automobiles. In order to live well and live properly, consumers need corporate producers to guide them. Consumers are taught personal incompetence and dependence on mass-market producers.

Are people worried about the security of their homes and families? No need to fear, Prudential or All-State will watch over them. Are people experiencing loneliness? Ma Bell brings distant loved ones to them with a telephone call. The corporate system knows what formulas to feed your infants, what foods to feed your family, what medication to feed your cold, what gas to feed your engine, and how best to please your spouse, your boss, or your peers. Just as the mass market replaced family and community as provider of goods and services, so now corporations replace parents, grandparents, midwives,

MEANWHILE, SOUTH OF THE BORDER

The sheer wealth and dynamism of American society clearly adds to Mexico's vulnerability, but United States business interests also play a key role in the Mexican economy. . . . United States investors dominate the more visible areas of automobile production, food processing and domestic appliances, which in turn shape consumption patterns.

Similarly, while the medium is controlled by Mexicans, the message of the American way of life dominates Mexican television, not only through the daily fare of Superman cartoons or live broadcasts of American football games, but also through a style of advertising where American blonds are used to sell Mexican beer, and slick spots, prepared by American advertising agencies, expound the virtues of everything from Pepsi-Cola to the Ford Mustang.

The cultural impact of television was underlined in a recent survey carried out by the National Consumer Institute. It showed that 85 percent of the children questioned recognized the trademark of a brand of potato chips but only 65 percent identified Mexico's national emblem. In another poll, only 14 percent recognized the Monument to the Revolution in Mexico City, but 70 percent identified the symbol of the brand of cornflakes.

Enrique Rubio Lara, the institute's director, noted recently: "Advertising is not only encouraging the sale of totally superfluous goods, but it is also stimulating aspirations, values and models of life that are not the best for Mexicans."

Alan Riding, "Mexico's Middle Class Turns to Disco and Burgers," New York Times, January 13, 1982.

neighbors, craftspeople, and oneself in knowing what is best. Big business enhances its legitimacy and social hegemony by portraying itself as society's Grand Provider.[4]

The world of mass advertising teaches us that want and frustration are caused by our own deficiencies. The goods are within easy reach, before our very eyes in dazzling abundance, available not only to the rich but to millions of ordinary citizens. Those unable to partake of this cornucopia have only themselves to blame. If you cannot afford to buy these things, goes the implicit message, the failure is yours and not the system's. The advertisement of consumer wares, then, is also an advertisement for a whole capitalist system, a demonstration that the system can deliver both the goods and the good life to everyone save laggards and incompetents.

SELLING THE SYSTEM

Along with products, the corporations sell themselves. By the 1970s, for the first time since the Great Depression, the legitimacy of big business was being called into question by large sectors of the public. Enduring inflation, unemployment, and a decline in real wages, the American people became increasingly skeptical about the blessings of the corporate economy. In response, corporations intensified their efforts at the kind of "advocacy advertising," designed to sell the entire capitalist system rather than just one of its products. Between 1971 and 1977, the spending on "nonproduct-related" advertisements more than doubled, from $230 million to over $474 million, showing a far greater growth rate than advertising expenditures as a whole.[5] *Today, one-third of all corporate advertising is directed at influencing the public on political and ideological issues as opposed to pushing consumer goods.* (That portion is tax deductible as a "business expense," like all other advertising costs.) Led by the oil, chemical, and steel companies, big business fills the airwaves and printed media with celebrations of the "free market," and warnings of the baneful effects of government regulation. "What this outpouring of eloquence seems to represent . . . is a sweeping reactionary movement that has outgrown its earlier roots in the special interests of particular firms and become really class-wide."[6]

Mobil Oil, probably the forerunner in this area, ran ad campaigns, with an annual budget of $5 million, to inform readers that Mobil "gave employment" to thousands of persons, contributed to charities, and brought prosperity to local communities. More significantly, as some of the Mobil ads note, business firms all across America do their part to create prosperity for all. One Mobil "Observations" column in the *Washington Post* put it this way:

> Business, generally, is a good neighbor, and most communities recognize this fact.
> From time to time, out of political motivations or for reasons of radical chic, individuals may try to chill the business climate. On such occasions we try to set the record straight . . . And the American system, of which business is an integral part, usually adapts.
> So when it comes to the business climate, we're glad that most people recognize there's little need to tinker with the American system.[7]

Thus capitalism and Americanism are inseparably joined in something called "the American system." A few faddish radicals or individual malcontents may criticize business but Mobil and the American system are pretty near perfect.

Newsweek ran a series of ideological advertisements sponsored by "The SmithKline Forum for a Healthier American Society." The November 9, 1981, four-page ad on "The Heroes of Growth" featured the headline: "SALUTE THE CAPITALIST ENTREPRENEURS, SAYS SOCIAL PHILOSOPHER GEORGE GILDER. THEY DREAM, THEN ACT, AND ENRICH OUR LIVES." The text has Gilder informing us that, contrary to Adam Smith's view, "capitalism is good and successful not because it miraculously transmutes personal avarice and ambition into collective prosperity but because it calls forth, propagates, and relies upon the best and most generous of human qualities. The process of capitalist investment, for all the obvious differences, bears a close relationship to the ritual gift-giving that anthropologists have discovered to be universal in primitive life."

Other ideological ads, like the one run by United Technologies, as an open letter to Ronald Reagan entitled "Godspeed, Mr. President," call for "a revitalized system of free enterprise" with more reliance on "the competitive forces of the marketplace," along with "controlling the growth and cost of government and its intrusion into our lives and liberties."[8]

One prime-time television commercial (October 1981) offers footage of a skier going down a beautiful mountain slope, with a deep, male, off-screen voice saying: "Freedom. We Americans have the freedom to choose. The freedom to live our lives the way we want as individuals. The freedom to take risks [skier leaps over a precipitous embankment]. The freedom to succeed [skier makes a skillful maneuver] and the freedom to fail [skier takes a mild spill into the powdery snow]. When government comes into our lives, things change. When people look to government for protection, they get protection but they lose some of their precious freedom [skier at the end of the trail on less precipitous ground, moving along slowly with his hands hanging down and his poles dragging behind him]. Just something to think about from the people at Getty."

Business as a providential social force was the theme of a full page ad by Conoco Inc. in the *Christian Science Monitor* (August 29, 1980). It read:

WHAT WILL CAPITAL BE DOING ON LABOR DAY?
Working.
Building new plants. Starting new businesses. Funding innovation and growth. Developing more energy to fuel the economy.
Part of the capital that creates jobs comes from the earnings of American industry . . .
Throughout the economy, stronger earnings can provide the capital to

create more and better jobs. So as we celebrate Labor Day, let's not forget capital.
It works, too.

American readers are not likely to be treated to an alternative view. No newspaper would run an advertisement pointing out that capital cannot build an industry, plant, or commodity without labor, and that when labor takes off on Labor Day, nothing is produced. Capital is the surplus value created by labor. "Putting one's money to work" means mixing it with labor to create more capital. Purely on its own, without labor, capital is incapable of building a woodshed, let alone "new plants." But the message we get is that capital creates, rather than *is* created.

Business is also depicted as society's Grand Protector. Defense companies spend millions in weeklies like *Time* and *Newsweek* and in the major newspapers to advertise their accomplishments in weaponry and to assure the reader that America's defenses are growing stronger thanks to the military hardware produced by this or that contractor. An advertisement in the *Washington Post* by "McDonnell Douglas, prime contractor," and "Northrop Corporation, principal subcontractor" displays a photo of the latest U.S. navy and marine corps fighter plane, along with the statement (reproduced here in its entirety): "We are convinced that we have in the F/A-18A a superior aircraft. One day we use it as a fighter, and that same afternoon we use it as an attack aircraft."[9] Fortified with this Dr. Strangelove pronouncement, Americans are supposed to sleep easier.

A full page advertisement in the *Washington Post,* paid for by Bath Iron Works Corporation, pictures a U.S. navy officer's hat sitting next to a Soviet navy officer's hat (complete with hammer and sickle emblem). The Soviet cap looks easily ten times larger. Under the picture is the headline: "When the other fellow's four times bigger, it's not enough to be right." The text warns:

> . . . U.S. naval strength has been declining while the Russians have been building in such numbers that they now have four times the number of ships we have.
> Our new administration has recently asserted that it's time to change the ratio. Quality ships in quantity are what we need. Ships like the guided missile frigates (FFGs) designed and built on a production line basis by Bath Iron Works.[10]

For the next few years, almost on a weekly basis, Bath Iron Works ran full-page advertisements in the *New York Times* and *Washington Post,* with variations of this same warning, accompanied by photos or illustrations showing a massive line-up of Soviet ships (each with hammer and sickle emblems) next to a few paltry American vessels, or a Soviet admiral dominating the entire page, peering through his binoculars at an American vessel that presumably is his intended prey.

Neither the *Times* nor *Post* expressed an obligation to inform their readers that these advertisements might be offering something less than the truth. According to the Center for Strategic and International Studies, the U.S. navy has twice the tonnage of the Soviet navy, with ships that are more modern, better equipped and designed to transport military forces anywhere in the world. As of 1984 the United States had thirteen operational aircraft carriers equipped with 1200 combat aircraft, the USSR had one full-size carrier, and a few miniature ones designed for antisubmarine warfare, specifically to try to locate U.S. nuclear missile submarines that target Soviet cities. The Soviet navy also has a very limited amphibious capacity, unlike the U.S. navy which is designed to deliver troops anywhere in the world.[11]

What the defense contractors sell to the public is an ideology, a fear of being harmed by some sinister foreign threat—most usually the Russian Bear, a promise of security through strength, an assurance that we can go on living safely as long as we don't skimp on military spending. The defense firms present benign facades: "Where science gets down to business," says Rockwell, whose business is making the plutonium triggers for atomic warheads. "We bring good things to life," says General Electric, who makes such good things as the neutron generators that activate thermonuclear devices. "We'll show you a better way," says Honeywell, whose electronic components show nuclear missiles a better way to designated targets.[12]

Another area targeted by corporate propaganda is environmentalism. The 1970s witnessed a surge in ecological consciousness in the United States. Industry responded by spending millions of dollars in a propaganda campaign designed to convince the public that business was caring for the environment. At the same time, the big corporations spent next to nothing on actual conservation and pollution controls. Were one to judge strictly from the ads, however, business does everything it can to avoid dumping raw industrial effusion and chemical toxins into our rivers and atmosphere. An ad by Chemical Manufacturer's Association in the *New York Times* (May 4, 1982) shows an attractive woman being hugged by a smiling little girl. The woman is saying: "My job is managing chemical industry wastes. What I do helps make the environment safer today—and for generations to come." Of the many similar ads that have appeared regularly on television and in various newspapers and news magazines, none alters the truth that the chemical industry has a dreadful record of poisoning the environment with toxic wastes.

SOMETIMES MONEY ISN'T ENOUGH

Advertisements by public interest groups and labor unions designed to counter the perpetual pro-business propaganda fail to gain exposure, mostly for lack of the millions of dollars needed to buy television time and print space. As of 1983 a full-page ad in the *Washington Post* cost $23,916 a day—and substantially more on Sunday.

On the infrequent occasions when unions and public interest groups muster enough money to buy broadcasting time or newspaper space, they still may be denied access to the media. Liberal-minded commentators have been refused radio spots even when they had sponsors who would pay. A group of scientists, politicians and celebrities opposing the Pentagon's antiballistic missile (ABM) program was denied a half hour on television by all three major networks even though they had the required $250,000 to buy time. On various occasions during the Vietnam era, the *New York Times* would not sell space to citizens' groups that wanted to run advertisements against war taxes or against the purchase of defense bonds. A *Times* executive turned down the antibond advertisement because he judged it not to be in the "best interests of the country."[13] In 1983, the American Council, a Washington-based public foundation concerned with foreign policy issues, tried to buy commercial time on local affiliates of the three networks in order to run a 28-second commercial critical of U.S. involvement in El Salvador. The ABC affiliate sold three spots, but the NBC and CBS affiliates refused to carry it.

Broadcasters and publishers can refuse to run any political message for any reason, or no reason at all, regardless of how factually accurate or important it might be. During the 1980 electoral campaign, the airwaves were crowded with political commercials, many sponsored by probusiness, conservative, and New Right organizations. In contrast, a citizen's group, Common Sense in National Defense, prepared a 99-word spot commercial dealing with the danger of nuclear war by computer error and calling for a freeze on nuclear weapons. In the last week of the campaign, the group set out to buy air time for the commercial in three senatorial and seven House races in an effort to defeat incumbents who had opposed the nuclear freeze. Some stations did not respond; others agreed to carry the spot then canceled at the last moment. In the end, voters in only three of the ten electoral contests got to see the commercial. Among the reasons given by broadcasters for turning down the message were:

"Too controversial."

"How an incumbent voted on the nuclear freeze does not constitute a controversial issue of public importance."

"Not in the best interest of the station to run it."

"I don't think this is the style that the people of Wyoming like. In my judgment it is not in the interest of the populace of Wyoming. They would not understand."[14]

All the stations were acting within their court-given rights: non-candidates have no guaranteed right of access to the airwaves. Broadcasters can run any political commercials they might want, no matter how emotionally raw and derogatory, and they can refuse to run any spot without having to give a reason.

PUBLIC SERVICE FOR PRIVATE INTERESTS

Not all air time is given to commercial gain. The Federal Communications Commission (FCC) requires broadcasters to set time aside for "public service announcements." The obligation is a vague one; the FCC has never denied any station its license for failing to live up to it, despite complaints from community and public interest groups. About 3 percent of air time, worth a half billion dollars annually, is given to public service announcements. This free time, like the millions of dollars worth of free space donated by newspapers and magazines, is monopolized by the Advertising Council, a nonprofit corporation funded and directed by corporations, bankers, and network officials. Its board of directors reads like a who's who of big business, with representatives from such major advertisers as Procter and Gamble, General Motors, General Mills, General Electric, and General Foods. A subcommittee of the Advertising Council, the Industries Advisory Committee (at one count composed of twenty-eight bankers and fifty-four major corporate executives), sets the ideological tone for all advertising campaigns. No public interest groups are represented on the Council's board.[15]

The Advertising Council is the second largest advertiser in the world (behind Procter and Gamble). Since its formation in 1941, it has used more than $10 billion worth of free "public service" advertising donated by radio, television, newspapers, and magazines. While supposedly nonpartisan and nonpolitical, the Council's public service commercials laud the blessings of free enterprise and urge viewers to buy U.S. Savings Bonds. The ads tell us that business is "doing its job" in hiring the handicapped, veterans, minorities, and the poor—when in fact, business makes little voluntary effort on behalf of such groups. Workers are exhorted to take pride in their work and produce more for their employers, but nothing is said about employers paying more to their workers.

The Advertising Council has waged a "Food, Nutrition and Health" campaign, whose ads urge viewers to send in for a free book-let entitled "Food is More than Just Something to Eat." The booklet fails to mention that Americans eat too much processed food, sugar, and junk food. Instead it cheerily announces: "Fresh or frozen? Canned or dried? Instant or from scratch? Which foods have the nutrients? Which do not? They all do."[16]

Council ads offer cosmetic solutions to serious social problems, thereby trivializing the nature of the problems. Unemployment? It can be reduced with "better job training." Crime? Lock your car after parking it and secure your front door. Hazardous and costly automobile transportation? Fasten your safety belts. Ecology and conservation? Listen to Smokey Bear and prevent forest fires. Industry's devastation of the environment? Do not litter. The Council's slogan is "People start pollution, and people can stop it." The ads blame pollution on everyone in general—thus avoiding placing any blame on industry in particular. The Council's "Keep America Beautiful" campaign of 1983 was coordinated by the public relations director of Union Carbide, a chemical manufacturer and a major polluter.

Throughout the Council's diverse range of messages runs one underlying theme: personal charity, individual effort, and neighborly good will can solve any mess; collectivist, class-oriented, political actions, and governmental regulations are not needed in a land of self-reliant volunteers.[17]

In the 1970s, with funds from the U.S. Department of Commerce, the Advertising Council launched campaigns to educate Americans about the blessings of private enterprise and the evils of inflation. Some 13 million booklets, distributed to schools, workplaces, and communities and reprinted in newspapers across the nation, informed readers that only *they* could whip inflation and make the system work better by themselves working harder, producing more, and shopping smarter. The anti-inflation campaign, reaching some 70 million Americans, listed government regulation as the primary cause of inflation. The solution was to keep the lid on wages and prices and roll back regulations.

The Ad Council's campaign seemed to have an effect on public opinion. In 1975, 22 percent of those polled thought there was too much government regulation; by 1979, 50 percent; and in 1980, 60 percent.[18] By the 1980 electoral campaign, "deregulation" had become a widespread, ready-made theme utilized to advantage by presidential candidate Ronald Reagan.

Those who wished to make monopoly profits, occupational safety, unemployment, and environmental protection the central themes of popular debate have no way of reaching mass audiences. The public service air time that could be used by conservationists, labor, consumer, and other public interest groups has been preempted by a business-dominated Advertising Council that passes off its one-sided, ideological ads as noncontroversial, nonpolitical, and in the public interest. As one liberal Congressman complained, "The Ad Council and the networks have corrupted the original intent of public service time by turning it into a free bonus for the special interests. The Ad Council is a propagandist for business and government, and with staggering control of the media, it not only makes sure its own side of the story is told, but that the other side isn't. The public has no meaningful access to the media."[19]

Notes

1. Charles Clark quoted in *City Paper* (Washington, D.C.), June 24, 1983.
2. For a good discussion of advertising and the creation of consumer culture, see Stuart Ewen, *Captains of Consciousness* (New York: McGraw-Hill, 1976).
3. Ibid.
4. Ibid.
5. J. S. Henry, "From Soap to Soapbox: The Corporate Merchandising of Ideas," *Working papers,* May/June, 1980, p. 55.
6. Ibid., p. 56.
7. *Washington Post,* October 25, 1981.
8. This appeared as a full-page ad in the *Columbia Journalism Review,* March/April 1981, and other publications.
9. *Washington Post,* October 25, 1981; similar kinds of McDonnell Douglas and other defense company ads have appeared in the *New York Times, U.S. News and World Report, Business Week,* and other such publications.
10. *Washington Post,* October 6, 1981.
11. Albert Szymanski, *Is the Red Flag Flying?* (London: Zed, 1979), pp. 114–115; also Center for Strategic and International Studies, *Soviet Sea Power,* cited in Szymanski.
12. Robert Friedman, "How America Gets Up In Arms," *Nuclear Times,* March 1983, p. 19.
13. Robert Cirino, *Don't Blame the People* (New York: Vintage, 1972), pp. 90, 302.

14. Philip Stern, "How TV Gagged Our Freeze Ads," *Washington Post,* November 21, 1982.

15. Bruce Howard, "The Advertising Council: Selling Lies," *Ramparts,* December 1974/January 1975, pp. 26–32; also "The State and Corporations: Public Service Ads," *Guardian,* May 26, 1976.

16. Howard, "The Advertising Council...," p. 31.

17. Keenen Peck, "Ad Nauseam," *Progressive,* May 1983, p. 44.

18. Ibid., p. 45.

19. Congressman Benjamin Rosenthal (D-N.Y.) quoted in Howard, "The Advertising Council...," p. 32.

5

Giving Labor the Business

In capitalist society, working people are the ones who get the least of what there is to get, while often paying a higher price. Their work is frequently dirty, mindless, dangerous, low paying, and lacking in job security and esteem. As compared to upper-income persons they are more apt to be victimized as employees, taxpayers, and consumers, and more apt to be slighted and negatively represented in the media.

SPEARHOLDERS, NONENTITIES, AND BIGOTS

The history of the working class is one of struggle, involving strikes, sit-ins, lockouts, blacklists and violent encounters with company goons and state security forces. That struggle continues to this day, but it is seldom mentioned in the schools or portrayed in the mass media.[1] The literature, poetry, songs, and sagas of working people, the great defeats and victories of labor, past and present, all part of working class culture, are pushed out of view by the business-dominated culture. Historians Herbert Gutman and Philip Foner point out that labor history has rarely been taught as part of American history except for an occasional reference to "strikes and violence."[2] Journalist Studs Terkel concurs: "Working people themselves have no understanding of their past, no idea where the minimum wage or the eight-hour day came from. There is no past."[3]

If working people have little sense of their great history, media people have even less. An extensive study of how labor is portrayed in prime-time television shows conducted in 1980 by the International Association of Machinists and Aerospace Workers (IAM) found that working people are consistently underrepresented and portrayed in denigrating and patronizing ways. In television stories, prostitutes outnumber machinists by twelve to one. There are twice as many witch doctors as welfare workers, eight times more butlers than miners, and twelve times more private detectives than production-line workers.[4] Factory workers are rarely seen and when so they are seldom depicted in workplace interactions.

Being the good-natured, simple sorts they supposedly are, laboring people are portrayed in television series and movies as more friendly, funny, and less selfish than nonlabor characters. But they are also shown as dumber, more foolish, less competent, less educated, less attractive, more given to drink and smoke, and less able to act as leaders.[5]

Another study finds that such service workers as bartenders, shopkeepers, and gas station attendants, appear frequently but in minor roles that are dispensable to the plot, doing jobs that support the central upper-middle-class characters. "Mostly silent and nameless, they serve and obey."[6]

This shadowy portrayal of working people is to be expected, for they actually do exist only on the silent service margins of the upper- and upper-middle-class world inhabited by the people who produce these shows. Furthermore, the business-owned media have an interest in avoiding any realistic portrayal of working people that might alert us to the existence of oppressive class realities in American society. The real tribulations of working people—their efforts to make ends meet, the specter of unemployment, the abuses suffered at the hands of bosses, the loss of pensions and seniority, the battles for unionization and occupational safety, the lives wrecked by work-connected injury and diseases—these and other realities relating to working life are given very little dramatic treatment in the commercial media.

A study of the twenty most popular prime time television entertainment shows during the fall of 1979 found that working-class characters express little inclination to bargain collectively. They are obedient to, even if slyly critical of, their superiors who, for comic effect, are often presented as bumbling and ineffectual—but basically benign. Serious work-associated difficulties "are virtually ignored or presented from an upper-middle-class management-oriented perspective."[7]

Television and film characters enjoy material abundance, good foods and beverages, fine clothing, and expensive houses. Economic want is not part of the script except when a character needs extra money for a special opportunity or event or is victimized by natural disaster. "Even in the very few instances of financial need, solutions brought about by individual ingenuity or heroics, are always forthcoming within the half-hour or hour framework of the show."[8]

THE WICKED UNIONS

Unions have a marginal and mostly negative image in television entertainment shows and movies. Despite the use of unionized occupations as the basis for an occasional plot, there are few depictions of the way unions have improved the worker's lot. Rare exceptions by independent producers are films like *Norma Rae* (1979), *Silkwood* (1983), and the TV drama, *A Matter of Sex* (1984). On occasions when union activity is a significant component of the plot, the portrayal is likely to be a negative one. In *Trapper John, M.D.*, a nurses' strike was shown as obstructing the critical routine of the hospital. In an episode of *Skag* union officials were cast as uncaring and brutal bullies. Generally, unions are presented as selfish, violent organizations that are likely to do their members no good.

The news media's treatment of labor unions is no less slighting and negative than the entertainment media's. For instance, years ago it was discovered that over 600,000 workers were exposed to an often fatal lung disease called byssinosis, or "brown lung," because they breathed the high levels of cotton dust in textile mills. Here certainly was the makings of a major news story. For more than ten years the textile unions and the Brown Lung Association (BLA) tried to draw public attention to the problem and get the government to impose protective standards, but the national and local press virtually ignored the story until the spring of 1977 when the Occupational Safety and Health Administration finally held national hearings on proposed rules to limit cotton dust in mills.[9] Even then, the news media usually ignored what the unions and the BLA had to say, preferring to quote industry sources. The press treated brown lung as a "problem" linked to the natural process of production, having little to do with safety conditions, speed-ups, and profits.[10]

The news media provide labor unions with few opportunities to present their side of the story. The network evening news regularly reports the Dow Jones average and other stock market news but offers no weekly tabulations on industrial accidents, housing evictions, or environmental violations. The major newspapers and weeklies have no "labor" section to go along with their "business" section. The Gross National Product (GNP) is reported but there is no "quality-of-life index" to tell us what the GNP takes away or fails to give us. Economic growth is assumed to be a beneficial phenomenon. The question of why we must increase production, especially of the private market variety, is never raised. Industrial plateau is called "stagnation." When the stock market has a good day this is presumed to be something beneficial to us all. One never hears the word "capital" or "capital accumulation" to describe the core process of our economy. There is seldom a reference to corporate economic power and its political influences. The economy itself is presented by the media as largely a business affair and not a creation of labor, as something government and business attend to, while organized labor tags along at best as a very junior and often troublesome partner, at worst as a threat to the system.

In 1980, when the president of the IAM, William Winpisinger, called a press conference to present the results of his union's study of prime-time TV entertainment, not a single representative of the national networks came to hear what he had to say. What labor had discovered about the entertainment media could not win the attention of the news media.

A month later the IAM released the second part of its survey, dealing with television news. This report concluded that network coverage repeatedly slights or ignores the issues of major concern to unions and union members, specifically, inflation, energy, foreign trade, health, unemployment, and tax reform. When these topics are touched upon it is usually from a management viewpoint.[11] Other concerns of labor, such as occupational safety, human services, and wage and work conditions receive little coverage. Reporters fail to enlist labor's views on national questions. Unions are most likely to be noticed when they go on strike, but the reasons behind the strike are seldom elaborated upon, the impression being that labor is simply insatiable in its demands.[12] A special report on CBS (November 21, 1983) thus concluded: "To a lot of Americans the unions have dug their own grave by being greedy. And management went along. Now things have caught up with them."

When the news media do mention unions (aside from strikes), it is to report on their links to organized crime, corrupt bosses, and the lack of internal democracy. (The media seldom raise the question of internal democracy in regard to corporations or most other social institutions.)

Few Americans get to hear what unions really are about. As Roberta Lynch puts it:

> Media coverage of trade union activities is restricted to superficial reports of major national strikes. Yet there is in unions of every variety a wealth of experience worthy of wider public attention. Local union members who know more than epidemiologists about cancer patterns. Union stewards who blow the whistle on secret hazardous waste disposal. Women in chemical factories who know first-hand the potential for causing birth defects of many commonly used manufacturing substances. Unions that face unscrupulous and high-paid consulting firms brought in

ONE HAPPY FAMILY

On May 5, 1983, ABC television ran an advertisement sponsored by the National Association of Broadcasters and narrated by Howard K. Smith. "The United States is a large richly endowed country," Smith says, "yet Japan, a country the size of Montana and with few resources is outcompeting us." (A shot of two Japanese workers in a motorcycle factory talking in a friendly manner to a supervisor.) "Why?" continues Smith, "Because they know how to work as a team. We have got to learn to work as a team. Government, management and employees must work together for the best performance." (Cut to a conference room of Americans talking earnestly together.) "They must work together as a team to get the best for all." (Fade out)

The ad's message denies there are antagonistic relations between labor and capital; instead, all differences can be reconciled by "teamwork" and better performance in the workplace. Management, it seems, is not compelled to exploit employees in order to maximize profits; workers are not subordinate to capital and do not have to struggle against bosses. There are no class conflicts. And to complete this fairy tale, government does not protect the hegemony of the corporate class but is a neutral evenhanded "partner" in a harmonious triad. Those who learn to cooperate and not make troublesome demands will succeed—like the Japanese supposedly have. The ad assumes that the Japanese worker is happily sharing in the economic success of the Japanese owning class.

not to negotiate with them but to break them. Unions that have joined in alliances with environmentalists to help clean up the air and the water. The list could go on.

The fact is that labor unions are on the whole among the most democratic institutions in American life. The local union represents one of the very few arenas in which ordinary people can come together to define their own concerns, to develop new skills and understanding, and to glimpse a sense of their own potential.[13]

The withholding of labor by workers is called a strike, but not the withholding of capital by employers. The latter is never treated as a controversial disruption of the production process. Corporations may close plants or refuse to invest because of low profit margins, or decide not to put money into maintenance and retooling, or they may milk a subsidiary for the highest possible profits and then close it down, or move to Taiwan or South Korea or some other country where labor can be even more ruthlessly exploited than at home—but such things are assumed to be management's prerogatives and are seldom treated by the press or anyone else as contributing to conflicts between bosses and workers.

Industrial strife is never characterized in the media as an expression of class struggle, with the capitalist relentlessly accumulating as much of the wealth created by labor as possible and workers fighting back in order to protect or improve their standard of living. Little attention is given to management's multimillion-dollar union-busting efforts and its tendency to coerce labor into giving back hard-won benefits and protections. The impression of who is giving and who is grabbing is inverted in a business-owned press that portrays management as making "offers" and labor as making "demands." The struggles between workers and bosses are called "labor problems" and "labor disputes," never "management disputes"—even when it is management that refuses to negotiate a contract—as is often the case.

In real life, the struggle between labor and capital is constant, not occcasional. Along with strikes and union organizing, worker resistance takes such forms as absenteeism, lateness, theft, deliberate inefficiency, sabotage, slow-downs and hostile expressions toward management and foremen. Management, in turn, will ignore safety regulations and grievances, habitually violate contract agreements, and impose speed-ups. Despite this constant strife, workers are seldom eager to strike. They do not wish to endure the hardships that come with loss of income and the possible loss of employment. Usually the strike is their weapon of last resort.

The business-owned news media, of course, do not mention class struggle as being the deeper cause of strikes. They say nothing about the incessant need of capital to extract as much profit from labor as possible. By ignoring the underlying causes of industrial conflict, the press finds it easy to represent strikes as irrational events, the outcome of some recalcitrant impulse on the part of workers.[14]

NICE BOSSES, CRAZY STRIKERS

Perhaps we can best illustrate how the press treats (and mistreats) labor struggles by providing a detailed account of a specific instance: the media's coverage of the 1977–78 coal strike. (What follows is drawn mostly from Curtis Seltzer's work on this subject.[15]) Newspapers like the *New York Times* and *Washington Post* blamed the collapse of contract negotiations on the union and warned that a long strike would plunge the nation into economic chaos. Management was described as making a wage offer that was "hefty,"[16] and "whop-ping,"[17] while, in exchange, asking only for "labor stability."[18] The press failed to explain that "stability" included the absolute right to fine or discharge any miner for strike activity or for encouraging strike activity. "Stability" also included the right to initiate "production in-centives"—in other words, speed-ups. The United Mine Workers' health care system would be phased out, miners were to be transferred to more expensive private insurance plans arranged by the coal bosses. Miners' health clinics were also to be cut back.

All of this was unreported or underplayed by the major news-papers and network newscasters throughout the strike.[19] The miners' wildcat strikes were treated as irresponsible, undisciplined actions by reporters who never worked a day in the mines and rarely bothered talking to the people who did. Wildcat strikes are often necessary protective actions against safety violations. When a foreman cuts the alarm system designed to warn miners of a dangerous gas build-up, such a violation cannot be overlooked for the week or two it would take for arbitration. The miners' only recourse is to refuse to enter the shafts. Miners also strike over cutbacks in their health benefits, black lung legislation, and compulsory shift rotation.[20] The right to strike can be a matter of life and death. None of this was made clear in the news coverage. Instead, wildcat strikes were characterized as wanton and self-defeating.

The press never reported that the mine companies had accumu-lated unprecedented stockpiles of coal at a time when demand was low, enabling them to sit out the entire winter. The owners rejected the UMW proposals out of hand and locked out the miners on Decem-ber 6, 1977, but the media kept describing the lock-out as a "strike" throughout the work stoppage. The press gave the impression "that it was the miners who were taking on their employers when the reverse was really the case."[21]

Having ignored the issues of takebacks, job rights, health insur-ance, safety, and real wages, the press had to find some explanation for why the miners had behaved so strangely and rejected a contract that had offered "substantial" wage increases. What was the matter with them? The miners, explained the New York Times, were "a breed apart" and "clannish."[22] Newsweek suggested that they were "in-bred" and "hell-raising and violent, promiscuous and enduring."[23] Time saw them as "traditionally quick to resort to violence," and "not addicted to regular work."[24] No such conjectures were offered regard-ing the mine owners, nothing about their "clannish" country clubs, and "inbred" and "promiscuous" social lives; their irregular, leisurely, and often nonexistent work hours; and the tradition of violence expressed in their reliance on goon squads, Pinkertons, gun thugs, state troopers, and National Guardsmen. No reporter wrote about management's "strange ways," nor would any editor or publisher have allowed such a story to pass.

Does the press influence what we think about things? Certainly in the 1977–78 coal strike there is reason to think so. Not only the general public—which is often unsympathetic toward unions—but, Seltzer observes, government officials also relied heavily on the *New York Times,* the *Washington Post* and the *Wall Street Journal* for information about the strike. The Carter Administration accepted the mine owners' view, propagated by the national media, and imposed a Taft-Hartley injunction against the miners.[25] In turn, the press uncritically served as "Washington's intelligence agency and propagandist,"[26] freely quoting government officials who charged that the final contract was "inflationary." But not a single story could be found that analyzed whether the charge was true. Neither the press nor the government mentioned that the coal companies were reaping high profits regardless of production costs. After-tax profits per ton of coal climbed 800 percent during the 1974–78 period, while miners' wages had risen only 160 percent in the previous twenty years.[27]

Years before, the miners had won the democratic right to vote on contracts negotiated between their leaders and the owners. When over 100,000 of them exercised this right in an orderly way, and voted down the contract by two to one, the *Washington Post* described the UMW as "in a state of virtual anarchy."[28] The failure of the UMW leadership to keep its membership in tow was, the *New York Times* said, "the main cause of this year's coal paralysis."[29] "As the weeks passed," writes Curtis Seltzer, "union-blaming became a substitute for thoughtful analysis." The "paralysis" supposedly caused by the union "could just as well be blamed on industry hardliners who hoped to use the union's weaknesses as a means of saddling its members with a punitive contract."[30]

Three years later when miners again voted down a takeback contract, the *Wall Street Journal* decided that "miners had wanted—and expected—a strike," and quoted one anonymous "union official" as saying: "it's fishing season in Appalachia, and a lot of miners are off in Fort Lauderdale on vacations they booked months ago."[31] Two weeks later, *Newsweek* echoed this fanciful story.[32] But neither publication could provide evidence of a mass exodus of vacationers from Appalachia, nor could they explain why a miner would forgo thousands of dollars in income and a supposedly generous new contract for the sake of a few catfish and bass.[33] In fact the 112-day strike in 1978 followed by the 72-day strike in 1981 had left many miners "deeply in debt."[34]

*   *   *

Far from being an anomaly, the media's treatment of the coal strike was characteristic of how the commercial press does its job. Consider another instance: press coverage of the 1982 contract negotiations between the steel industry and the United Steelworkers of America (USWA). The industry demanded not only a suspension of cost-of-living allowances but substantial wage cuts amounting to about $3,700 for each steelworker in the first eight months alone. The workers rejected this "offer." But the media gave no indication that the owners were pushing the workers into a corner and forcing them into a fight. Instead, they presented "the companies' proposals as reasonable and the workers' rejection as greed pure and simple. To paint this picture, the press had to lie," writes David Bensman.[35] The *New York Times* ran an editorial (November 26, 1982) condemning the unyielding attitude of the union and its inability to accept the "gravity of the steel industry's present plight," followed two days later by a *Times* business feature that blamed the steel industry's troubles on the workers' excessively high wages. The *Times* presented a chart showing that steelworkers earned 60 percent more than other U.S. blue-collar workers. Bensman notes acidly that this was a powerful argument, "but it was false," for the *Times* had compared the hourly wages of employees in other industries to the steelworkers' *total* hourly compensation including wages *and benefits*.

The *Wall Street Journal* headlined its story of November 22: "US RECOVERY IS SEEN SET BACK BY UNION'S VOTE." Based on information provided by the steel companies, the story failed to mention that steelworkers would lose twenty cents an hour in incentive pay. The *Journal* noted that the workers would have to contribute to a fund for laid-off employees but failed to report that part of this sum would actually have gone to the companies to repay them for payments they had previously made to the unemployed. Also unmentioned was that more than half the jobless members would have received nothing from the fund.

The overall impression from the mainstream press was—as in the case of the coal strike—that the greedy, stubborn steelworkers were inexplicably intent upon cutting their own throats while bringing ruination to the industry and possibly to the entire economy.

Let us venture a few generalizations about the media's treatment of labor's struggles:

1. As previously noted, by ignoring how strikes are part of the larger class struggle between labor and capital, an outgrowth of

capital's perpetual need to extract the highest possible profit from the labor it employs, the media are able to present labor struggles as something of senseless origin, readily avoidable if only some good will were shown. The media regularly portray *labor* as unwilling to negotiate in good faith, even when it might be management who refuses all compromises and forces a strike.

2. The press generally publicizes those portions of a company's "offer" that might reflect most favorably on management (for example, the higher pay raises offered to a select stratum of employees), while making no mention of such takebacks in the areas of job security, seniority, pensions, health insurance, and safety protections that may actually be the central issues of the strike. By repeatedly omitting or underplaying employee grievances, the press makes workers appear as irrational and greedy, self-indulgent to the point of being self-destructive.

3. While emphasizing the supposedly fat wage labor would enjoy if the union would only accept management's "offer," the press usually says nothing about the enormous increases management awards itself. If the high salaries, million-dollar bonuses, juicy stock options, and other such goodies were better publicized, this would cast serious doubt on management's argument that employees must make concessions lest the company go broke.

4. While the business-owned press has little to say about the deeper causes of strikes, it greatly emphasizes their impact— as in the coal and steel disputes—noting the supposed damage they might do to the economy and the inconveniences inflicted on the public.[36] The overall impression created is that strikers are indifferent to the well-being of the larger public.

5. While playing up the real or imagined damage the strike might do to the economy, nothing is said about the damage to *workers'* interests if they give up the strike and accept management's terms.

6. The mutual support that strikers provide for each other, and the aid that unions sometimes extend to other unions, is seldom reported by the news media. During the coal strike there was almost nothing on how farmers were bringing food to the miners. By ignoring the existence of worker solidarity and mutual assistance within and between occupations, the press denies the class dimension of the strike and underplays the support strikers have among other sectors of the public.

7. The news media unfailingly portray the government as a neu-

SAME STORY NORTH OF THE BORDER

The overall effect of the coverage of labour relations in the Canadian media is to present an image of an institution that has no moral or legal right to exist, and which has no positive contribution to make to our economy. Unions and their leaders are treated by newspapers, TV and radio stations as greedy, irresponsible, anti-social and disruptive. It is not surprising that public opinion polls reflect such a low opinion of the labour movement. Nor is it surprising that, given this persistent media distortion of labour's image, governments' anti-union legislation should be so widely endorsed. The standard of labour reporting in Canada—with only a few notable exceptions—is atrocious.

A recent survey of newspaper stories about unions (Ray Sentes, *Trade Unions and the Press,* an unpublished thesis) disclosed that the same unfavourable words keep recurring. High on the list are strike, picket, demands, helpless public, breakdown, inflationary, labour unrest, held to ransom, inconvenience, labour bosses, callous, irresponsible, violence, contempt, lawless agitators, greedy, blackmail, and abuse of power . . .

In sharp contrast to the negative language associated with unions, the language used in describing the activities of business organizations is the exact opposite. Words such as growth, income, investment, capital gain, entrepreneurship, employment, and so on, are used to portray a generally favorable image of companies and their executives.

Ed Finn, "Labour Reporting in Canada," The Facts, *June 1983, p. 20; (publication of the Canadian Union of Public Employees).*

tral arbiter in the struggle between capital and labor, acting on behalf of the "national interest"—which itself is assumed to be best served by getting the workers back into production as soon as possible, regardless of the terms of settlement. The press seldom comments on the role of the state troopers and police who guard the company's property, escort scabs safely to work, and enforce injunctions against picket lines. The police—along with the courts, the president, and the rest of the government—are presented as neutral guardians of the peace and defenders of the public interest rather than as protectors of corporate property and bodyguards for strikebreakers.

Small wonder the American public, including many progressive people, has such a negative image of organized labor and persons who are critical of racist, sexist, and antigay attitudes themselves still harbor anti-working-class and anti-union sentiments of the kind propagated by the media and other institutions of the business dominated culture. The continual anti-labor, anti-union media propaganda helps to divide organized labor (which consists of less than 20 percent of the work force) from unorganized labor. A negative image of unions discourages workers from unionizing and leaves them suspicious of labor organizations. With its monopoly over mass communication, business has been able to present a largely unchallenged picture of "Big Labor" as an avaricious, narrowly self-interested, and often irrational force that does itself, the economy, and the public no good, driving up prices with its incessant demands, making gains only for itself while creating costs that must be passed on to the rest of the public. Labor has no direct means of countering this negative image among the general public. If there exists for labor a free market of ideas, it is not to be found in the mass media.

Notes

1. For excellent accounts of that history see Richard Boyer and Herbert Morais, *Labor's Untold Story* (New York: United Electrical, Radio and Machine Workers, 1972); Howard Zinn, *A People's History of the United States* (New York: Harper & Row, 1980); Philip Foner, *History of the Labor Movement in the United States* (New York: International Publishers, various volumes: 1947, 1955, 1964, 1965, 1980, 1981).
2. Their comments were carried in the *New York Times*, September 8, 1981. The *Times* generally has nothing to say about how the media, including the *Times* itself, neglect contemporary labor concerns.
3. Ibid.
4. "Television Entertainment Report Part II: Conclusions and National Summary of Occupational Frequency in Network Primetime Entertainment for February 1980." International Association of Machinists and Aerospace Workers, June 12, 1980. For an earlier study see Mil Lieberthal, "TV Images of Workers—Reinforcing the Stereotypes," *Labor Studies Journal*, 1, Fall (1976).
5. "IAM Television Entertainment Report . . ."
6. Ralph Arthur Johnson, "World Without Workers: Prime Time's Presentation of Labor," *Labor Studies Journal*, 5, Winter 1981, p. 203. The same conclusion is drawn in the IAM survey.
7. Johnson, "World Without Workers . . . ," p. 203.
8. Ibid.
9. See Bob Hall's report in the *Columbia Journalism Review*, March/April 1978. The brown lung story was news in the radical press, however.
10. Ibid.
11. "Network News and Documentary Report," International Association of Machinists & Aerospace Workers, July 30, 1980.
12. Janet Coffman in *TV Monitor*, August 1, 1980.
13. Roberta Lynch, "The Media Distort the Value of Labor Unions," *In These Times*, July 15–28, 1981, p. 17.

14. John Downing, *The Media Machine* (London: Pluto Press, 1980), p. 35.

15. Curtis Seltzer, "How the Press Covered the Coal Strike," unpublished study, August 1979; and Seltzer's "The Pits: Press Coverage of the Coal Strike," *Columbia Journalism Review,* July/August 1981.

16. *Wall Street Journal,* March 16, 1978. This citation and most of the following ones are from Seltzer's "How the Press Covered the Coal Strike."

17. *Time,* March 20, 1978

18. *Washington Post,* February 13, 1978.

19. Seltzer, "The Pits . . ."

20. Seltzer, "How the Press Covered the Coal Strike."

21. Ibid.

22. *New York Times,* December 4, 1977, and March 5, 1978.

23. *Newsweek,* March 20, 1978.

24. *Time,* March 6, 1978.

25. Seltzer, "How the Press Covered the Coal Strike."

26. *Ibid.*

27. Michael Parenti, *Democracy for the Few,* 4th ed. (New York: St. Martin's Press, 1983), p. 19.

28. *Washington Post,* March 6, 1978.

29. *New York Times,* March 29, 1978.

30. Seltzer, "How the Press Covered the Coal Strike."

31. *Wall Street Journal,* April 2, 1981.

32. *Newsweek,* April 13, 1981.

33. Seltzer, "The Pits . . ."

34. *Daily World,* July 22, 1981.

35. David Bensman, "The Press Joins the Steel War on Labor," *In These Times,* January 12–18, 1983.

36. Downing, *The Media Machine,* p. 35.

6

Creating Moods
Left and Right

There exists not only public opinion but opinions about public opinion. What the people think is one thing; what is *publicized* about what they think can be quite something else. The media cannot mold every political feeling we have, but they can fill the air with pronouncements about what our feelings allegedly are. The press may not be able to create a conservative mood within us but it can repeatedly announce that a conservative mood exists, thereby doing much to create the impression of such a mood and encouraging conservative forces to come to the fore. The press cannot stop protests, but it can discredit them, ignore them, and declare them to be things of the past, of no interest to people nowadays, thereby discouraging popular political actions. In short, even more than manipulating actual opinions, the media have a great deal of power in controlling *opinion visibility*. They create a media image of public opinion that often plays a more crucial role in setting the issue agenda than does actual public opinion and which has a feedback effect on actual opinion.

The institutions of this society whose job, among other things, is to socialize people into patterns of conventional belief and acceptable behavior, do not operate with perfect effect. Despite persistent conditioning, some people will still become disaffected. Longstanding grievances can erupt at unexpected moments. Sometimes extraordinary events play on the public's discontents, galvanizing a kind of protest that not even the most skillful media propagandist, the smoothest educator, or the slickest political leader can mollify.

The Vietnam War was just such an extraordinary event. While the news media are often credited with, or damned for, making the war unpopular by providing daily accounts of its carnage, in actuality, during the early years of the conflict the press reported the war largely the way the U.S. government wanted it reported, raising no serious objections about U.S. intervention. Nevertheless, sectors of the public developed an opposition to U.S. intervention through means other than the mainstream press; these included campus teach-ins, lectures, radical publications, progressive unions, and religious groups. Eventually the small groups grew into large demonstrations, and the demonstrations into sit-ins, civil disobedience, draft resistance, and even riot. Criticism turned into protest and protest into confrontation. Opposition to the war evolved into opposition to the system that conducted such a war. By 1966 or so, the antiwar movement had become a political force to be reckoned with.

After initially downplaying the war and the protests, the media began giving serious attention to both. Unable either to prevent or to ignore mass protests, the opinion manufacturers set about to misrepresent, discredit, and contain a political movement that was raising serious questions about "democratic capitalism." The story of how that was done is expertly told in a book by Todd Gitlin and will not be repeated here.[1] Suffice it to say that during the 1960s the media commentators spent more time attacking those who protested the enormities of this world than those who perpetrated such enormities. The news media did not always speak with negative uniformity about what became known as the "New Left." As Gitlin notes there were "exceptional moments of coverage," especially in the early stages when protesters were occasionally treated with some sympathy and insight. But the *cumulative impact* of press coverage was to create the impression that these "kids" were crazy, violent, extremist, and dangerous to society. Thus the protesters were made the issue rather than the things they were protesting. These discrediting techniques were to be repeated against other protesters in the years to follow.

CREATING A "CONSERVATIVE MOOD"

In the aftermath of the antiwar movement of the 1960s, the press was quick to announce a return to normalcy. Supposedly protests were passé and everyone had gone back to their private pursuits. By the mid-1970s the news media were going so far as to proclaim that the nation was in a "conservative mood." "The country is moving in the conservative direction . . . surely," intoned *Washington Post* columnist David Broder. And the *New York Times* talked about opinion "swinging to the right."[2]

Press commentators pointed to students who now struggled for grades instead of for revolution. They noted the conservative victories in a number of state legislatures against the Equal Rights Amendment, against abortion, and for the death penalty, and the widespread resistance in local communities to school busing for racial balance. Ultra-right leaders like Jerry Falwell, Richard Viguerie, and Phyllis Schlafly became familiar faces in the news. New conservative columnists and TV and radio commentators were hired to bolster the old stock. Some liberal intellectuals now declared themselves to be neo-conservatives. The Iranian hostage crisis and the Soviet intervention into Afghanistan caused a temporary public upsurge in jingoistic fervor. As far as the news pundits were concerned, these developments demonstrated that the country was on an increasingly conservative trajectory.

In discovering a "conservative mood," the news media had to overlook a great deal about the 1970s and 1980s including the various polls conducted during that period—which showed a shift in a *progressive* direction (even among many who labeled themselves conservative) on such issues as military spending, environmental protection, care for the elderly, tax reform, and race relations.[3] Surveys showed that by the end of the 1970s *fewer* people called themselves "conservatives" (more choosing the "moderate" designation) than at the beginning of the decade. Throughout the 1970s and early 1980s the number of Americans who thought the government spent too much on education, health, and environmental services remained at a low 10 percent, while over two-thirds approved of liberal programs for jobs, housing, occupational safety, and equal opportunity.[4] At the same time the public was against increased spending for defense, the space program, and highways—favorite conservative spending projects.[5]

Even on "social" issues Americans were not becoming all that conservative. Attitudes toward crime and capital punishment did harden, and busing remained highly controversial; but there was also increased support for minority rights, women's rights, gay rights, and the legalization of marijuana, while support for abortion and gun control held firm.[6] After sifting through the available survey data, Paletz and Entman conclude, "The ability of conservatives to mobilize effectively around some social issues should not be minimized. But the social mood was by no means conservative, and much of the drift was to the left."[7]

In the area of political activism, differences between the flaming sixties and slumbering seventies were not what the media opinion molders would have us think. In various parts of the nation there were large demonstrations against South Africa, Chile, Somoza's Nicaragua, the shah's Iran, and a half-dozen other dictatorships. Citizens groups took to the streets to protest cuts in human services. There were mass rallies in New York, Washington, and other cities against nuclear power, and large civil disobedience actions at nuclear sites in various states. College campuses throughout the country witnessed rallies, demonstrations, strikes, sit-ins, and arrests over such issues as

COLLAPSING RIGHTWARD

The liberal-left ardor of some prominent New York-based, intellectual magazines had chilled, even frozen. These periodicals are sources for some of the ideas and insights purveyed by columnists and editorial writers. . . . The mutually reinforcing musings of rising Republican stars, reborn social reactionaries, former liberals, and uninspired editorialists combined to give an illusory picture of public opinion.

Many liberal politicians collapsed before the rightist assault. There was a void (or an echo) in the places where journalists were accustomed to finding liberal responses to conservative voices. Farther left, the activist groups of the 1960s had ceased being newsworthy. No longer did the news feature a continuing crescendo of radical demands that made it seem to reporters that the country was moving rapidly left.

The conservative myth reinforced itself by affecting reporters' choices of sources. In a time of putatively surging conservatism, journalists may have perceived spokespersons on the left as irrelevant or naive. As these delegitimized sources were consulted less frequently, liberal proposals and interpretations received less coverage, and those on the right obtained relatively greater emphasis. Moreover, the location of the all-important center, to which editors cleave and by which reporters set their bearings, was perceived as having shifted rightward. Positions and politicians once thought too conservative became a part of the respectable mainstream; contrast the treatment of Barry Goldwater during the liberal heyday of 1964 with Ronald Reagan 16 years later.

David Paletz and Robert Entman, Media Power Politics *(New York: Free Press, 1981), p. 201.*

university investment policies, the firing of radical professors, cuts in minority studies and women's studies, and questions of governance. The national media slighted all these events.

In the 1970s there were major strikes by steelworkers, truck drivers, farmers, farm workers, teachers, and newspaper, hospital and utility workers. In 1978, some 50,000 coal miners stayed off the job for three months. Environmental, consumer, and other public interest groups continued to pit themselves against the giant companies, while peace organizations and religious groups launched protest actions against military spending. During one week in November 1981, over 150 college campuses across the nation held rallies and teach-ins to protest the nuclear arms escalation.

These activities either went unreported in the national media or were given only passing and sometimes negative mention.[8] In the face of substantial evidence to the contrary, and with a singlemindedness that, were it to occur in a country with a leftist government, would be taken as evidence of a controlled press, the media treated protests and activism as pretty much a thing of the past.

With the election of Ronald Reagan to the presidency in November 1980, along with a number of conservative victories in the U.S. Senate, the media now talked not only of a conservative "mood" but of a conservative "mandate," giving essentially the same interpretation to the election results as did the Reaganites themselves.

Polls conducted during the first two years of Reagan's White House occupancy showed that by a margin of 80 to 13 percent, Americans felt the tax system favored the rich at the expense of the average person. By 72 to 20 percent they judged that "too much money was going into wars and defense." An overwhelming four to one majority, supported a freeze on nuclear armaments and approved a 50 percent cut in arms by the United States and the Soviet Union. In scores of communities and municipalities and in a number of states, nuclear freeze referenda passed by wide margins. Despite the cold-war alarms repeatedly sounded by the Reagan administration and the media, fear of "the threat of communism or aggression by a communist power" declined from 29 percent in 1964, to 13 percent in 1974, to 8 percent in 1981.[9]

If people desired a change, there was no evidence they wanted to move still more precipitously in the direction Carter had been going—which is the way Reagan went. The claim that a conservative mandate existed was highly debatable—but the debate never occurred in the press.

By giving uncritical credence to the myth of a conservative mood and mandate the press not only happened to misreport public opinion but helped frame issues in a way favorable to conservatives. By crediting conservative policies with a popular support they did not have, the press did its part in shifting the political agenda in a rightward direction. Public opinion is not just an expression of sentiment; it is a democratic power resource that sometimes constrains and directs policymakers who otherwise spend their time responding to the demands and enticements of moneyed interests. "By misrepresenting public opinion, by emphasizing some opinions at the expense of others, the press deprives the unorganized masses of some of their potential power. The media short-circuit the process by which public preference may otherwise be translated into government policy."[10]

In addition, the myth of a conservative mood helps create a self-fulfilling prophecy. If the media keep telling us that times are favorable for conservative politics, people begin to believe it and act accordingly. Right-wing candidates thrust themselves forward more aggres-sively, readily attracting volunteers and big contributions. Liberals are perceived, and maybe even perceive themselves, as out of step with the times. In January 1984, for instance, Congressman Richard Ottinger (D.-N.Y.), when announcing his decision to resign form the House after sixteen years, noted: "The [House] leadership seems to have adopted the basic premise that the country has gone conservative and that [social welfare] programs . . . are no longer acceptable."[11] Liberal politicians shy away from "risky" issues and drift to the right. Given the media-created climate of opinion, fewer political leaders become willing or able to challenge the "conservative mood"—even if they suspect it to be only a myth.[12]

HOW TO DISCREDIT PROTESTERS

On those infrequent occasions when the media took the trouble to report on protests during the seventies and eighties, the coverage was reminiscent of the disparaging treatment accorded demonstrations during the sixties. The *Washington Post's* story of the May 3, 1981, "March on the Pentagon" can serve as a typical example of how the press treats protests on the left.[13] Buried in Section C along with local news, obituaries, and classified ads, the story, written by Mike Sager, begins by describing the demonstrators as a "loose coalition of groups whose causes range from gay rights to Palestinian autonomy." At the outset one might wonder why the *Post* singled out these two groups— in a march protesting U.S. intervention in El Salvador and Reagan's cuts in social programs—unless it was to typify the event as a pot-pourri of marginal, off-beat characters or in other ways to play upon the negative prejudices of certain sectors of its readership.

The story seems more concerned with describing the protesters than with telling us anything about the content of their protests, about why they were out there in the first place. So we read that the "youth-ful crowd formed a colorful river of jean-and-tee-shirt-clad humanity" and that "they marched carrying banners for their causes while licking ice-cream bars and taking pictures of each other with complicated camera gear." Furthermore, "Yesterday's minions carried a few plac-ards and repeated a few chants, but some also took time to eat picnic lunches, smoke marijuana, drink beer and work on their tans." These images suggest a frivolous, festive atmosphere that denies the pro-testers the seriousness of their concerns. It might be noted that a "minion," according to Webster's Unabridged Dictionary is "a term of contempt" describing "one who is a servile follower."

Two fairly large photographs of the event, accompanying the story, show no one consuming picnic lunches, pot, beer, or ice cream, nor is anyone sunbathing. And the photos reveal not "a few placards" but what must be hundreds of placards and banners. To be sure, some of the participants may well have paused to refresh themselves—in a demonstration that continued for some seven hours under the hot Washington sun. What might be questioned is why the *Post* writer treated these minor activities as central to the event.

Judging from the photographs accompanying the story and observations by persons like myself who witnessed the day-long event, the atmosphere was a serious political one and not that of a carnival. But the *Post* had its own scenario to spin: "Many of those interviewed yesterday—from long-haired hippie hold-outs with painted faces to L. L. Bean-clad outdoorsmen to health-conscious joggers who had stopped by to witness the spectacle—said they had come not so much to protest U.S. intervention in El Salvador as to voice their disapproval of the state of the nation under Reagan and the state of the world in general." (No danger of encountering any earnest and knowledgeable political intentions in this crowd.) "In all," continued the *Post*, "the demonstration took on a flea market atmosphere—something for everyone." It was a "hodge-podge collection." Even the headline noted: "25,000 PROTESTERS MARCH FOR MIXED CAUSES."

One could just as readily, and more accurately, see the diversity of issues as a sign of unity and maturity among progressive-minded people joined in struggle against a common enemy. The *Post* story assumed there was an incongruous mix of issues, when in fact the demonstration sought to link a range of domestic and foreign policies. Such issue linkage is somewhat alien to a press that treats political issues as unrelated events and dismisses large popular coalitions as hodge-podge collections.

The crowd was described as "youthful" and the event little more than a rerun of "the Vietnam antiwar rallies of a decade ago." (For years the press repeatedly described, or rather dismissed, demonstrations as tiresome repeats of the Vietnam era.) The emphasis on the supposedly "youthful" quality of the demonstrators plays on the stereotype of youth as not very responsible or rational, making it easier to treat the protest as a product of their immature spirits than as a justifiable response to political reality. But a few columns later we read that participants included trade unionists, retired elderly, lawyers, Hispanic migrant farm workers, feminists, and government employees—certainly a crowd of more than just youthful protesters.

The *Post* reporter accepted the police estimate of the crowd at 25,000, making no mention of the 100,000 claimed by the march organizers. A counterdemonstration, counted by me at 100 to 110 people, was reported in the *Post* story as 300 "clean-cut protesters" from "Rev. Moon's Unification Church which is calling for U.S. intervention in El Salvador to rid it of Russian and Cuban communist influence . . ." (Here the *Post* is accepting as established fact the Moonie charge that the Salvadoran revolutionaries are puppets of Moscow and Havana; a less biased statement might have read: "to rid it of *what the counterdemonstrators claim* is Russian and Cuban communist influence.") While the Moonies were only a minute fraction of the people present, they and their concerns were accorded about one-fifth of the story.

Speakers from a wide range of political groups made statements about U.S. policies at home and abroad, yet nothing about these speeches appeared in this rather lengthy article except for a few mocking lines describing one speaker's plea for funds to pay the demonstration costs. In sum, in most of its tone and content the *Post* article was belittling. Readers who had no direct experience with the demonstration might easily have come away thinking they had exercised good sense in choosing not to participate in what must have been a rather inane, circuslike affair.

The *Washington Post* outdid itself a few months later when it reported—or failed to report—the huge Labor Day parade that took place in New York City in September 1981. The parade organizers estimated the marchers at 200,000; the police said 100,000. In either case, the turnout was quite impressive in size and militancy. The *Post's* story, choosing instead to concentrate on President Reagan's visit to Mayor Edward Koch of New York, allowed only passing reference to the parade, buried toward the end of the article, describing it as a "disappointingly small crowd of less than 100,000 union workers."[14] Actually the parade organizers were jubilant at the enormous size of the turn-out.

The next month a series of civil disobedience actions at the Diablo Canyon nuclear site in California resulted in over 2,000 arrests. For years the protesters had argued that the plant was not sufficiently earthquake-proof, that human error made no nuclear plant safe, that there was no sufficient technology to deal with nuclear waste, radiation leakages, and a serious accident. Television news coverage of the Diablo Canyon protests, ignoring the arguments and evidence offered by the demonstrators, concentrated on the personal appearance of the marchers, their chants and songs, and the confrontation with the police—with much footage devoted to the arrests. Again, the *reason* why people were taking this extraordinary action was lost in a superficial recording of the action itself.

A *Washington Post* editorial did its part in making the Diablo Canyon protesters the issue rather than the thing they were protesting, referring to them as "the mindless school of nuclear protest" and the "quintessentially California happening of underworked TV actors and overgrown flower children complete with folk songs and 'affinity groups' . . ." (not Americans who were willing to put their bodies on the line to oppose a human and environmental menace).[15]

The media make a regular practice of undercounting the size of demonstrations. The Solidarity Day march of organized labor on September 19, 1981, in Washington, D.C., was reported at 240,000 by the *New York Times* and 260,000 by the *Washington Post,* both far below the police estimate of 400,000. (And police estimates are usually notorious for undercounting).

On July 2, 1983 the People's Anti-War Mobilization, a broad-based coalition of several hundred peace groups around the country held a demonstration in Washington, D.C., to protest the U.S. intervention in Central America. Parade organizers claimed 20,000 participants. (I and two assistants counted about 14,000 as the demonstrators marched to Lafayette Park; this did not include the substantial numbers who had departed during the previous two hours of speeches to escape the stifling 95-degree heat.)[16] The police estimate of 7,500 was the only one reported in the *Washington Post.*[17] A local evening television news report referred to "several thousand," and showed a brief 30-second clip of the march.

A right-wing counterdemonstration of Moonies, Vietnamese exiles, and a Christian group held on the same day numbered about 200 people by my count. The *Post* reported the police estimate of 500, then added that "unofficial estimates" were much higher. The article did not identify who made the unofficial estimates. This reporting of the counterdemonstration stands in marked contrast to the way the *Post* ignored the "unofficial estimates" of the larger major event and printed without question the low count of the police. Similarly, the story gave almost as much coverage to the tiny pro-war, pro-Reagan group as to the antiwar rally and more photo space. The networks gave *equal* time to both the 14,000 who marched against U.S. intervention in Central America and the 200 or so who gathered in support of it. The *New York Times* carried no story at all but ran a picture of a portion of the congregated crowd on page 12, captioned, "Rally Opposes U.S. Role in Carribbean." The *Times* made no estimate of the crowd size, but noted in the caption that the rally "prompted criticism from Government supporters, who held a rally nearby. No violence was reported."[18] The reference to the absence of violence carried the implication that violence might have been expected—thus continuing the media association of protest with violence. The absence of any reference to crowd size allowed the *Times* to describe the mass rally and the very minor one in equal terms.

Not all protests are slighted or ignored by the U.S. news media. The 1981 crisis in Poland won the rapt attention of the U.S. business-owned press for days on end in a way that no strikes or demonstrations in the United States have ever done. Western sympathizers designated January 30, 1982, as "Solidarity Day" and planned demonstrations in support of Polish Solidarity in various cities. Unlike most demonstrations these were well publicized beforehand in the media. Also widely publicized was the International Communication Agency-produced television show "Let Poland Be Poland" featuring songs and appearances by Hollywood celebrities and statements by political leaders of various countries, offered for prime-time viewing on "Solidarity Day" to some 50 broadcast services around the world. Few political events had ever received such massive and favorable prepublicity, but the turnout on "Solidarity Day" itself did not live up to the media hype preceding it. The *Washington Post* story, bravely headlined: "THOUSANDS HERE AND ABROAD TURN OUT FOR 'SOLIDARITY DAY,' " reported rallies held in cities in the United States and a few foreign capitals, the largest being in Chicago, the city with the biggest ethnic Polish population outside Warsaw, where Secretary of State Haig spoke to a crowd reportedly of 8,000 (no source was given for that figure). In Boston, the three biggest names in the state, Governor Edward King, Senator Edward Kennedy, and Humberto Cardinal Medeiros attracted a crowd reported at 300. In Washington, the *Post* reported "more than 1,000" marched to Lafayette Park (although I counted about 570). The story gives no figures for the rallies in other cities. While the press usually does not cover the speeches made at protest rallies, the *Post* devoted substantial space to the statements made by the speakers at the Chicago, Boston, and Washington gatherings.[19] The evening news programs of all three commercial networks covered the story, offering clips of speakers making statements in support of freedom in Poland, with no mention of the disappointing size of the crowds. (Left demonstrations of such small numbers seldom, if ever, make the evening news of national television.)

In May 1983 the *Post* gave front page play to the "tens of thousands of protesters" in Poland who "boycotted official May Day ceremonies and staged counterdemonstrations."[20] The story noted that the Warsaw government estimated the number of protesters at 40,000 and the number of participants in the pro-government demonstrations at 6.5 million. The *Post* however claimed that "estimates by western correspondents placed the number of demonstrators in Warsaw and

Gdansk combined at more than 40,000"—but does not say how much more. Nor does the story refute or comment on the massive 6.5 million turnout in support of the Polish government! This latter, somewhat astonishing figure would seem to have been the real story, but it received only one bare mention buried in a story headlined: "POLES PROTEST IN 20 CITIES ON MAY DAY." In a country where the mass of the populace was reported as in a state of rebellion against the government, how was it that 6.5 million ignored the Solidarity marches and participated in the government-sponsored demonstration? The *Post* leaves us to our own conjectures.

Drawing on what has been said so far and on Gitlin's study of how the media covered the New Left, we can come to the following generalizations regarding the methods used by the press to discredit leftist protests:

Scanting of Content

Usually unmentioned are the meaning and political content of the event, the reasons why so many thousands feel impelled to risk arrest at a nuclear site or travel long distances to Washington to stand for hours in the stifling heat. The event itself is depicted as something of a "spectacle" connected to little more than its own surface appearances and not as part of a democratic struggle over vital issues.

One way content is scanted is through "single-issue reductionism." The indictments made against the practices and institutions of class power itself—against poverty, racism, sexism, economic exploitation, capitalism, and imperialism—are reduced to just one or two specific complaints by the press, for example, "end the war." While the demonstrators are sometimes branded as extremists intent upon disrupting orderly society, the truly radical content of their message is reduced in media reports to a minimal reformist demand.[21]

Sometimes the political content of a protest is slighted not by denying the scope of issues but by treating them as a jumble of complaints conveyed by a "hodge-podge collection" marching for "mixed causes." Thus, the media may sometimes acknowledge the multiplicity *but not the linkage* of issues in order to emphasize the supposed lack of focus within the protest movement.

Trivialization

By directing our attention to surface appearances and ignoring the substance of the protest, the press is free to ascribe irrational and frivolous motives to the demonstrators, using selective details to make light of their dress, age, language, styles, presumed lack of seriousness, and self-indulgent activities.[22]

Marginalization

The protesters are portrayed as a deviant and unrepresentative sample of the American people (hold-out hippies, underworked TV actors, gays, PLO supporters, youths), marginal groups presumably lacking in credible politics. As with trivialization, the marginalizing features are presented in a general tone of mockery that makes it difficult to take the protesters seriously or have much respect for their cause.

Another way to marginalize a group is to portray it as violent and irrational, or linked to groups thought to be violent, or in some way threatening and disloyal.

False Balance

Under the guise of evenhandedness and objectivity, the press will give disproportionate attention to counterdemonstrations and unsympathetic authorities. The mass demonstration, with its great investment of time, money, energy, and sentiment, is afforded about the same reportorial impact, or only a little more, and disproportionately less than the minuscule right-wing opposition.[23] Sometimes the protesters get absolutely less coverage than their opponents. The *New York Times* account of the April 1983 demonstration in Great Britain against nuclear weapons, in which thousands linked hands to form a 14-mile human chain across the English countryside, carried none of the political views of the participants, the only quote in the article being from Britain's defense secretary, Michael Heseltine, who denounced the peace marchers for following a "naive and reckless road. Every mile they march, every yard they stretch, they strengthen the Kremlin case." Mr. Heseltine was described as having "begun a campaign of his own to counter the peace movement."[24] Given the generous exposure he receives from the *Times,* his campaign should not languish for want of publicity.

Gitlin offers this example of how the *New York Times* reported the New Left:

> Despite the conventional claim that news objectivity requires a balance of opposing views, few of the *Times's* stories turned to antiwar or New Left voices for conflicting opinions, even when the subject of the story was New Left activity itself. In the first two weeks of October

[1965] . . . the *Times* ran seven pieces touching on student antiwar action. Four of these consisted entirely of antagonistic statements by authorities: two university presidents . . . [a] police chief, and the attorney general of the United States. The composite effect was that students produce actions while authorities have thoughts.[25]

Often, then, there is not even an attempt to maintain the appearance of balancing a story with opposing viewpoints.

Undercounting

Another way to discredit demonstrations is by undercounting the protesters; "disparagement by numbers" is what Gitlin calls it.[26] Conversely, right-wing counterdemonstrators are overcounted, thus enhancing their legitimacy and diminishing the effect of the larger protest. Undercounting is regularly achieved by: (1) dismissing or ignoring the estimates offered by rally organizers; (2) failing to make an independent estimate from the number of chartered buses, trains, and the auto flow that brings participants to the rally site, or by direct counting of parade flow or "grid" counting from aerial photographs; and (3) treating as accurate and "official" the figures provided by police, while raising no question about how they arrive at their estimates. However, should a police count prove too favorable, the press is capable of providing a lower figure: recall how the *Times* and the *Post* estimated the labor protest of September 1981 at far below the police figure.

Just as important as the crowd count is the way it is framed for the reader. Recall how the *Post* reported the anti-Reagan Labor Day parade as a "*disappointingly small* crowd of *less* than 100,000." But in upbeat fashion, the same newspaper described the Washington, D.C., march for Polish Solidarity as "*more* than 1,000," proclaiming that "*thousands* marched" in various cities. Adjectives like "small" and "disappointing" are rarely if ever used to describe counterdemonstrators who are anticommunist and supportive of existing policies. Adjectives like "dedicated" and "massive" are rarely, if ever, used to describe left protests, no matter how dedicated and massive they be. Imagine if the governor, the cardinal, and the senator of Massachusetts had appeared to speak at an antinuclear rally in Boston after a week of intensive publicity, and only 300 people showed up. The crowd would have been described as "disappointingly minuscule" or maybe "stunningly sparse." But, as we saw, when that number came to hear these three illustrious personages in support of Polish Solidarity, it was reported without any minimizing adjectives.

Omission

Perhaps the most common and complete form of distortion is nonreporting. As noted, most media stories about popular protest, as with press coverage of strikes, simply omit what the struggle is about. The reader or viewer is left again with the question: "Why *are* these people behaving this way?" The suggestion that they "just like to hear themselves holler in the streets" becomes almost plausible in the absence of any reporting of the criticisms, analyses, and information that protesters provide either through the radical press, or in press releases, leaflets, and speeches at the rally.

Not only is the content slighted but the event itself may go unreported *in its entirety*. Protests are no longer news. Even if what is being protested against is new, the *act* of protest eventually runs into what Gitlin calls the media's "we've done it" syndrome.[27] Another way to discredit radical protests, and even not-so-radical protests, is by *red baiting*. As we shall see, this method has been used persistently since the nineteenth century by the press with much success.[28]

RED BAITING THE PEACE MOVEMENT

In October 1982, President Reagan described the U.S. nuclear freeze campaign as "inspired by not the sincere, honest people who want peace, but by some who want the weakening of America . . ." At a November 11 televised White House press conference, Reagan was asked if he had any evidence of foreign involvement in the peace movement. He answered "plenty." "There has been, in the organization of some of the big demonstrations, the one in New York, and so forth, there is no question about foreign agents that were sent to help instigate and help create and keep such a movement going." When asked to elaborate about the Soviet agents who supposedly were manipulating U.S. citizens, Reagan backed off because "I don't discuss intelligence matters and that's what I would be getting into now." The next day White House spokesman Larry Speakes said the State Department had issued reports on Soviet infiltration of the peace movement and that further "documentation" was contained in two conservative publications, *The American Spectator* and *Commentary* and in the October issue of the *Reader's Digest!*[29]

Reagan was immediately criticized by members of Congress, peace activists, and segments of the press for resorting to McCarthyite tactics in order to discredit the peace movement. But there were others in the press who propagated the President's view. On the eve of the antinuclear weapons rally that brought a million people into New York on June 12, 1982, the *Wall Street Journal* ran a major article attempting to link the U.S. peace movement to the Soviet KGB. In an October editorial, the *Washington Post* criticized Reagan for his remarks but then referred to Women Strike for Peace and the Women's International League for Peace and Freedom as "Soviet stooge groups."[30] The editorial sparked protests from peace and civil rights groups, enough to cause the *Post* to publish a retraction a few days later.[31] A number of other newspapers and radio commentators cited the original *Post* editorial—but not the retraction.

After an extensive investigation, which included testimony by members of the U.S. intelligence community, House Intelligence Committee Chair Edward Boland (D.-MA) concluded that "the hearings provide no evidence that the Soviets direct, manage or manipulate the nuclear freeze movement."[32] This did not prevent *New York Times* columnist Flora Lewis from asserting, without a speck of supporting evidence: "No doubt the KGB has a vast masterful network to spread disinformation among us."[33]

The absence of evidence did not prevent the "KGB menace" from becoming all the rage. In July 1983 the *Times* ran a three-part series alleging that the KGB had infiltrated the European peace movement and was going to use the protesters to block the deployment of U.S. missiles in Europe. An anonymous "American intelligence specialist" is quoted as saying, "The question then will be how hard the KGB pushes. We know it has catalogues of shouters, marchers, street fighters, bomb throwers and killers it could turn loose.[34] This fantasy about agitator-killer "catalogues," from an unidentified source, was duly treated by the *Times* as news that was fit to print. The article found evidence of KGB direction in a slogan used by the antimissile campaign: "No New Missiles in Europe." As the *Times* explained it, "experts said the slogan was first seen in 1981 on placards distributed by Communist front organizations in West Germany." And if this wasn't enough, the *Times* asserted that the same supposedly KGB-inspired slogan was also spotted in Williamsburg, Virginia, during a summit meeting of Western leaders.[35]

Several months later the Sunday *New York Times Magazine* ran a cover story by John Vinocur (chief of the *Times* bureau in Paris) entitled "The German Malaise," which explained that the massive peace movement in West Germany was the symptom of a national "malaise" resulting from the tendency of Germans to see themselves "as victims" and to fall into a "sour and Angst-ridden" mood, arising "in part from an insufficient exercise of authority at all levels."[36] Once more the protesters were the problem and not the thing they were protesting. The Germans, it seems, were agitated not because they were fearful about nuclear war and having their country made into a prime target by the deployment of American missiles that would be controlled and fired by Americans, as Americans so decided, without regard to German safety or sovereignty. No, they were agitated because of some deficiency in themselves, in their personal, social, or cultural situation, the kind of agitation caused by "insufficient" authority.

Probably the most egregious examples of red baiting in recent years came when CBS's *60 Minutes* devoted forty minutes on January 23, 1983, to attacking the National Council of Churches (NCC) and the World Council of Churches (WCC), charging the two organizations with having funded arms supplies to Marxist-Leninist revolutionary groups around the world. Entitled "The Gospel According to Whom?," the program opened with the camera on a church service in Indiana and host Morley Safer's voice saying:

> This congregation is as generous as any—money to do God's work, at home and abroad. But what if some of that money is used to do *this* man's work [cut to picture of Fidel Castro speaking to a crowd] or *these* people's [Soviet crowds carrying a portrait of Lenin]?

Safer interviewed conservatives who charged that the two church organizations were guilty of "a pattern of support of totalitarian leftist regimes across the country and the world." When interviewing the two WCC and NCC representatives, Safer posed hostile, skeptical questions and challenged everything they said. But to the right-wing critics he fed gentle, supportive questions, leading them along to the most damaging conclusions. For instance, when Salvation Army commander John Needham accused the WCC of aiding "a good many extremely radical causes around the world," Safer coached him with: "But [the WCC's attempt] to help the common man *could* mean money for weapons . . ." Taking his cue, Needham answered: "That's right."[37]

The unexamined premise was that revolutionary groups in places like El Salvador and Namibia were inherently evil and any assistance to them was indefensible. Representatives of the NCC and WCC pointed out that, in any case, their funds had not been used for such purposes and that there was no evidence to support such a charge. Safer airily dismissed the search for evidence: "It is nearly impossible to follow church money in any precise way." Especially if one doesn't bother to investigate.

Anticipating criticism of his methods, Safer tried to cover himself early in the program: "One is careful in this kind of report to not make the suggestion of guilt by association, to not use what are generally described as McCarthy tactics." In the denial we sometimes find the admission, for he then went on to make the following McCarthyite guilt-by-association comments: "A great deal of the World Council and National Council would seem to—don't exactly *belong* to the Marxist system, but speak much the same language;" and "You are often judged by the company you keep." (At no time was any thought given to the possibility that keeping company with Marxists, even Marxist revolutionaries, might not be grounds for a denunciatory judgment.) In what might be considered a rather good imitation of Senator McCarthy claiming he had documented evidence of subversion, Safer showed the camera a number of publications and fliers which he described as communist inspired and supported by the NCC.[38]

There is no denying that the NCC and WCC backed egalitarian causes at home and abroad and that *this*—rather than the nonexistent "guns for revolutionaries"—was their real sin. The 60 *Minutes* program criticized them for supporting an ecumenical group concerned with human rights in Latin America, a literacy program in Nicaragua, and two research groups that were respectively critical of U.S. counterinsurgency activities and U.S. agribusiness in Latin America. Regarding the agribusiness project, Safer criticized the NCC for financing research that was "an indictment of capitalism and American agricultural corporations," revealing his own loyalties. Throughout the program Safer reproached the NCC and WCC for meddling in politics, asking in scandalized tones: "Is *this* the sort of thing church people should be doing?"

When not red baited, peace activists are routinely ignored by the U.S. press. When representatives from over a hundred Western, Eastern, and Third World nations met at peace conferences in Prague in June 1983 and in Vienna in November 1983 to support resolutions for nuclear disarmament and a nuclear free Europe, the broadcast and print media carried not a word about these deliberations; but they did give eager attention to a small group of Czech right-wing dissidents who demonstrated outside the Prague conference.

Except for an occasional vote taken in response to an unusual crisis, the United Nations has become something of an invisible organization for the U.S. press, especially the UN's special disarmament meetings and regular General Assembly sessions. During its 1983 session the UN General Assembly adopted by lopsided majorities seventeen antinuclear war resolutions sponsored by socialist nations, including support for a nuclear freeze, a nuclear weapons-free zone in the Middle East, and a condemnation of any "first-use" doctrine of nuclear weapons. On one occasion, the United States was left in stark isolation in a 147 to 1 tally, casting the only vote against a resolution to ban the arms race from outer space. (Britain abstained.)[39] These resolutions, the accompanying deliberations, and the actual votes went virtually unreported in the U.S. mainstream press. The American news media are not about to give much attention to an arena of world opinion that, by overwhelming majorities, repeatedly challenges and denounces U.S. foreign policies while favoring peace stances taken by Communist nations.

PRESSURE FROM THE RIGHT

As already noted, well-financed conservative groups became more active on "backlash" issues during the seventies and eighties but the press did more than merely report this development; it helped activate it by treating conservative sentiments as representative of a widespread mood overtaking the nation. In its efforts at muting the left and bolstering the right, the press got a little help—or a big shove—from its conservative friends and bosses.

Both the left and right try to extend their influence into the political mainstream. The left, by mobilizing large numbers of people, hopes to gain greater visibility, win more adherents, and create a ground swell for social change. The right usually does not have that kind of popular support for its political agenda, there being no mass of people out on the streets demanding still more funds for the Pentagon, still more favorable banking laws for Chase Manhattan or wider tax loopholes for Exxon, no elderly agitating for cuts in Social Security, no workers demonstrating for higher corporate profits and wage slashes. So the right attempts to channel popular grievances into non-economic issues such as busing, school prayers, pornography, and abortion, issues that might cut into the support of progressive causes and candidates while strengthening conservative ones.

Organizations like the Moral Majority, the New Right, and the Christian Voice operate as well-financed pressure groups rather than mass movements, drawing from affluent sources like the multimillionaire Richard Mellon Scaife, who alone has donated $100 million or so to right-wing causes in recent years. The John Olin Foundation gives over $5 million a year. Big corporations give many millions more. The conservative Christian Broadcast Network (CBN) brings in an annual $22 million from members around the country.[40]

Conservatives, and religious New Rightists make over 17,000 weekly television and radio broadcasts across the country, with much

KEEPING IT QUIET FOR THE MORAL MAJORITY

Although groups like the Moral Majority were sometimes chided by the press for their excessive self-righteousness and prudery, the press did not raise any serious questions about the right's claim to widespread popular support. Indeed in 1980 when a Harris Poll showed that most Americans (including persons who had voted for Reagan that year) were diametrically opposed to the conservative views of right-wing groups like the Moral Majority, the media suppressed the results as unnewsworthy. The Harris Poll is distributed to 200 newspapers across the nation, but this particular poll appeared only in the *Boston Herald American* (December 5, 1980). When questioned about this, Carmen Hudson of Louis Harris Associates could give no explanation as to why material about such a topical issue had not been picked up by the national media.

Based on Robert Dobrow, *"Media ignores poll refuting right-wing claims,"* Workers World, *January 2, 1981.*

of the air time donated by sympathetic station owners. Hundreds of radio and TV stations are owned outright by conservative organizations.[41] Over 1,100 radio and TV outlets beam a fundamentalist evangelical message around the nation.[42]

The right is not seeking changes of a kind that burden or threaten the interests of the dominant corporate class. If anything, it advocates a view of the world that wealthy media owners look upon with genuine sympathy, unlike the view offered by left protesters. The centrist media is, in a word, more receptive to the right than to the left because its owners and corporate heads share the right's basic feelings about free enterprise, capitalism, communism, labor unions, popular protest, and U.S. global supremacy, even if not always seeing eye-to-eye with it on specific policies and certain cultural issues. In addition, the right has the money to buy media exposure and the left usually does not.

Aside from outright bannings and boycotts, the right influences the mass media by generating rightist themes in its ultra-conservative publications and then working these into the communication mainstream. The attack on the World and National Councils of Churches by CBS, for instance, did not just happen. Months before, red-baiting criticisms and assaults against the WCC and the NCC had appeared in the *American Spectator, Commentary, Conservative Digest,* and the *New Republic,* and in newsletters issued by the Institute on Religion and Democracy (IRD), a group of conservative labor leaders, evangelical religionists, and intellectuals, financed in large part by the Smith

107

Richardson Foundation and Scaife Foundation.[43] In January 1983, just before the *60 Minutes* program appeared, the *Reader's Digest* published an attack on the two church organizations which drew heavily from IRD sources. In sum, beginning as red-baiting fulminations in far-right publications, the attack against the two church organizations was picked up by a large circulation conservative magazine, then aired on a highly respectable mainstream investigative news show that is beamed into more American homes than almost any other news or documentary program.

To say that in such cases the right simply outplays and outpressures the left, getting to network producers with more ammunition than the left can muster is to overlook the built-in advantage the right enjoys in propagating its anticommunist procapitalist viewpoint within a communications system and a society that is owned by anticommunist capitalists. For this reason alone, pressures from the right will seem more imperative and less easy to ignore than pressures from progressives of any stripe. Long before CBS's attack on the NCC and WCC, persons connected with *60 Minutes,* like Mike Wallace, had complained privately about the pressures coming from right-wing groups like Accuracy in the Media. The attack on the two church organizations, favorite bogies of the conservatives, must have taken some of the heat off CBS— or certainly was in response to that heat. During the program Safer did interview at friendly length two members of the Institute on Religion and Democracy.[44]

The rise of the "KGB menace" in America provides another example of how the right feeds into the center. The first time I heard of this updated version of the Red Menace was when the conservative columnist M. Stanton-Evans, whom I happened to be debating at a college campus in 1980, announced that "KGB agents had infiltrated our American institutions" and were "walking the streets of our nation's capital." The claim brought skeptical smiles to faces in the audience, so outlandish did it sound. First germinating on the far-right fringe, then repeated again and again by right-wing propagandists like Robert Moss, Arnaud de Borchgrave, Claire Sterling, and Michael Ledeen, the KGB charge began to slowly seep into the center. Through the process of repetition and dissemination it began to sound less outlandish. William Preston and Ellen Ray provide a good summary of how a determined right feeds a receptive center:

> A theme which is floated on one level—a feature item on VOA about Cuba for example—will appear within record time as a lead article in *Reader's Digest,* or a feature in a Heritage Foundation report, or a series of "exposés" by Moss and de Borchgrave or Daniel James in some reactionary tabloid like *Human Events* or the *Washington Times* or *In-*

quirer. Then they will all be called to testify by Senator Denton's Subcommittee on Security and Terrorism, repeating one another's allegations as "expert witnesses." After that they are given credibility by the "respectable" Cold War publications like the *National Review, Commentary,* and the *New Republic.* And finally, since they have repeated the theme so many times it must be true, they are given the opportunity to write Op-Ed pieces for the *New York Times* or the *Washington Post.*[45]

Not only are they given the opportunity to write guest pieces, but as we have already observed in the case of the KGB bogey, regular mainstream columnists like Flora Lewis begin asserting that "the KGB has a vast masterful network to spread disinformation among us," and the president of the United States begins to claim that the KGB has taken over groups that oppose his nuclear escalation policies.

AN ANTIBUSINESS BIAS?

If the mass media are owned by capitalists who can translate their financial dominance into control over media content, injecting that content with a bias against organized labor, antiwar protesters, socialists, Communists and all progressive causes, then why do business people and conservatives repeatedly complain that the media are hostile toward business and toward conservative values?[46]

In the kinds of issues covered by the news, the mainstream national media do sometimes seem almost liberal when compared to the narrow conservatism of most regional and local media owners, "persons of hard right-wing bias . . . ."[47] These owners often see the national media as dominated by Eastern, liberal elites who are allegedly indifferent to, or even subersive of free enterprise and the patriotic virtues.

While the news media never challenge the capitalist system, they do occasionally report things that seem to put business in a bad light. Media coverage of poisonous waste dumpings by industrial firms, nuclear plant accidents, price gouging by defense contractors, the bribery by corporations, of public officials at home and abroad, and the marketing of unsafe consumer products usually just scratches the surface of these problems; but even these limited exposures are more than business elites care to hear and are perceived by them as an antibusiness vendetta.

By treating business wrongdoings as isolated deviations from the socially beneficial system of "responsible capitalism," the media overlook the systemic features that produce such abuses and the regularity with which they occur. Business "abuse" is presented in the national press as an occasional aberration, rather than as a predictable and common outcome of corporate power and the business system. The exposé *that treats the event as an isolated and atypical incident implicitly affirms the legitimacy of the system,* just as the exposé of the massacre of the Vietnamese village of My Lai by American troops established the false notion that such atrocities were rare deviations from higher standards by which the war was supposedly being conducted. Nevertheless, there were persons in the U.S. army command who saw the press's exposure of My Lai as an attempt to undermine the war effort. Similarly with the business community: any particular exposé is seen as an attack on the integrity of the corporate system in general. What business wants is for these matters to be left entirely alone.

But the press can ignore or distort social reality just so much before losing its credibility. People expect the news to say something about the major events that affect their daily life. Why are people out of work? Why do things cost so much? Why are we building so many nuclear missiles? Why is there so much pollution? Why are American soldiers being sent overseas and coming back in plastic sacks? Why must our sons register for the draft?[48] That the media cannot ignore these questions does not mean they come up with revealing, truthful explanations. But there are limits to how reality can be brushed aside. As Peter Drier puts it:

> As the nation faces the system's contradictions at home and abroad, the media bring the "bad news." . . . Big Business gets part of the blame, but (as polls show—and the media reports), they share the blame with labor unions, big government, the President, the Congress, and the media itself. Still, the nation's business and political leaders blame the messenger, rather than the system, for the nation's crisis of legitimacy.
>
> Because business cannot expect to take a fundamental look at its own assumptions, and cannot see the systemic causes of inflation, unemployment, foreign policy setbacks, and so on, it blames the news media for distorting and simplifying these problems . . . and attacks the media for its "emotional" and "sensational" reporting.[49]

If reporters go too far too often in a muckracking direction, they are reined in, as we noted earlier. Yet limited leeway is allowed on some issues, mostly for the reason just mentioned: The press cannot completely ignore the realities that affect the daily lives of millions of people and hope to retain the public's trust. A press that does nothing more than propagate a narrow, right-wing ideology, ignoring economic problems to give only sunny reports on the health of the economy and sing hosannahs to the blessings of private enterprise, a press that did not bother to explain away systemic injustices as the incidental flaws of a basically good system, would earn less criticism from conservatives but would not have much credibility in the public eye and would do a poor job of legitimating the existing system. The owners and executive heads of the mainstream press can manipulate and ignore reality only so much. They cannot go beyond what the public will swallow. In their hearts, many media owners would like to put an end to *all* critical information about business and other such issues, but they do not think they can go that far. It is not a matter of being unable to control their liberal reporters, which they can do well enough when they put their minds to it; rather it is a matter of not superimposing a viewpoint that is so blatantly at odds with popular experience as to be rejected for being the propaganda it is. A press governed solely by the desire to avoid all critical news that might reflect negatively upon dominant class interests reveals itself as an obvious instrument of class domination, loses popular support, and generates disbelief and disaffection.

Notes

1. Todd Gitlin, *The Whole World is Watching* (Berkeley: University of California Press, 1980).

2. *Washington Post,* July 20, 1975; *New York Times,* December 4, 1977. Sources are cited in David Paletz and Robert Entman, *Media Power Politics* (New York: Free Press, 1981), p. 196.

3. William Watts, "Americans' Hopes and Fears," *Psychology Today,* September 1981; Gallup Poll, *Washington Post,* December 22, 1981; Peter Hart Poll, *Ithaca* (N.Y.) *Journal,* September 5, 1975.

4. Polls cited in the *New York Times,* January 22, 1978, January 13, 1982, February 3, 1981.

5. See the citations in footnote 3.

6. Paletz and Entman, *Media Power Politics,* pp. 198–99.

7. Ibid., p. 199.

8. See the discussion of the press's treatment of the coal and newspaper strikes in chapter 5.

9. Gallup Poll, *Washington Post,* December 22, 1981; Yankelovich, Skelly, and White Survey, *New York Times,* January 13, 1982; also *Washington Post,* September 23, 1981.

10. Paletz and Entman, *Media Power Politics,* p. 197.

11. *New York Times,* January 26, 1984.

12. Paletz and Entman, *Media Power Politics,* p. 203.

13. *Washington Post,* May 4, 1981.

14. *Washington Post,* September 8, 1981.

15. Editorial, *Washington Post,* October 6, 1981.

16. The method we used was to make a count of five hundred marchers, estimating the portion of the street block they occupied, then using that measurement to count out additional blocks of five hundred as subsequent marchers passed by.

17. *Washington Post,* July 3, 1983.

18. *New York Times,* July 3, 1983.

19. *Washington Post,* January 31, 1982.
20. *Washington Post,* May 2, 1983.
21. Gitlin, *The Whole World . . .*, p. 35.
22. Ibid., 27, passim.
23. Ibid., pp. 47–48 for an example drawn from the *New York Times* and earlier examples described above.
24. *New York Times,* April 2, 1983.
25. Gitlin, *The Whole World . . .*, p. 289; and the *New York Times,* April 8, 1979.
26. Gitlin, *The Whole World . . .*, pp. 80–81.
27. Gitlin, *The Whole World . . .*, p. 234.
28. See chapter 7 for an account of the press's red-baiting campaigns earlier this century.
29. *New York Times,* November 13, 1982.
30. *Washington Post,* October 6, 1982.
31. *Washington Post,* October 9, 1982.
32. *Organizing Notes* (Washington, D.C.), January/February 1983.
33. *New York Times,* July 18, 1983.
34. *New York Times,* July 26, 1983.
35. Ibid.; see also *Guardian* editorial, August 10, 1983.
36. *New York Times Magazine,* November 15, 1981, pp. 40–45, 116–125.
37. John Wicklein, "The Gospel According to '60 Minutes'," *Progressive,* April 1983, p. 49; see also Alexander Cockburn and James Ridgeway, "CBS Sees Red," *Village Voice,* February 22, 1983.
38. Wicklein, "The Gospel According . . ."
39. Tom Foley, "UN Says No to Nuke War," *Daily World,* December 17, 1983.
40. Karen Rothmyer, "The Mystery Angel of the New Right," *Washington Post,* July 12, 1981; also Jeremy Rifkin with Ted Howard, *The Emerging Order: God In the Age of Scarcity* (New York: Putnam, 1979).
41. Report by In the Public Interest; statistics by Group Research, Inc., Washington, D.C., n.d.
42. Bob Brewin, "God and Mammon in Washington," *Village Voice,* February 14, 1984, p. 33; also Rifkin and Howard, *The Emerging Order.*
43. Steve Askin, "Institute Says It Reveals Threat—Others Say It Is Threat—to U.S. Church," *National Catholic Reporter,* February 4, 1983, pp. 1, 7–8, 18–19; Wicklein, "The Gospel According to . . ."; Walda Katz Fishman, "The Political Economy of Ideology: The Case of the Attack on the NCC and WCC," unpublished paper, Washington, D.C., 1983.
44. Wicklein, "The Gospel According to . . ."
45. William Preston, Jr., and Ellen Ray, "Disinformation and Mass Deception: Democracy as a Cover Story," *Covert Action,* Spring-Summer 1983, p. 8. As an example of this end process see Arnaud de Brochgrave, "The KGC's Bead on the Media," *Washington Post,* April 14, 1981.
46. See for instance the Mobil advertisement "Does the TV Camera Distort Society?" *Washington Post,* May 17, 1981.
47. Les Brown, *Television, The Business Behind the Box* (New York: Harcourt Brace and Jovanovich, 1971), p. 214. Brown is referring to broadcasting but the same can be said of print media.
48. Peter Drier, "Business and the Media," unpublished paper, 1983.
49. Ibid. Ever faithful to the business viewpoint, *Time* joins in the controversy with a cover story to explain why the media has become the object of public criticism; see "Journalism Under Fire," *Time,* December 12, 1983, pp. 76–83.

7

The Media Fight the
Red Menace

Rightwing governments that deny their people basic human and political rights but which are accommodating to Western corporate investments generally are subjected to a benign neglect or at most an occasional criticism by the U.S. news media. But communist governments and any revolutionary or leftist movement at home or abroad which proffer a competing way of using the land, labor, resources, and capital of a nation are treated with a fairly persistent hostility by the U.S. government, business and the media. Anticommunism has long been an unremitting media theme, an ideological bias that pervades both the news and entertainment sectors. Here we will concentrate on the news.

LOOKING BACKWARD

While American anticommunist sentiment is often portrayed as a defensive response to the threat of Soviet aggrandizement, the truth is it is older than the Soviet Union, going back to the earliest struggles within the United States between industrial workers and owners. Throughout much of the nineteenth century, the business-owned press, joined by the pulpit, the politicians, the police, the professors, and the plutocracy itself, alerted the public to the dangers of syndicalism, socialism, anarchism, and Communism—lumping all these radical tendencies together as one great danger to the American Way of Life.[1]

Any proposed departure from the capitalist social order was characterized as an end to *all* social order and a descent into chaos and anarchy. Thus as early as 1880 Roscoe Conkling could hail President Ulysses S. Grant as an eternal foe of "communism, lawlessness and disorder."[2] Opposition to the privileged institutions of power was treated as opposition to America itself. Capitalism was called "free enterprise" and equated with true Americanism, while socialism was depicted as an alien virus infecting the American body politic.

Labor struggles were portrayed as attacks upon society itself. The great Pullman strike outside Chicago in 1894—in which 60,000 workers, led by Eugene V. Debs, ceased work along the Western railway lines in a well-organized, disciplined, and orderly mass action—was greeted with shrieking headlines like "MOBS IN CONTROL OF CHICAGO" and "CHICAGO FACES FAMINE" and was dubbed the "Debs Rebellion." At about that time, to whip up public alarm about radical disorder, the *New York Tribune* "discovered" and alerted its readers to an "ANARCHIST PLOT TO BLOW UP THE CAPITAL."[3]

The propaganda war against the Red Menace intensified soon after the Russian Revolution of 1917. The specter of Bolshevism sent a shudder through the wealthy classes of the Western world, for here was an emerging economic system that seemed to fundamentally challenge their own social order. In 1919, a 14-nation expeditionary force, including British, French, and American troops, invaded the Soviet Union in what proved to be an unsuccessful campaign to overthrow the new Bolshevik government. The anti-Soviet campaign was quickly taken up by the press. Forgetful of who had invaded whom, the *New York Times* ran story after story about imminent Bolshevik invasions of Europe, Asia, and America, with headlines like "LENIN THREATENS INDIA" and "REDS SEEK WAR WITH AMERICA."[4]

As one historian describes it:

> Anti-Bolshevik testimony was played up in the columns of the nation's newspapers and once again the reading public was fed on highly colored tales of free love, nationalization of women, bloody massacres, and brutal atrocities. Stories were circulated that the victims of the Bolshevik madmen customarily had been roasted to death in furnaces, scalded with live steam, torn to pieces on racks, or hacked to bits with axes. Newspaper editors never tired of referring to the Russian Reds as "assassins and madmen," "human scum," "crime-mad," and "beasts." Russia was a place, some said, where maniacs stalked raving through the streets, and the populace fought with dogs for carrion.[5]

During this same period, in the aftermath of World War I, strikes swept the major industries of the United States. In the autumn of 1919 two million workers walked off their jobs, including 500,000 coal miners and 350,000 steel workers. Immediately the press began to link worker unrest at home to the "Soviet menace" abroad with sensational headlines like "RED PERIL HERE," "PLAN BLOODY REVOLUTION," and "WANT WASHINGTON GOVERNMENT OVERTURNED."[6] A special Justice Department publicity bureau was set up to plant stories in newspapers about a Moscow-directed plot to overthrow the U.S. government, issuing press releases with such headings as "U.S. DEPARTMENT OF JUSTICE URGES AMERICANS TO GUARD AGAINST BOLSHEVIK MENACE" and "PRESS, CHURCH, SCHOOLS, LABOR UNIONS AND CIVIC BODIES CALLED UPON TO TEACH TRUE PURPOSE OF COMMUNIST PROPAGANDA."[7]

On January 2, 1920, under the direction of Attorney General A. Mitchell Palmer, the Justice Department, assisted by state and local police, conducted raids in twenty cities, arresting thousands of leftists, including many trade union militants. *The New York Times* hailed the "Palmer raids" with this headline: "REDS PLOTTED COUNTRY-WIDE STRIKE—ARRESTS EXCEED 5,000—2,635 HELD." The *Times* also ran an editorial that heaped praise on the government's action and promised that the raids were "only the beginning" in the war against Communism. In a similar vein, the *Philadelphia Public Ledger* greeted the Boston police strike with the observation: "Bolshevism in the United States is no longer a specter"—meaning it was a reality. Headlines in the *Wall Street Journal* cried "LENIN AND TROTSKY ARE ON THEIR WAY."[8]

The American public was bombarded with lurid press stories of an impending Red take-over. In truth, "the nightmare was not revolution but reaction, and it was real: the job had been done. Under the pressure of the combined forces of industry, government, and press, the major strikes had been broken, wages driven down, the open shop restored and the ranks of the unions decimated."[9]

The government-industry-press campaign against the Red Menace continued throughout the 1920s. Socialists elected to the New York state legislature and to the U.S. Congress were denied their seats. Legislative committees conducted witch-hunting investigations. Radicals and union organizers were harassed and arrested by state and local authorities. Immigrant leftists were summarily deported. And the Federal Bureau of Investigation (FBI), under the directorship of J. Edgar Hoover, grew in size and activity. These developments earned little criticism and much praise from the business-owned news media.

In marked contrast to the horror stories about the Soviet Union that continued to flood the American press was the treatment accorded fascist Italy and Nazi Germany. In the 1920s, major publications like the *New York Times, Wall Street Journal, Fortune, Saturday Evening Post, Chicago Tribune,* and *Christian Science Monitor* hailed Mussolini as Italy's savior, the man who had suddenly brought his nation from poverty and unrest to harmony and prosperity, rescuing his people from the perils of anarchy and radicalism.[10] Likewise the stories that greeted Hitler's ascension to power in 1933 were strikingly different from the shrill and hysterical press treatment of Lenin and the Bolsheviks. With a few notable exceptions like the *Baltimore Sun* and the *Boston Globe*, American newspapers and radio news reports were optimistic about Hitler. In an editorial entitled "The Tamed Hitler," the *New York Times* (January 30, 1933) told its readers to expect a "transformation" in Hitler as he begins "softening down or abandoning" "the more violent parts of his alleged program."

There swiftly arose the give-Adolph-a-chance press claque. The *Houston Post* pleaded, "Let Hitler try his hand." CBS national radio interviewed the *Times* Berlin bureau chief, Frederick Birchall, who said the Nazis were not intending "any slaughter of their enemies or racial oppression in any vital degree." While the Soviets were being portrayed as ever on the edge of launching aggressive attacks against any and all, Birchall reassured listeners that the Nazis had no desire to go to war and Hitler could not be called a dictator. With that keen eye for the irrelevant that is the hallmark of American journalism, he observed that Hitler was a vegetarian and a nonsmoker, attributes that were supposedly indicative of a benign nature. And he noted that Hitler had taken upon himself "the hardest job that ever a man could undertake." The *Los Angeles Times* (April 4, 1933) also looked at the brighter side of things, seeing Hitler as a stern opponent of Communism. And even though violent attacks had begun against the Jews, Nazi anti-Semitism was "understood to have been mainly rhetorical."[11]

While denouncing the Soviet Union as a menace to civilization, the U.S. press could manifest an open admiration for fascism in Italy and a hopeful tolerance of Nazism in Germany because Mussolini and Hitler, unlike the Soviets, were attacking not the capitalist system but its enemies. Both dictators murdered leftists, imprisoned dissenters, and destroyed labor unions and all other democratic political organizations. Henry Ford, Thomas Watson, and press moguls like Hearst and McCormick looked with approval on both Hitler and the many profascist organizations sprouting in the United States during the 1930s. Some business leaders accepted decorations from Mussolini and Hitler and others longed to emulate their rule. As former president of the National Association of Manufacturers, H. W. Prentiss, announced, "American business might be forced to turn to some form of disguised Fascistic dictatorship."[12] However, when Hitler gave indications that he would challenge the interests of the Western capitalist nations, he became an object of media criticism (as was true of Mussolini when he unsettled the West by invading Ethiopia in 1936).

The Red Peril continued to be paraded out by the media whenever labor militancy gathered momentum. In 1934, some 35,000 maritime workers went on strike in San Francisco, Seattle, Portland, San

Diego, and other Pacific coast ports. The police brutality directed against the strike eventually galvanized a general strike of 127,000 San Francisco workers. Newspapers, radio commentators and clergy joined together to whip up anticommunist hysteria against the strikers. A typical sample, the front-page story in the *San Francisco Chronicle* headlined "RED ARMY MARCHING ON CITY," announced that Communist forces were nearing the Northern California border, and a Communist army planned the destruction of railroad and highway facilities and intended to take San Francisco.[13]

Organized labor won some important victories during the struggles of the 1930s. The Congress of Industrial Organizations (CIO) grew from less than a million to nearly four million by 1938. Massive strikes, sit-ins, and agitations swept across the country in the period between 1935 and 1941. The eight-hour day, fought for since 1866, was at last won by millions of workers. The wage gains achieved by unionized employees, along with the indirect wage increases that went to millions of unorganized workers as a result of the unionization struggle, increased the national purchasing power of wage-earners in the United States by an estimated $5 billion each year.[14]

Despite its victories—or because of them—the CIO was attacked as an agent of the "Communist conspiracy" with "all the power of 98 percent of the nation's press and radio."[15] By the late 1930s American corporations were spending huge sums for spies, thugs, and propaganda to prevent unionization and to spread anti-Red propaganda among the rank and file. The hysteria emanating from the corporate class and their representatives in the press was so persistent as to move Senator La Follette's committee to declare in 1939 that business saw "Communism behind every move designed to improve the lot of labor." The committee added that the employer "cloaks his hostility to labor" under "the pretext that he is defending himself and the country against Communism."[16]

Communists did play a crucial role in organizing the CIO. But they were targeted by the press and business not because they threatened to take over the nation but because their organizing efforts were helping to cut into the profits of the industrialists. The Communists would be the first victims of union purges, but equally troublesome to the bosses were the noncommunist employees who were organizing and redirecting billions of dollars of would-be profits into the workers' pay envelopes.[17] It would not be until the postwar Truman and Eisenhower administrations, the "McCarthy era," that the ruling elites and the press would be able to generate enough anticommunist phobia to hunt out the leftists and divide and tame the labor unions.

THE COLD WAR

Anticommunist propaganda was muffled during World War II as the United States found itself allied with the Soviet Union against Nazi aggression. But as hostilities came to a close, President Harry Truman asserted to a White House visitor that the Russians would "soon be put in their place" and that the United States would then "take the lead in running the world in the way that the world ought to be run . . . "[18] With the war's end in 1945, the longstanding antilabor, anticommunist, and anti-Soviet attitudes of government, business, and media once more came to the fore with dire warnings about Soviet plans for "world domination" and the internal threat of "Communist spies and saboteurs."

No one was more instrumental in creating a crisis atmosphere than President Truman himself. In 1947 he declared in his Truman Doctrine that the United States was locked in a mortal contest defending world freedom from "Soviet expansionism" and that huge amounts of American money and arms would be used to fortify pro-U.S. regimes in Greece, Turkey, and elsewhere. The inseparable advances of the dollar and the flag were hailed in publications like *Business Week* with headlines and captions that read, "New Democracy, New Business. U.S. Drive to Stop Communism Abroad Means Heavy Outlays for Bases, Relief and Reconstruction. But in Return American Business is Bound to Get New Markets Abroad." And the financial editor of the *New York World-Telegram* wrote, "All of this is a much safer and profitable state of affairs for investors. It is good news of a fundamental character."[19]

A few newspapers expressed concern about Truman's bellicose challenge to the Soviets. The *Chicago Daily News* said the United States was "asking for a war with Russia." But the great majority of the press hailed Truman's cold war declarations with an avalanche of articles and stories about the "international communist menace."[20]

As the press continued to propagate the cold war, downplaying Soviet overtures for negotiation, public opinion responded in kind. In 1945, 32 percent of the public thought the U.S. would be involved in a new world war within two decades or so; by 1947 it was 63 percent and by March of 1948, 73 percent, according to a Gallup poll. Joseph and Stewart Alsop wrote in the *New York Herald Tribune*, "The atmosphere in Washington today is no longer a post-war atmosphere. It is, to put it bluntly, a pre-war atmosphere."[21]

In 1950, *U.S. News & World Report* offered this revealing observation:

PROMOTING THE SOVIET MENACE

With the press properly briefed and oriented by [Secretary of Defense, James V.] Forrestal [a former Wall Street executive], it was not long until . . . every newspaper teemed with the alleged doings of the devilish foe at home and abroad. . . . The most alarming news began to appear. In the press and over the air the American people were told that the Red Army was mobilizing for the invasion of Iran one day, Turkey the next, and western Europe on the third. Red submarines were seen off the coast of California. There were Red Army plots to seize Yugoslavia and even Detroit, according to a witness at a later trial of alleged reds. The only thing that saved us was our monopoly of the atomic bomb and there was increasing talk of dropping it on Moscow and thus solving all.

No improbability was too wild for serious treatment by the press or radio, particularly just before the Army or Navy asked for additional billions before Congressional appropriation committees.

Richard Boyar and Herbert Morais, Labor's Untold Story, *p. 346.*

Government planners figure they have found the magic formula for almost endless [economic] good times. . . . Cold War is the catalyst. Cold War is an automatic pump-primer. Turn the spigot and the public clamors for more arms spending. Turn another, the clamor ceases. . . . Cold War demands, if fully exploited, are almost limitless.[22]

The real formula for "good times," *U.S. News* was saying to its corporate readers, was big defense spending: It brought huge contracts, guaranteed markets, and the highest profits available. Armaments spending did not compete with the consumer market, nor did it expand the nonprofit public sector of the economy as did some human services, yet it gave a much needed boost to a sluggish economy. And how do you get the public to go along with the huge deficits and high taxes that big defense budgets bring? Turn on the cold war spigot. Create a state of alarm about the "Soviet threat."

The anticommunist witch hunt continued against labor. Faced with high profits, high prices, and frozen wage levels, organized labor—now grown to some 16 million by the end of World War II—embarked on a series of strikes. In 1947 Congress passed the Taft-Hartley Law (written word for word by representatives of the National Association of Manufacturers, according to Congressman Donald O'Toole of New York). The new law reinstituted injunctions to break strikes, and the court's power to impose heavy fines. It outlawed mass picketing, secondary boycotts, and the closed shop. It authorized employer interference in workers' attempts at unionizing and "right-to-work" anti-union laws at the state level. It prohibited unions from ejecting company spies as long as they paid their dues. Owners now could refuse to bargain collectively, even by shutting down their plants, and could destroy union treasuries with expensive court suits. In sum, the new law repealed many of the hard-won gains of the prolabor legislation of the previous decade.

Taft-Hartley also required union officials to sign noncommunist oaths. Those who refused were ejected from their positions. Communists who might sign risked perjuring themselves and going to jail. Thus many unionists were deprived of one of their most precious liberties, the right to work.[23]

With the exception of a few liberal publications, the news media applauded the new law for its anticommunist features and because it supposedly redressed the power balance between management and labor. Succumbing to pressure from business, government, and the press, the CIO expelled many of the more militant and pace-setting unions from its organization, then launched membership raids against them. As a result, CIO membership declined by one-fourth. Burdened also by the strictures of the Taft-Hartley Act, a much weakened, divided, and red-baited union movement never regained the momentum and effectiveness of previous years.[24]

The anticommunist witch hunt reached into other areas of life. Government employees and private citizens had their careers ruined and their personal lives and opinions scrutinized by legislative committees, the FBI, local police—and the press. Millions were required to sign loyalty oaths. Prosecutions of U.S. Communist Party members under the Smith Act, state sedition trials, and contempt proceedings during the 1950s, gave the United States a growing number of political prisoners. (By 1952, 110 persons had been indicted or imprisoned under the Smith Act, about half of them trade unionists.) A Democratic-controlled Congress overwhelmingly passed the McCarran Internal Security Act of 1950; it called for the registration of "communist-front" and "communist-action" groups, and authorized the construction of concentration camps for purposes of interning without trial or hearing all suspected "subversives," should either the president or Congress declare a "national emergency." Of the six camps built in 1952, several were maintained on a standby basis through the 1950s and into the 1960s. The attorney general and congressional and state legislative committees periodically published lists of "Communist front" organizations. The House Un-American Activities Committee called the front groups "communism's greatest weapon in the country today." Generally, these groups supported such causes as world disarmament, peace, organized labor, and greater racial and economic equality.

Despite these repressive measures, Republicans in Congress and the Republican-dominated press repeatedly charged that the Truman administration was "soft on Communism." Truman reacted to these pressures by taking an increasingly bellicose line toward the Soviets abroad and setting up "loyalty boards" to screen the political views of federal employees at home.[25] Such measures did not stop the conservative-dominated press from continuing to fault the Democrats for being insufficiently vigilant against the Red Peril. If anything, a more strident cold war policy toward Moscow and a government-sponsored purge in Washington only strengthened the view that Communists and "Communist-sympathizers" were terribly lethal persons who had infiltrated all American institutions.

THE CREATION OF JOE McCARTHY

One of the more notorious figures to emerge during the anticommunist mania of the 1950s was Senator Joseph McCarthy (R.-Wisc.). Using innuendo, nonexistent "documents," and outright fabrication, McCarthy rose in 1950 from an obscure Senator to national prominence with a series of alarming charges about "communist subversives" who supposedly had infiltrated the State Department, other branches of government, the universities, the clergy, and the press itself. McCarthy's accusations have been described as "sensational," but they would have been nothing more than ludicrous had not the press given them such sensational play.

McCarthyism was hardly a creation of McCarthy alone. Well before he burst upon the national scene, as we have seen, the press was filled with lurid tales of how the Kremlin was planning to subvert and conquer the world, and how "spies" were lurking in our government. Since they were the targets of his charges, Democrats condemned McCarthy for his wild charges of "Communists in government" and his use of anonymous testimony, professional informers, and guilt by association. But they themselves had instituted these same practices with their loyalty boards well before the Senator from Wisconsin made his debut.[26]

Although many reporters came to hate McCarthy as a cynical liar and power manipulator, they treated his attacks as straight news, failing to report that supporting evidence was nonexistent. Under the rule of "objectivity" the press reported the senator's character assassinations about treasonous Reds and pinkos who were subverting our country in front-page stories with banner headlines, while the refutations from his victims were buried on inside pages or lost under the next wave of charges. As Aronson acidly notes:

> The portrait of the press of the United States as an objective entity is a myth. There is nothing in the Canons of Journalism that compelled reporters to accept and editors to publish information allegedly contained in uninspected documents waved at them by a Senator. Such reports, if their content proved to be false, might have been excused once or twice on the ground of deadline or overzealous reporting. But when this happened day in, day out for four years, when every reputable Washington correspondent knew that the disseminator of this information was a proved liar, there was no shred of an excuse. Objectivity was mocked when almost every story was weighted in favor of McCarthy's fraud.[27]

More than cowardice and uncritical sensationalism lay behind the press's role in the making of McCarthyism. Active complicity and sympathy for his goals played a major part, if not among most of the working press, certainly among many media owners and editors. Some publishers entered directly into the red-baiting game, sending reporters out to conduct their own investigations to "expose" Communists or ex-Communists and stigmatize progressive persons, organizations, and ideas. Not only did they do the senator's work by publishing his attacks but they sometimes copied his methods, purging individuals from their own staffs who had been affiliated with groups of leftist persuasion—as did the *New York Times*.[28]

Liberal editors and news commentators who opposed McCarthy were always careful to do it on cold war anticommunist grounds, contending that he was "giving comfort to our enemies" or was "playing right into the hands of the Communists" because he was disrupting our institutions and "demoralizing loyal Americans." This was "not the best way to fight Communism." The unchallenged assumption was that Communists were our treacherous, mortal enemies and *should* be hounded, hunted out, and even jailed for their political affiliations and beliefs—as many had been before McCarthy. Ben Hibbs, editor of the *Saturday Evening Post,* when commenting on McCarthy's crusade, offered a view shared by most centrist and liberal editors and politicians:

> My own guess is that there are some pinks in the State Department and in other government departments and agencies, and of course they should be found and ousted; but it seems to me that this can be done without besmirching innocent people and without making such broadside charges that people will lose faith in all government.[29]

Hibbs's observation is revealing. McCarthy's critics defended the rights of noncommunists only. The liberal's complaint about McCarthy was that he was attacking liberals, "besmirching innocent people," in Hibbs's words, "innocent" meaning anticommunist like themselves. Anyone who harbored political beliefs to the left of liberalism ("pinks"), who preferred socialism and rejected capitalism, who thought there might be positive things to say about existing socialist societies, who thought Communists should be allowed their political freedom not so they can be better exposed and defeated but because it was their right as Americans and human beings and because they had good things to say—such a person was implicitly judged guilty, a worthy target of purge and attack. The liberal complaint against McCarthy was that he was attacking the wrong people. Also his wild attacks against government, as Hibbs notes, might make people "lose faith in all government"—something the established powers did not relish. Indeed, this danger proved to be McCarthy's undoing.

McCarthy made his big mistake in 1954 when he undertook an investigation of the Army loyalty-security program. The probe was a veiled assault on the Eisenhower administration and was McCarthy's bid for leadership of the Republican party and dominance over national politics. This time the Senator went too far:

> Most of the nation's newspapers . . . supported McCarthy during the first four years of his campaign against "Communists in government." As long as the people McCarthy was accusing of treason were Democrats, they approved. But when it became obvious, in the early months of 1954, that those being accused of tolerating Communists in government were part of the Republican administration of President Eisenhower, Republican publishers, with the notable exceptions of the publishers of the *Chicago Tribune* and the Hearst newspapers, began to see McCarthy in a new light. . . . Scripps-Howard executives . . . simply decided that McCarthy was harming rather than helping the Republican party and that it was time to get rid of him.[30]

Aronson reports, "The forces that had set McCarthy in motion back in 1950 now moved in unison to stop him. The White House took up the challenge and defended the Army; the Senate ordered an investigation of McCarthy; and the press cried 'Enough!' "[31]

In short time McCarthy's activities were no longer given headline coverage; his charges were ignored or buried in the back pages, and the same reporters who once obligingly gave copious coverage to his every utterance now failed to show up for his press conferences. He was finished. The personal instrument of McCarthyism, the senator himself, had been consigned to oblivion. But not before McCarthyism had accomplished much of its task, having stigmatized as "traitors" persons and organizations of progressive opinion in all walks of life, including labor unions, universities, and newspapers.

NIKITA CONQUERS AMERICA

In the late 1950s anticommunism showed no signs of disappearing as a politically repressive force, although some of its more hysterical expressions and legislative vigilantism began to wane. In 1959 the Soviet leader Nikita Khrushchev was invited by President Eisenhower to visit the United States. Immediately after the invitation, editorials and full-page ads appeared in the press, including the *New York Times* and *Washington Post* urging a "National Day of Mourning" and offering warnings against Khrushchev's "effort at brainwashing" the American public. Most of the reporters assigned to cover Khrushchev's tour took pains to demonstrate their hostility toward the Soviet leader in print and in person. "Yet there was a curious quality to the hostility; it was as if they were adopting this conforming attitude because each thought the other expected it of them,"[32] writes Aronson.

The Soviet premier was described as both a clown and a menace. He "waddled" and "talked incessantly." According to the *San Francisco Examiner,* he was trying to act "more like a peace-loving peasant than the most dangerous man in history."[33]

Khrushchev was also accorded a great deal of television coverage. For years the public had been told that Soviet leaders, presiding within the foreboding chambers of the Kremlin, were plotting aggression and world domination. Now here was the ebullient Soviet premier, supposedly the Monster from Another World, manifesting an unmistakable resemblance to ordinary mortals, interested in seeing America, courting its politicians, trade unionists, farmers, and businessmen, eagerly campaigning for "peaceful coexistence" (a phrase that was eventually to become acceptable and even popular in the West).

While television news commentators were no less disdainful toward the Soviet leader than the rest of the press, the public was able to get a direct glimpse of Khrushchev on TV and could observe that he was not acting or speaking in his reputedly menacing and threatening manner. His very act of visiting the United States, complete with an extensive and often admiring tour of its cities and farmlands, seemed to belie the image of an aggressor intent upon burying us. The American people's impression of Khrushchev, his family, and colleagues, left them less suspicious of him than of the press that presented the visit "in a manner which bore little resemblance to what they were seeing."[34] Indignation at the press treatment of Khrushchev was expressed in an outpouring of letters to newspapers across the country, "and its impact on the working press was demonstrated in the changing quality of their reports, particularly after spectacular welcomes for the Soviets at several railroad stops en route from Los Angeles to San Francisco."[35]

Not only was television giving direct coverage to the Khrushchev visit but also to the warm and enthusiastic response of large numbers of Americans. It was becoming evident from the crowds who greeted the premier that much of the public did not share in the cold war anticommunism that was the stock-in-trade of establishment opinion makers. The American people were judging for themselves what the Soviet leader's intentions were and what the opportunity for peaceful coexistence might be. The judgment was generally a positive one. Immediately after Khrushchev's departure a Gallup poll showed that 52 percent of the public thought the visit had been a "good thing," while only 19 percent had a negative view.

The media wasted no time in attempting to undo the positive opinions held by the public. As Aronson observes, teams of experts were gathered to discuss the visit, and no aspect of the tour was too large or too small for disparagement: The premier's personality ("unstable and emotional"); his world disarmament proposal before the United Nations General Assembly ("unrealistic and utopian"); his approach to the American farm and business communities ("Machiavellian").[36]

RATIONAL HYSTERIA

Here are a few things that might be worth reiterating and expanding upon: American anticommunism did not recently emerge as a response to the threat of a "superpower" Soviet Union but has existed since at least the first great industrial struggles of the nineteenth century—before the advent of a single socialist state. There was no evidence that the immigrant union organizers and agitators who were deported during the red scare of 1920 were anywhere close to taking over the Republic. There was no evidence that subversives had infiltrated the State Department or other branches of government or that the CIO was plotting revolution or that the Russians were getting ready to march on Paris or drop an atomic bomb on Washington. Yet these fantasies were cultivated as realities by the U. S. press.

The red scare of 1920, McCarthyism, the cold war, and anticommunism in general were not products of a mass hysteria that gripped the populace like some strange mania from the Dark Ages. Anticommunism was consciously and strenuously propagated by government leaders, business representatives, and the business-owned news media. No doubt large numbers of people were enough influenced by the propaganda to provide an additional momentum and feedback to the various anticommunist campaigns. Yet the evidence suggests that when the propaganda subsided so did popular fears about the Red Menace. And when the propaganda intensified so did the fears. Although it probably never worked that automatically, the important point is that *such campaigns were generated mostly from above, more in the service of elite interests than in response to popular passions.*

The Red Menace was not a foolish fantasy or hysteria of the opinion makers and officials who propagated it—although its central aim was to produce fantasy and hysteria. While anticommunism may manipulate irrational images and play on irrational feelings, it, itself, is not a product of irrational politics. *It serves a very real and rational purpose: It creates a climate of opinion and a political atmosphere that makes it easier to discredit and repress labor militancy and progressive and anticapitalist viewpoints at home and abroad.* So much of politics is the rational use of irrational symbols, and this is what media-created anticommunism is. Because the propaganda proves to be ill-founded, and therefore foolish-sounding when refuted, does not mean the propagandists are fools. Because arguments and alarms, charges and headlines, are false does not mean the purveyors don't know what they are doing. Because the anticommunist opinion makers are misleading, does not mean they are themselves hopelessly misled.

Time and again the Red Peril theme propagated by the governmental-industrial-media complex played an effective part in (1) setting back or limiting the struggles and gains of labor; (2) distracting popular attention from the recessions and crises of capitalism by directing grievances toward interior or alien foes; and (3) marshaling public support for huge military budgets, cold war policies and—as we shall see in more detail—Third World interventions to make the world safe for corporate investment and profits.

Did the corporate, political, and media elites believe what they said about the Red Menace? There is evidence to suggest that in some cases, anticommunist opinion leaders were consciously and deliberately manipulative. Certainly Joe McCarthy's entire career was a monument to a self-serving, mendacious, and totally cynical anticommunism. We've already noted how *U.S. News & World Report* cynically remarked to its business readership that cold war attitudes could be turned on and off like a spigot to coincide with the dictates of the defense budget and the profit needs of the economy. In the 1964 electoral campaign, when Republican presidential candidate Barry

Goldwater attempted to revive the "Communists in the government" charge against the Democrats, he indicated that if it did not catch on, he would drop it—which he did, apparently untroubled that the country had not been alerted to the latest and most passing Red Peril. In politics, as in advertising, truth is often purely instrumental: if it sells, it's true; if it doesn't sell, it isn't true.

Yet there is no doubt that many elites believed what they said about the Red Menace and were themselves gripped by anticommunist fears, sometimes even pathologically so. One of the foremost architects of the cold war, Defense Secretary James V. Forrestal was tirelessly obsessed with the Communist threat and thought of little else right up until the day he jumped to his death from the window of a hospital to which he had committed himself. Most corporate-political-media elites hated and feared Communism as the enemy to their own class privileges and powers. This itself may have been enough to convince them there was truth in all they said about Communism. That a belief serves an ulterior class interest does not mean it is insincerely held. If anything, the congruence between material interest and ideology makes the ideology much easier to embrace wholeheartedly.

In any case, we cannot always presume that a belief gains or loses merit depending on whether its advocates are sincere. Even many fascists are sincere in their views, but this says little about their beliefs. Whether the propagators of the dominant ideology believe in their own arguments is not the point, sometimes they do, sometimes they don't. The important thing is that they are able to mass distribute these images and realities, thereby preempting the symbolic environment and severely limiting political discourse and consciousness.

As we have seen from the account of Khrushchev's visit, media elites do not exercise perfect and automatic control over the communication universe. The media sometimes tell the truth in spite of themselves, being unable to manipulate reality in a limitless way. Liars can use the camera, but short of doctoring the film, the camera cannot lie (which is why the film often has to be doctored). When the Soviet leader—in a friendly visit to the United States—smiles, eats a hot dog, hugs a farmer, speaks admiringly of U.S. technology, praises the beauty of San Francisco, angrily walks out of a Hollywood can-can performance announcing that the face of humanity is more lovely than its backside, and does it all before news cameras and in the public eye, there are limits to how much the media can dehumanize and demonize him—especially when the public lacks the same commitment to cold war militancy that the ruling elites have. Instead, the people saw Khrushchev's travels as something more than "antics" and subversion; they responded to the humanity of his presence.

Like the people, the media themselves are to some degree resistant to total manipulation. Reality seeps in unexpectedly into the packaged communication environment. And reality—the hope for peace and prosperity—sometimes has a stronger hold on the people than the rulers' propaganda. So the cold war mentality and anticommunist dedication must be repeatedly reinforced, for despite all propagandistic efforts, the people keep drifting off into reality, thinking of jobs, peace, and their own human needs.

Notes

1. See William Preston, Jr., *Aliens and Dissenters* (Cambridge, Mass: Harvard University Press, 1963); Sidney Fine, *Laissez-Faire and the General-Welfare State* (Ann Arbor: University of Michigan Press, 1964).

2. Matthew Josephson, *The Politicos* (New York: Harcourt, Brace & World, 1938), p. 284.

3. Ibid., pp. 570, 577.

4. Walter Lippmann and Charles Merz, "A Test of the News," *New Republic*, August 4, 1920, p. 39.

5. Robert Murray, *Red Scare* (New York: McGraw-Hill, 1955), pp. 95–98.

6. Ibid., p. 98.

7. James Aronson, *The Press and the Cold War* (Boston: Beacon Press, 1973), p. 29.

8. *Ibid.*, pp. 29–30; also Murray Levin, *Political Hysteria in America* (New York: Basic Books, 1971).

9. Aronson, *The Press and the Cold War* , p. 30.

10. John Diggins, *Mussolini and Fascism: The View From America* (Princeton, N.J.: Princeton University Press, 1972).

11. M. R. Montgomery, "The Press and Adolph Hitler," *Boston Globe Magazine*, January 30, 1983, pp. 11–13.

12. Richard Boyer and Herbert Morais, *Labor's Untold Story*, 3d ed. (New York: United Electrical, Radio & Machine Workers of America, 1972), pp. 320–21.

13. Boyer and Morais, *Labor's Untold Story*, pp. 283–84.

14. Ibid., p. 317.

15. Ibid.

16. Ibid., p. 324.

17. Ibid., p. 321.

18. William Appleman Williams, *The Tragedy of American Diplomacy* (Cleveland: World Publishing, 1959), p. 168.

19. Aronson, *The Press and the Cold War*, p. 35.

20. Ibid., p. 36.

21. The above quotations from *Business Week*, *New York World-Telegram*, *Chicago Daily News*, and *New York Herald Tribune* are all taken from Aronson, *The Press and the Cold War*, pp. 35–37.

22. Boyer and Morais, *Labor's Untold Story*, p. 349.

23. The discussion on Taft-Hartley is drawn from Boyer and Morais, *Labor's Untold Story*, p. 348, passim.

24. Ibid., pp. 350–70.

25. Edwin Bayley, *Joe McCarthy and the Press* (New York: Random House, 1982), p. 6.

26. Ibid., p. 7.

27. Aronson, *The Press and the Cold War*, p. 71.

28. Ibid., pp. 77, 133–52.

29. Bayley, *McCarthy and the Press*, p. 163.

30. Ibid., pp. 173–75.

31. Aronson, *The Press and the Cold War*, p. 83.

32. James Aronson, *Packaging the News* (New York: International Publishers, 1971), p. 21. This account of Khrushchev's visit is from Aronson's eyewitness report.

33. *San Francisco Examiner*, September 22, 1959.

34. Aronson, *Packaging the News*, p. 22.

35. Ibid.

36. Ibid., p. 25.

8

The Russians Are Coming, The Russians Are Collapsing

To justify military intervention in places like Vietnam and Laos, the United States found another Great Red Menace to go along with the USSR, now accusing the People's Republic of China of being the purveyor of something called "Asian Communism." By the 1960s the word was out: "Red China," an awesome giant, armed with nuclear weapons and bent on regional and world domination, was U.S. public enemy number one.[1] This image was fortified by pronouncements emanating from Peking itself. While Soviet leaders tirelessly advocated peaceful coexistence and said relatively little about Third World revolutions, China called for "wars of national liberation" and denounced the United States as an "imperialist paper tiger."

In lockstep with official policy, the U.S. news media began depicting China as a menacing "extremist" nation populated by hundreds of millions of Communist fanatics. By the early 1960s newspaper political cartoons no longer caricatured Khrushchev as a threatening figure but as a pudgy almost benign personage overshadowed by an awesome slanty-eyed giant labeled "Red China."[2]

GOOD CHINA, BAD RUSSIA

In the mid-1970s, after suffering setbacks in Indochina, Angola, and Mozambique, and confronted with a deepening recession at home, U.S. policymakers once more began to portray the Soviet Union as a growing menace to U.S. security and as a purveyor of Third World revolutions. While the actual material assistance the Soviets gave to liberation struggles was (with the exception of Vietnam) not all that great and in some cases nonexistent, Moscow did offer political and moral support, and did aid nations like Cuba which, in turn, directly assisted leftist insurgents in places like Angola. In contrast, the Chinese attacked the Soviet Union for being the great aggressor and

130

purveyor of "social imperialism." At the same time Peking cultivated sympathetic relations with reactionary governments and counterrevolutionary forces in various countries.

The U.S. media again mirrored the shift in official policy, discovering that China was no longer a menacing giant nor a mindless ant-hill but was inhabited by human beings who liked to play ping-pong, sip soda, and even fall in love and do a turn on the dance floor.[3] The "fanatical Asian communists" were now described as "moderate." According to *Newsweek*, Peking's post-Maoist leaders were putting "China's house in order" and presiding "over a strongly entrenched and resolutely pragmatic government."[4] In 1978 Peking's top-man, Vice-Premier Deng, appeared in a cover portrait as *Time* magazine's "Man of the Year."

Press reports also talked of mass discontent, poverty, instability, lagging production and other "signs of political and economic disarray" in China.[5] As a *national entity*, China was accorded a more favorable representation in the U.S. media, but *Chinese socialism* was still described in essentially negative terms. The American public was not to mistake the improvement in U.S.-Sino relations as a sign of approval for China's economic system.

In contrast, the Soviet Union was once more the Red Menace. Almost on cue, alarmist stories appeared in the news media about the superiority of Soviet military capabilities. During this period Soviet advisers were kicked out of Egypt and Somalia; a massive country like China seemingly switched over to the Western camp; Poland experienced widespread unrest; and the revolutionary government in Afghanistan proved so unstable as to cause the Soviets to commit themselves to a politically and militarily costly intervention. Yet the USSR was portrayed in the press as an inexorably successful foe winning victory after victory, posing a mounting threat to U.S. security.

The Soviet intervention into Afghanistan in December 1979 lent much needed fuel to the image of "Soviet expansionism." In the months to follow, commentators, columnists, and reporters inundated the media with speculations that the Afghanistan venture was merely a prologue to more serious aggressions, including an impending invasion of Iran, an invasion of the entire Middle East to cut off the U.S. "oil lifeline," and an invasion of Yugoslavia—which supposedly would come during the instability caused in that country by Tito's death. The media pundits offered no subsequent explanations as to why these invasions never happened. Even if proven false, the alarming anticipations of Soviet aggression had their conditioning effect, creating a climate of opinion that left their propagators all the more free to market such speculations as "news analysis."

The accession of Ronald Reagan to the White House guaranteed that the new cold war begun by Jimmy Carter would continue but *fortissimo*, with a confrontational belligerency not displayed by American policymakers since the 1950s. In his very first press conference as president of the United States, Reagan declared that the Soviet Union's goal was to impose "a one-world Socialist or Communist state" over the entire globe. "The only morality they recognize is what will further their cause: meaning they commit any crime; to lie, to cheat, in order to obtain that." The United States, Reagan observed, had no choice but to counter the USSR's aggrandizing moves wherever possible.[6]

A *Newsweek* story on "REAGAN'S DEFENSE BUILDUP" offered the following phrases repeated with no documentation: "America must redress the Soviet gains of recent years," "aggression by Moscow . . . ," "Soviet . . . expansionist actions," "offset Soviet gains in the Third World."[7] Similarly bald assertions cluttered the news stories, opinion columns, and editorials of the *New York Times, Washington Post*, and *Time* and were repeated on the major network evening news shows.

The years of détente were now forgotten by officials and opinion makers. The press seldom mentioned Moscow's calls for rapprochement; instead references were to "Soviet global expansionism" by a "totalitarian" Soviet system that "poses the most serious military threat and political challenge facing the West."[8] The news media revived cold war stereotypes that had been dormant for over a decade of détente. Soviet concerns were now "Soviet designs." The Soviet Union was again the "Soviet empire." "Soviet defenses" were now "Soviet attack capabilities." Soviet leaders were once more "ruthless Kremlin powerbrokers" whose main interest in life was "power for power's sake."[9]

Media pundits and columnists speculated with chilling calm about the likelihood of nuclear war with the Russians. Within a short period during 1981, officialdom and the press put World War III back on the agenda, treating the public to a steady diet of "delivery systems," "civil defense evacuations," "throw weight," and "retaliatory capability."[10] All the grotesque Dr. Strangelove imagery that had been considered an aberration of the nuclear minded 1950s again became part of the mainstream media's vocabulary.

In early 1982 President Reagan proposed a "zero option" plan which called for the dismantling of all Soviet intermediate-range missiles in Europe. In exchange, the U.S. would refrain from deploying its new Pershing 2 and cruise missiles and since the U.S. had no missiles in Europe, the continent would then be nuclear-free. But the Soviets rejected the offer. So it was reported in the press for the next fifteen months.[11] The news media usually neglected to point out that the U.S. offer was confined to *land-based* missiles and excluded the hundreds of forward-base sea and air missiles that the U.S. had around Europe. It also excluded the land-based and air and sea missiles of Great Britain and France which were aimed at the USSR. In effect, Reagan's zero-option called for the total dismantling of the entire Soviet medium-range missile arsenal while leaving the American and European medium-range forces intact. But it was never spelled out that way in radio, television and newspaper accounts.

Nor did press commentators point out that all the American medium-range missiles were in effect strategic in that they could hit Soviet ICBMs in a first strike, while none of the Soviet SS20s could cross the Atlantic. The implacement of an additional 500 Pershing 2 and cruise missiles, eight minutes away from Soviet soil, was a big step in giving the United States a first-strike superiority—with missiles that were within an eight-minute striking range of the USSR. Instead, the impression left by most of the press was that the Soviets had turned down an offer to eliminate warheads from Europe in order to maintain a numerical superiority.

The media willingly went along with Reagan's next move. In March 1983 he offered to reduce the number of new missiles he intended to install in Europe, if the USSR would scrap some of its existing SS20s—even though a rough parity already existed between the Soviet land-based missiles and the U.S., British and French missiles. In effect, Reagan was offering to increase the U.S. strike force above parity, if the Soviets would decrease their force below parity.

Yet the *New York Times* greeted the proposal with these headlines: "REAGAN OFFERS CUT IN U.S. MISSILE PLAN FOR WEST EUROPE. PROPOSES WARHEAD LIMIT. MOSCOW IS URGED TO REDUCE ALL MIDDLE-RANGE WEAPONS TO LEVEL OF AMERICANS" (March 31, 1983). The story went on to say, as a statement of fact that recognized no other interpretation: "The cutbacks by the two sides would leave each with the same number of warheads on [medium-range] missiles." On the same day the *Los Angeles Times* headlined the story: "REAGAN OFFERS INTERIM EUROPE MISSILE ACCORD. URGES SOVIET CUTS MATCHED BY U.S. CURBS." The *Washington Post* made the same assertion: "REAGAN OFFERS SOVIETS PARTIAL ARMS CUTBACK." Smaller city papers like the *Orlando* (Fla.) *Sentinel* marched in step with headlines that read: "REAGAN TO SOVIETS: LET'S LIMIT MISSILES IN EUROPE." Except for a passing nod by the *Times* to the Soviet "claim" that parity already existed, none of the major news media gave any exposure to the idea that the Reagan offer might be deceptive. All seemed to accept the president's proposal at face value, treating it as a step toward arms limitation.

In the early 1980s the Soviets (1) asked for another round of arms limitation agreements, (2) unilaterally supported a no first-strike nuclear pledge and repeatedly invited the United States to do likewise, (3) offered to reduce the number of their medium-range missiles in Europe from 600 to 162, (4) unilaterally put a freeze on any further deployment of their updated medium-range SS20 missiles, (5) urged the Americans to refrain from deploying their more advanced Pershing 2 and cruise missiles, (6) called for a ban of all weapons in outer space, and (7) proposed a 25 percent cutback in intercontinental strategic missiles. These kinds of conciliatory gestures were either ignored by the press or dismissed as "initiatives" in "a propaganda war."[12]

A commentator on the ABC evening news (Nov. 20, 1982) brushed aside Soviet proposals with the comment: "The rhetoric sounds good but it remains to be seen if the Kremlin is really interested in better relations." The commentator then asserted that previously "friendly overtures" by the United States "in the 1970s" intended to "improve Soviet behavior" had brought no results. Perhaps better trade relations "would convince the Soviets to change their behavior." One would have to look hard and long to find a columnist, reporter, or editor in the mainstream media who questioned the assumption made about a benign United States and an ill-intentioned, ill-behaved USSR. News reports and analyses seemed limited to discussions of how the U.S. might best deter Soviet aggressiveness.

While the Soviets were calling for arms cutbacks, U.S. News and World Report (Nov. 22, 1982) was alerting its readers to "an unremitting Soviet arms buildup." A CIA report released in December 1982 contradicted the "arms buildup" charge, noting that the share of Soviet GNP devoted to the military had "increased slightly since 1965." But this datum went largely unreported in the press. On December 22, 1982 both the Supreme Soviet and the Central Committee of the Soviet Communist Party unanimously approved a nuclear weapons freeze resolution virtually identical to the version that had been passed by numerous municipalities and states throughout the United States— an action that went unreported by the New York Times, the Washington Post, Time, Newsweek, the major networks, and just about all the mainstream media.

On February 10, 1983, CBS radio announced: "The Soviet people say they want peace. Yet they are obsessed with war and their society is permeated with a military presence. Hear a report this evening on why the Soviet people are so belligerently insecure." The evening report itself created the impression that the Soviet government and citizenry were addicted to militarism and that the USSR was little more than a massive armed camp.

The officially condoned peace movements that conducted massive demonstrations in the Soviet Union and other Eastern European nations during 1981–1983, received no coverage in the mainstream American news media, but much media attention was given to the small dissident groups that were organizing in these countries and were running into official interference. The erroneous impression left by the press was that no peace demonstrations were tolerated in socialist countries. In fact during 1982 millions of people in the USSR and other Eastern European nations had marched in support of a nuclear freeze and an end to the arms race, events that were reported in the *Daily World*, organ of the Communist Party USA, and directly by Western observers, but ignored by the U.S. mainstream media and by much of the U.S. peace movement itself.

EXTERNAL THREATS FOR INTERNAL CONSUMPTION

The campaign against the Red Menace was not exclusively a media creation but reflected the interests of the dominant corporate-political class of which the media is a part. The twists and turns of media anticommunist alarmism largely parallel similar shifts in official policy. This anticommunism can change its direction and its targets but it can never be put to rest for it is a necessary component in making life safe for corporate capitalism both at home and abroad. Just when we think the cold war is a thing of the past, it reappears like some epic cinematic rerun. It is not enough to denounce it as a product of wrong thinking. Such thinking has been around for many decades. We must also try to understand why it continues to be so functional to the interests that nurture it.

In truth the real threat to the "American Way of Life" has come not from without the system but from within, in the form of poverty, inflation, recession, unemployment, a decline in the real wages of American workers, urban blight, pollution, and a deterioration in housing, transportation, education, and health care. In propagating the image of a Soviet menace, the ruling elites have tried to convince people that in times of recession it is necessary to tighten their belts and support increasingly titanic military expenditures and budget deficits. With economic crises and material injustices there often come popular unrest, strikes, demonstrations, riots, sit-ins, agitations, resist-

ance to the law, and a threatened disruption of class order. The Red
Menace image propagated by the government and the media attempts
to direct popular discontent and anxieties away from domestic realities and toward imaginary foes. Rally around the flag, for the Republic is threatened by alien forces. The crisis within the system is trans-
formed into an external threat against it. Just as Hitler sought to
blame German's misery on the Jews, so U.S. political leaders, with the
help of media opinion makers, target the Reds.

In addition, the United States is engaged in an intense struggle to
make the world safe for capital accumulation, to retain control of the
markets, natural resources, and cheap labor of poorer countries, and
to prevent the emergence of anticapitalist social orders. To justify the
use of American public funds and military personnel in a global counterinsurgency program, the U.S. government and the news media talk
about defending freedom and protecting our national security. How is
tiny El Salvador a threat to our national security? It is a tool of
Nicaragua, which is a tool of Cuba, which is a tool of "Soviet expansionism." Behind the Little Red Menace lurks the Giant Red Menace—or so the opinion merchandisers would have us believe. And
even if not a tool of the Soviets, the Central American guerrillas are
"Marxists" or "leftists," hence, evil enough on their own and in need
of eradication.[13]

As in the 1950s, so in the 1980s: the Red Menace theme so
saturated the mass media that even left-leaning and progressive publications felt obliged to lay down an anti-Soviet barrage of a kind they
would have not found necessary to do during détente. Skittish liberal
and leftist intellectuals, concerned above all with their credibility, once
more shifted with the prevailing tide and tone—as defined by mainstream media—and tried to outdo each other in displaying their anti-
Soviet (or anti-Marxist, anticommunist, or even just anti-left) credentials. Sometimes the display permeated an entire article or review, even
one that supposedly dealt with the iniquities of the right. More often
the writer flashed his or her anticommunism in a parenthetical, almost
casual aside, just enough to cover himself or herself.

The ploy is familiar and dates back to the McCarthy era, when
one sought to establish one's political respectability by anticommunist
genuflection. However, this outpouring only strengthened the very
cold war mania and anticommunist orthodoxy that intellectuals ostensibly opposed. Rather than creating more space for themselves, they
created less.[14]

Far less responsive to Cold War II have been the American people
themselves. To be sure, after a century or so of propaganda from the
press and the other dominant institutions of this society, anticommu-

nism permeates the American political culture. "Communism" is a fear word eliciting, without benefit of explanation or definition, a negative response from millions of Americans. For instance, President Reagan's repeated pronouncements about the belligerent nature of what he called the Soviet "evil empire," well-publicized and unchallenged by the mainstream media, had a discernible effect on public opinion. A New York Times/CBS poll in April 1983 found that by a 3 to 2 margin the public backed Reagan's view that the USSR was a growing threat and an immediate danger.[15]

Yet it is remarkable how anticommunist *sentiment* does not always translate into popular support for anticommunist *policies*. The same *Times* poll found that an even larger majority (2 to 1) felt that the American arms buildup would only induce a similar buildup from the Soviets and was not the right road to peace. By a 64 to 25 percent margin, respondents supported a mutual freeze of nuclear weapons rather than a military buildup. Other polls and referenda in the 1980s indicate that decisive majorities of the American people supported substantial cuts in military spending and did not believe the Russians wanted nuclear war. By lopsided majorities they opposed sending U.S. troops to foreign countries to fight against "Communist aggression" and they strongly preferred a nonintervention policy toward countries like Nicaragua and El Salvador.[16] In the face of all propaganda to the contrary, the American people, while far from immune to the anti-red calumny, showed themselves unwilling to go along with military interventionism and nuclear confrontations. Yet, except for brief mention in an occasional poll, this public opinion was kept out of the public eye. The press filled the airwaves and the dailies with *official* opinion and with the deliberations of commentators who did not stray all that far from the official perspective and who readily mistook their own expert pontifications for the last word.

"THEIR ECONOMY IS A FAILURE"

The media work tirelessly to paint a negative picture of alternative societies, letting us know that "no matter how bad we have it, they have it even worse." Be it a mixed economy as in Nicaragua, a social democratic welfare state as in Sweden or Great Britain (before Thatcher), or a socialized state as in Cuba and the Soviet Union, the press goes after any system which begins to use a substantial portion of its wealth and resources in "statist" or "collectivist" ways. Likewise the news media are quick to point out anything that looks like backsliding, chortling over every instance of "capitalism" in China, Hungary, or Cuba (such as small service businesses and private market farms), and inviting the American public to see in these experimentations a confirmation of the superiority of the corporate profit system. Here I will concentrate on the press's treatment of the Soviet Union as an especially important and persistent example of how socialism is presented to the American people.

Judging from the news photos and film footage that appear in the U.S. media, life in the Soviet Union consists of (1) Kremlin leaders reviewing military parades in Red Square; and (2) citizens waiting on long lines for scarce goods. Certainly these images faithfully reflect the two basic and somewhat contradictory themes American political leaders and the media have long been feeding the American public about the USSR: It is a robust and dangerously powerful nation, but its productive capacity is falling apart. It has a sophisticated, highly advanced military-industrial formation, but its economy has failed.

As the American economy sank deeper into the stagflation of the 1970s and 1980s, the old game of celebrating the deterioration of the Soviet system enjoyed a revival in the press. First came reports, beginning in 1974 and extending into the 1980s, in such publications as the *New York Times, Wall Street Journal, U.S. News and World Report,* and *Washington Post,* announcing that the Soviet economy was plagued by inflation. The *Post* headlined a report in 1981: "SOVIETS JOINING THE 'REST OF THE WORLD' WITH BALLOONING INFLATION."[17] All these stories had one thing in common: a close reading reveals that the inflation was mostly in such luxury items as cars, gasoline, alcoholic beverages, furs, and the like. Not until thirteen paragraphs into the *Post* story do we discover that the "skyrocketing prices" did not affect basic staples; the prices for potatoes, beef, bread, milk, and rents have remained fixed for two decades. And "Moscow residents still enjoy subsidized subway rides for seven cents, just as they did in 1961."

A *New York Daily News* story headlined "SOVIET PRICES SOARING. GAS, BOOZE COST COMRADES A PRETTY KO-PECK" offers an identical treatment, waiting until the very last paragraph to note that prices were actually "lowered for antibiotics, synthetic fabrics and clothing and a variety of recreational and household goods."[18] In 1983 the *Washington Post* was at it again, this time with a front-page story assuring inflation-ridden Americans that in the USSR "well-informed sources" said prices were going to be increased on construction materials, tools, mail services, and other items. Again not until the thirteenth paragraph, back on page 11, do we discover that basic foodstuffs were not affected.[19]

While the U.S. press offered numerous stories about inflation in the Soviet Union, it had little to say about unemployment—most likely because there was none to speak of in that country. An American public enduring 20 million unemployed and underemployed might be interested in learning how the Soviet Union and most other socialist nations have achieved full employment in a planned economy. Certainly, here is a story at least as newsworthy as the ones about price increases in cigarettes and gasoline. But the business-owned U.S. media have managed to avoid the subject. The media's operational rule when reporting on socialism is: good news is no news; bad news is the only news.

As our opinion makers would have it, the entire Soviet economy is bad news. According to the *Washington Post*, throughout the "Soviet Bloc," "the symptoms of decay are visible . . . from widespread political apathy to ill-lit streets and empty shops to massive corruption."[20] A couple of months later, the *Post* told its readers, "After a decade of growth" the Soviet economy is "on a severe decline."[21] *Time* magazine struck the same note, claiming that the Soviet economy was "slipping into deep trouble. Factories are faltering . . . Oil production is peaking and may soon fall."[22] *Newsweek* joined the chorus, with a headline proclaiming that the Soviet economy was "A SYSTEM THAT DOESN'T WORK."[23] NBC's Garrick Utley announced on the evening news: "The Communist system is a failure. It can't deliver the goods . . ." Dan Rather of CBS referred to "an economic system that doesn't work."[24] And the *New York Times* announced that the USSR was suffering from severe "domestic economic stagnation."[25]

In fact, the Soviet Union *was* having problems with productivity, but they were hardly indicative of systemic failure and impending collapse. Even *Time* had to admit that "the Soviet standard of living nearly doubled during the last two decades."[26] The purchasing power of the Soviet citizen was increasing. In 1965 only 11 percent of Soviet citizens had refrigerators, by 1980 84 percent had them. In that same period the number who had television sets grew from 24 to 85 percent, and annual per capita meat consumption went from 41 to 58 kilos.[27] Public transportation in Soviet cities is inexpensive and superior to what is found in the United States. Housing conditions have improved greatly since the devastation of World War II, and housing costs have been steadily reduced. By law, Soviet citizens now expend not more than 4 percent of their income on rents.[28]

A CIA report released by the Joint Economic Committee of Congress in 1982 concluded that the Soviet economy has been growing at a faster rate than the U.S. economy and that "the level of living of the Soviet people has improved rapidly during the past 30 years . . . Real consumption per capita nearly tripled," while the Soviet diet "improved greatly." Furthermore the increases in consumption were not confined to goods. The CIA report found major gains in services and "a particularly rapid expansion . . . in the provision of transportation, communication and utilities."[29]

What little the U.S. media have to say about the condition of labor in the Soviet Union is largely negative. The image is of a cruelly disciplined work force, represented by powerless unions, suffering in silence and exploited by a new elite class. Throughout the 1950s and 1960s the American press talked about how Soviet workers did not have the right to change their jobs. As late as 1983, a liberal journalist like John Judis could write that the condition of labor was better in "democratic capitalist countries" because, among other things, "labor is mobile," while in communist countries, "labor lacked mobility."[30] In fact, the prohibition against changing employment without permission became a defunct law in the USSR after World War II. Because of the labor shortage and the availability of a wider employment choice, Soviet workers tend to voluntarily change jobs with greater frequency than in the United States where work opportunities are scarce and employment competition is keen. Generally, in Communist countries it is much more difficult for a manager to fire a worker than for a worker to quit.[31]

Far from lacking in benefits and rights, Soviet workers have a guaranteed right to a job; relatively generous disability, maternity, retirement, and vacation benefits; an earlier retirement age than American workers (60 for men, 55 for women); free medical care; free education and job training; and subsidized housing and transportation. If measured by the availability of durable-use consumer goods such as cars, telephones, lawnmowers, and dishwashers, the Soviet worker's standard of living is lower than the American worker's. If measured by the benefits and guarantees mentioned above, Soviet workers enjoy more humane and secure working and living conditions than their American counterparts. "In relation to national income," notes the American Sovietologist Alex Nove, "the Soviet Union spends far more on health, education and so on, than highly industrialized Western countries do."[32]

A NEW CLASS?

If we are to believe our commercial press, there exists a "Soviet ruling class" whose average member resides in splendor, owns expensive foreign cars and a palatial dacha (summer home), and enjoys every other possible luxury. In fact, while it cannot be claimed that Soviet citizens live under conditions of perfect equality, most of the millions of dachas are fairly modest abodes (except for a few of the more elaborate ones used to entertain foreign guests of state); and the living conditions and consumption levels of the Soviet political and managerial strata are not dramatically different from those of other Russians. Soviet leader Yuri Andropov, as *Time* magazine reported, lived in a simple five-room apartment in the same housing project near the Kremlin that once accommodated Leonid Brezhnev. Soviet political leaders, managers, and intelligentsia cannot amass great wealth from the labor of others. They cannot own the means of production nor pass ownership on to their progeny. When they retire, it is to modest living quarters on modest pensions. This hardly constitutes a "new class."

Top-level state ministers and enterprise managers earn only about 2.7 to 4.0 times above the average industrial wage.[33] (However, small numbers of prominent artists, writers, university administrators, and scientists make close to 10 times more.) Such income differences are not great when compared to the United States, where top entertainers, corporate owners, and other wealthy individuals annually take in several hundred times more than the average American wage earner. In addition, the American worker must rely on his salary for a range of services that the Soviet worker receives free or at heavily subsidized prices. As one American specialist in Soviet affairs notes:

> Western newsmen going to the Soviet Union always seem to discover to their shock that income and privileges are distributed unevenly, but in reporting that "news," they have totally missed the real news of the last decade in this realm: a continuation of the sharp reduction that began after Stalin's death in the degree of inequality of incomes in the Soviet Union. . . . The wages of members of the working class have been growing much more rapidly than those in the managerial-professional class.[34]

The American Sovietologist Samuel Hendel lists a number of egalitarian measures adopted soon after the postwar recovery:

> These included currency devaluation (which had a particularly adverse effect on high income groups as well as black marketeers), the ending of the tuition system (making education generally available to the talented, at all levels, without tuition fee), an increase in minimum wages and pensions, extension of the pension system to farm workers, special tax concessions for low-income groups, and reduction in the use of the piece-work system—all of which have been of special and substantial benefit to those at the bottom of the economic scale. Labor benefited, too, from a shorter work week and from reform and liberalization of the labor code. In addition, the Soviet people for many years have had access to cultural

opportunities and to hospital and medical facilities on a widespread and generally egalitarian basis.[35]

These reforms received no attention to speak of in the American press.

THE RUSSIANS ARE STARVING, THE RUSSIANS ARE STARVING

In trying to convince the American public that the Soviet economic system is not working, the U.S. press has pointed to the alleged "failure" of the agricultural sector. *Time* announced in 1982 that Soviet "farms cannot feed the people"; and a year later the *Washington Post* reported "Soviet agriculture [is] simply not able to feed the country."[36] The *New York Times* correspondent, Flora Lewis, claimed that Brezhnev's "ice age has accumulated terrible failures," among which are "feeding the people."[37] Writing in *Parade Magazine*, Robert Moss designated "the collective farms" as "the prime reason for Russia's inability to feed herself."[38] None of these assertions was accompanied by any supporting documentation.

The press has made U.S. grain exports to the Soviet Union the most highly publicized international sales agreement in human history. Western Europe annually imports far more grain than does the USSR, yet no one in the U.S. media or government accuses West Germany or the Benilux countries of being unable to feed their people. In contrast, every Soviet grain deal with the United States is front page news, a reminder to the American public of the allegedly superior productivity of U.S. agribusiness and the failure of collectivism. The truth is something else.

Today the Soviets produce more than enough grain to feed their people. They import foreign grain to help feed their livestock and thereby increase their meat and dairy consumption. (This is seen in both the East and West as an "improved" diet, even though there is evidence suggesting that a high meat and dairy intake is not necessarily the best diet.) It takes between seven and fourteen pounds of grain to produce one pound of meat. And *that* is the cause of the Soviet "grain shortage." In actuality, per capita meat consumption in the USSR has doubled in the last two decades and exceeds such countries as Norway, Italy, Greece, Spain, Japan, and Israel. Milk production has jumped almost 60 percent in twenty years so that today the USSR is by far the largest milk-producing country in the world.[39]

According to the 1982 CIA report on the Soviet economy, "The Soviet Union remains basically self-sufficient with respect to food."

These are the accomplishments of an agrarian labor force that decreased from 42 percent in 1960 to 20 percent in 1980, working in a country where over 90 percent of the land is either too arid or too frigid to be farmed. Still, the press continues to tell the American public that the Soviet system cannot feed its people.

THE PRESS GANGS UP ON BILLY GRAHAM

For years the U.S. media have circulated the notion that "behind the Iron Curtain" people cannot worship freely. The press not only propagates this view, it seems ready to defend it with wolf-pack ferocity. In May 1982, while visiting Moscow with other church leaders, the noted evangelist the Reverend Billy Graham remarked, "The churches that are open, of which there are thousands, seem to have liberty to have worship services." He described his visit as "an enlightening experience." While there were differences in religious practices between our two countries, "that doesn't mean there is no religious freedom" in the USSR, concluded Graham. This one positive comment drew heavy fire from editorialists and columnists in the United States, who suggested that Graham had been duped by the Russians or, worse, had turned soft on Communism. (The many other comments Graham made in the Soviet Union regarding the arms race and nuclear holocaust were ignored.)

The *Washington Post* reported the Baptist minister's return to the United States with the headline "BILLY GRAHAM: 'I AM NOT A COMMUNIST'." The opening paragraph of the *Post* story by Joyce Wadler reads, "In the time-honored tradition of Christians going bravely before the lions, evangelist Billy Graham faced a crowd of snarling reporters here today in his first public appearance in this country since remarking in Moscow that he had seen no evidence of religious repression in the Soviet Union."[40] Outdoing each other in displaying their anticommunism, the reporters asked: Had Graham made a deal with the Soviets to say nice things in exchange for the opportunity to conduct a religious crusade? (Graham had been allowed to preach to religious congregations in the USSR and other Communist countries.) Was he aware some Russian clergy might be KGB agents? Did he really think there could be such a thing as freedom of religion in the USSR? Wasn't there more freedom here?

The *Post* noted that Graham "seemed to spend much of his news conference repenting." Indeed, it appeared to be less a news conference than a McCarthyite investigation with the reporters acting as a gang of little McCarthys. The confrontation got close enough to a witch hunt to cause the Baptist leader to exclaim at one point, "I am not a Communist and have not joined the Communist Party."

Graham did try to explain the comment he had made in Moscow. He believed that in the Soviet Union, people had the freedom to worship. "Churches have some measure of freedom to hold public worship services on church properties if they agree to abide by government regulations. Families are free to teach their children the Bible and to have prayer in their homes. . . . " The evangelist added that "freedom is relative. I don't have freedom in the United States to go into a public school and preach the Gospel, nor is a student free in a public school to pray . . . "41

In a written statement intended as a response to his critics, the minister pointed out that "in China, there are many restrictions and yet leaders in the United States seemed to be applauded for going to China. Perhaps less than 200 churches are open in a population of about one billion. In the Soviet Union, there are an estimated 20,000 places of worship of various religions open. Each year hundreds of permits are granted for new churches."42 Graham's explanations were either downplayed or suppressed by the U.S. press.

UNDER THE TOTALITARIAN YOKE

According to the U.S. press, the Soviet people are a muted, intimidated mass, afraid to speak their minds and denied their basic freedoms. This picture is fortified by the lavish media exposure given to the small number of Soviet dissidents who, like A. I. Solzhenitsyn, Vladimir Budovsky, and Andre Sakharov ally themselves with conservative anticommunists in the West and who seem to have little concern for, nor support from, Soviet workers. To be sure, there is no freedom in the USSR to attack the fundamental assumptions of the Soviet politico-economic system, specifically the Communist Party as an institution, its predominant role in society, and the legitimacy of socialism as an economic system; and there is no freedom to advocate a fundamentally divergent political ideology, nor to engage in organized political opposition outside the framework of such institutions as the party, the unions, the soviets, and various other official state and local organizations and federations.

Nevertheless, for a more balanced picture than offered by the U.S. press, we should note that there is a great deal of public debate and criticism—much of it carried out in the unions, work places, and local soviets. The Soviet press is full of critical letters and exchanges on a wide range of issues, including economic, educational and legal reform, city planning, crime, pollution, women's role in the economy, corrupt or incompetent bureaucratic management, and farm problems. There is even criticism of specific abuses committed by middle-level Communist Party officials and of the ideas and programs of the top leadership (but not of the top leaders themselves). Relying largely on the research of western scholars, Albert Szymanski concludes:

> Observers otherwise hostile to the Soviet Union claim . . . there is considerable freedom of discussion and there exist sharp differences of opinion on a wide range of issues. Basic policies are increasingly formulated, discussed and challenged in public speeches, forums and editorial statements . . . The different Soviet papers and periodicals more or less openly take sides on public issues.[43]

This reality hardly fits the U.S. media's image of mute masses suffering under the yoke of Communism.

The U.S. media's encompassing negativity in regard to the Soviet Union might induce some of us to react with an unqualifiedly glowing view of that society. The truth is, that in the USSR there exist serious problems of labor productivity, industrialization, urbanization, bureaucracy, corruption, and alcoholism. There are production and distribution bottlenecks, plan failures, consumer scarcities, criminal abuses of power, suppression of dissidents, and expressions of alienation among some persons in the population. What is needed, and what is not provided by the U.S. press, is a measured evaluation of this vast, changing, complex, and most unusual Soviet society. The predominance of an anti-Soviet orthodoxy makes a balanced analysis not only difficult but *unnecessary*. Without benefit of extensive inquiry and sometimes without any actual familiarity with the subject being disparaged, the opinion makers "know" and repeatedly make *us* "know" that the Soviet system is a "failure." They may or may not believe it; usually they do. In any case, they get paid for saying so and are rarely inclined, or allowed, to say otherwise.

Notes

1. See the remarks by Secretary of State Dean Rusk, *New York Times*, October 13, 1967.

2. See the reportage and cartoons in *Time*, *Newsweek*, and the *New York Times* "News of the Week in Review" throughout 1963–1965.

3. *Time*, January 15, 1979; also more recently James Sterba, "The Sense of Beauty Shriveled in China, Buds Again," *New York Times*, March 18, 1981.

4. *Newsweek*, August 29, 1977.

5. *New York Times,* December 31, 1978.
6. *Washington Post,* January 31, 1981.
7. *Newsweek,* June 8, 1981.
8. *Time,* November 22, 1982.
9. *Time,* November 22, 1982; also the citations and discussion in William Dorman, "The Image of the Soviet Union in the American News Media," paper given at a New York University conference on news media, March 19, 1983.
10. See the regular and guest columnists that appeared through 1981 and into 1982 in the *New York Times* and *Washington Post.*
11. See for instance the *Washington Post,* February 2, 1983.
12. See the Associated Press release, December 24, 1982.
13. See chapters 10 and 11 for a more detailed discussion of the media's treatment of Third World struggles.
14. For an analysis of how intellectuals performed during an earlier period, see Michael Rogin, *The Intellectuals and McCarthy* (Cambridge, Mass.: M.I.T. Press, 1967).
15. *New York Times,* April 15, 1983.
16. See the survey reported in the *Washington Post,* May 25, 1983.
17. *Washington Post,* December 4, 1981; also *New York Times,* October 6, 1974; *Wall Street Journal,* August 19, 1974; *U.S. News and World Report,* September 16, 1974.
18. *New York Daily News,* September 15, 1981.
19. *Washington Post,* February 8, 1983. See the study done by *Social Policy* editor Roy Bennett and economist Lyn Turgeon, which concluded that inflation in the Soviet Union was a relatively minor or nonexistent problem: Roy Bennett, "All the Inflation News That's Fit to Print," *Social Policy,* November/December 1974, pp. 2–3.
20. *Washington Post,* December 12, 1982.
21. Ibid., February 20, 1983.
22. *Time,* November 22, 1982.
23. *Newsweek,* April 12, 1982.
24. NBC evening news, November 11, 1982; CBS evening news, November 16, 1982; cited in William Dorman, "The Image of the Soviet Union in the American News Media War," Peace and News Media Conference, New York University, March 18–19, 1983.
25. *New York Times,* November 12, 1982.
26. *Time,* November 22, 1982.
27. See Jerry F. Hough, "The Brezhnev Era and Citizen Participation," in Samuel Hendel, ed. *The Soviet Crucible,* 5th ed. (North Scituate, Mass.: Duxbury Press, 1980), pp. 221–26; also the interview with E. H. Carr and accompanying comments by Alexander Cockburn and James Ridgeway in the *Village Voice,* November 23, 1982.
28. Mike Davidow, *Cities Without Crisis* (New York: International Publishers, 1976).
29. *New York Times,* December 26, 1982.
30. *In These Times,* January 19–25, 1983.
31. Albert Szymanski, *Is the Red Flag Flying?* (London: Zed, 1979), pp. 53–56; also Margrit Pittman, *Encounters in Democracy, A U.S. Journalist's View of the GDR* (New York: International Publishers, 1981) for a view of labor conditions in East Germany.
32. Alec Nove, "Reply to My Critics," in Hendel, *The Soviet Crucible,* p. 427.
33. Hough, "The Brezhnev Era . . . "; also Robert Osborn, *Soviet Social Policies* (Homewood, Ill.: Dorsey Press, 1970), p. 176.
34. Hough, "The Brezhnev Era . . . "

35. Samuel Hendel, "The Role of Theory," in Hendel, *The Soviet Crucible*, pp. 447–48.

36. *Time*, November 22, 1982; *Washington Post*, February 20, 1983.

37. *New York Times*, November 12, 1982.

38. *Parade Magazine*, May 8, 1983.

39. The *Christian Science Monitor*, December 13, 1982, printed these facts in an excellent guest column by economist Harry Schaffer. This information has been ignored by almost all the mainstream media.

40. *Washington Post*, May 20, 1982.

41. *Daily World*, May 21, 1982.

42. See comments by Edward Plowman in *Christian Century*, June 23–30, 1982, and Arie Brouwer in *Christianity and Crisis*, June 21, 1982, on the way the press misreported the conference and distorted Graham's visit to the USSR.

43. Szymanski, *Is the Red Flag Flying?*, p. 84; see also H. Gordon Skilling and Franklin Griffiths, *Interest Groups in Soviet Politics* (Princeton, N.J.: Princeton University Press, 1971); Osborn, *Soviet Social Policies*.

9

Soviet Terrorists, Bulgarian Pope Killers, and Other Big Lies

The press does more than merely transmit the government's anti-communist crusade to the public; it tells us what to make of things; it lends credibility to the official message by providing "expert" testimony, judicious summations, half-truths and outright fabrications, some of which go beyond even what political leaders are claiming. The press looks the other way when embarrassing truths threaten to surface; it directs our attention back to the invented reality; it commits blatant omissions and maintains a stony silence about many urgent things. The press fleshes out the Big Lie, bringing it to life with alarming images and on-the-spot "eyewitness reports." If the news media do not always succeed perfectly in manipulating the public, it is not for want of trying. What follows are some major examples of the Big Lie.

THE INVISIBLE HAND OF "SOVIET TERRORISM"

In January 1981, Secretary of State Alexander Haig—soon followed by President Reagan and other high officials—announced there existed a network of "international terrorism," directed by the Kremlin, involving everything from airline hijackings to Third World insurgencies.[1]

With a few scattered exceptions, the mainstream press quickly echoed the cries of the secretary of state. A *Washington Post* editorial accused the Soviets and their allies of being the "principal source of terror in the world" and urged the United States and other Western countries "to improve intelligence and counterterror measures" so that Moscow would no longer have "a free ride for being the hatchery of international terrorism."[2] The *Post* offered no evidence to support these sensational charges and admitted it was difficult to cite actual instances of Soviet terrorism. But if it was so difficult to do so, whence the certitude that the Soviets were culpable? Equally unencumbered by evidence, a *Wall Street Journal* editorial asserted that the Soviet Union has set up Libyan and Palestine Liberation Organization (PLO) training camps for terrorists and might be doing the same in the United States and that "Cuban intelligence" might have a "deep involvement in American terrorism."[3]

Soon after Haig's press conference there appeared a book, *The Terror Network*, by Claire Sterling, a journalist who had once worked for a CIA-funded newspaper in Rome. Sterling might have been dismissed as the author of just another ultra-right conspiratorial potboiler were it not that the two most prestigious newspapers in the United States, the *New York Times* and the *Washington Post*, gave their imprimaturs by running lengthy excerpts and adaptations from her book as cover stories in their Sunday magazines, complete with sensational photographs and headlines.[4]

The *Times* selection was accompanied by nothing less than twelve photographs of terrorists or terrorist acts, including a grisly picture of a NATO employee lying in a pool of blood, with the caption stating that he was one of four Americans killed by "Marxist terrorists" in 1979. Both the *Times* and *Post* Sterling articles referred to Arab, Irish, Basque, Japanese, West German, and Italian terror groups and repeatedly asserted that they were linked to Moscow. Missing from these selections, as from Sterling's book, was any evidence connecting the terrorists to the Soviet Union. "It's just not that simple," Sterling admitted in the *Times* story. "Such direct control of terrorist organizations was never the Soviet intention. All were indigenous to their countries. All began as offshoots of relatively violent movements that expressed particular political, economic, religious, or ethnic grievances,"[5] But if there was no intention of direct control from Moscow, what was the Soviet intention? And how did Moscow exercise its influence over such indigenous, self-willed, nationalistic groups? And why then call it an "international force" of terrorism?

To prove Moscow's involvement, Sterling asserted that the terrorists had money and had been "moving about the world in yachts and helicopters."[6] In a perfect example of fallacious *post hoc* reasoning, she argued a reverse cause and effect. Moscow provided money to terrorists. Proof? The terrorists had money. Moscow directed the terrorists all over the world. Proof? There were terrorists committing violent acts all over the world. By first showing that the effect existed, she then concluded it must be "proof" of the cause she ascribed to it.

In fact, nothing was proved. The Moscow "link" was established only by repeated assertion and conjecture.

At one point Sterling maintained she needed no evidence to support her thesis: "I rely on the historic position taken by the Soviet Union."[7] She asserted that Soviet leaders placed their faith in terror, and quoted what she called "Lenin's definition" of terror: "The purpose of terror is to terrorize," thus leaving the false impression that Lenin was an advocate of terrorism. In fact, Lenin and the Bolsheviks waged a persistent campaign against terrorism, calling it an "infantile disorder" that ruptured contact between the revolutionary organization and the populace, while diverting party activists from the real task of organizing a mass revolutionary movement. "The experience of the entire history of the Russian revolutionary movement," Lenin writes, "warns us against such methods of struggle as terrorism."[8] Today the Soviets admit to giving support to Third World national liberation movements, as in Vietnam; but they and all the Western Communist parties have denounced the terrorist groups in Western Europe as frenzied, isolated, and even "fascistic."

In 1981 ex-CIA director William Colby testified before the Senate Subcommittee on Security and Terrorism that there was little evidence that the Kremlin masterminded terrorist acts around the world. FBI director William Webster declared "there is no real evidence of Soviet-sponsored terrorism within the United States."[9] Most acts of terrorism in the United States, as Webster testified on a subsequent occasion, have involved Croatian and Armenian nationalists, anti-Castro Cubans like the murderous Omega 7 group, and Puerto Rican nationalists.[10] None of these has been linked to the Soviet Union. These testimonies were reported in the press, although on the back pages, and failed to keep the *Times,* the *Post,* and numerous other media from giving sensationalist coverage to the Reagan-Haig-Sterling terror fantasies.

In less than a year, however, by the end of 1981, the "Soviet terrorism" theme receded from the news as quickly as it had appeared, with no explanation as to why the public was no longer being alerted to this menace and no demand from the press for an explanation. Only three years later, in January 1984, did the *Washington Post* let the truth peek through; it ran a series of articles entitled "The Terror Factor," which concluded that there could be found no "significant information of Soviet involvement in terrorist enterprises."[11]

The pattern of propaganda displayed in the government-media "Soviet terrorism" escapade is one that has been repeatedly used since the early days of anticommunist propaganda. First, a publicity campaign is launched to alert the public to an alien threat. Then the threat suddenly disappears as mysteriously as it appeared. Except for one or two skeptical voices, the press unquestioningly goes along with the whole thing, energetically publicizing the threat, then offering no comment about its evaporation. Nor, as we shall see, does the press offer any comments about its mysterious reappearance after a substantial lapse of time.

Journalists are supposed to report opposing viewpoints, guard against manipulation by their sources, check stories against available evidence, and seek out new sources of information. They often fail to do these things and in this instance they failed miserably. The reasons are worth pondering. Stories about "Soviet terrorism" deal with sensational, highly secretive events—or nonevents. The official sources are often anonymous, although in this case they were far from that, being the secretary of state and the president of the United States. But these visible officials can claim a reliance on "top secret" sources that are not accessible to questioning or to demands for hard evidence. In a word, officials can say whatever they please, and sympathetic journalists can embellish as they please, even if what they say is unfounded, alarmist, and implausible. When the subject is the Red Menace the press throws caution to the wind and jumps in with both feet.

YELLOW RAIN AND OTHER DROPPINGS

The story about Soviet chemical warfare that first appeared in 1975 is still being sold to the public ten years later as I write this. In 1928 the Soviet Union signed the 1925 Geneva Protocol, which prohibits the use of chemical and bacteriological warfare (CBW). The United States became a signatory fifty years later in 1975 after much public pressure. That same year, also in response to public pressure, the United States agreed to enter into negotiations with Moscow to ban all chemical weapons. From that time on, however, U.S. government officials began accusing the USSR of waging chemical war, a charge that, if proved true, would give Washington enough justification to continue to expand its own CBW program.

Washington initially accused the USSR and Vietnam of using an unidentified lethal gas (later dubbed "yellow rain") in Laos and Cambodia. On the basis of these charges, and little else, Congress in 1979 passed a resolution condemning both countries. The next year, the Carter administration charged that the Soviets were using nerve gas in Afghanistan. The news media obligingly reported these unsubstantiated accusations, giving little play to disclaimers (some of which came from official U.S. sources). A small article in the *New York Daily News* did report that "government specialists were skeptical of reports that the Russians had used lethal nerve gas against the Afghans."[12]

The next big propaganda push came in September 1981 when Secretary of State Alexander Haig, speaking in West Berlin, charged that there was "substantial," "compelling," and "overwhelming" evidence that the Russians were engaging in illegal "germ warfare in Afghanistan, Cambodia, and maybe elsewhere."[13] The evidence? A single leaf supposedly taken from the Thai-Cambodian border, containing trichothecenes, a toxin found naturally in many fungus-ridden plants including spoiled grain. Such were the claims of a U.S. government that had sprayed over five million acres of Vietnam with twelve million gallons of Agent Orange, containing dioxin, a substance so poisonous that its use has been banned in fifty-eight countries.[14]

On December 21, 1981, ABC television aired a special "documentary" entitled "Yellow Rain," which provided no additional evidence and ignored the arguments accumulating within the scientific community against the government's case. The program did interview a number of "intelligence experts" and "defectors" from "Communist Indochina" who said, yes, the Soviets and Vietnamese were using chemical sprays to kill people in Laos, Cambodia, and Afghanistan.

In 1982 the State Department reported it had stalks and leaves from an unidentified plant allegedly brought from Cambodia that showed abnormally high traces of mycotoxins, also water samples and blood samples from "victims" that supposedly confirmed the possibility of trichothecene poisoning.[15] The State Department also maintained that Soviet chemical attacks were responsible for 10,000 deaths in Southeast Asia.

Typical of the propaganda role played by the media was an article appearing in 1983 in *Parade* magazine, a Sunday supplement carried by newspapers across the country, including the *Washington Post*.[16] Written by Al Santoli and entitled "How the Soviets Use Chemicals to Wage War," it talked of aerial attacks against hill tribes by "Laotian and Vietnamese Communists," killing "thousands upon thousands of people," with thousands more showing "the same horrifying medical symptoms" of bleeding from every bodily aperture, nausea, skin lesions, and convulsions. The accompanying pictures did not exactly fit the story. One is of a roomful of seemingly healthy persons purported to be Laotians being interviewed about yellow rain attacks at a "holding center" in Thailand. Another was of three men reclining on blankets, identified as "Three yellow rain victims following attack in Cambodia on March 11." From the photo, taken at a distance of about ten feet, there was no way to determine the condition of these men. Most of the article was given over to descriptions of the Soviet CB arsenal rather than to chemical war in Southeast Asia. The photograph on the first page of an armed figure in a gas mask was said to be "from a Soviet military journal" showing "Communist bloc troops wearing full chemical warfare gear as they attack." (Attack whom?) The article made much of the fact that the Soviets had developed CBW weapons but failed to mention that the United States had done the same.

Meanwhile leading American mycotoxin and CBW specialists were offering evidence and arguments of a different kind, summarized as follows:

· The material evidence provided by the government was unconvincing because of its paucity. Massive chemical war campaigns extending over nine years and killing thousands of people would have produced more than a few leaves and twigs. There should have been indisputable proof: many contaminated corpses, a large number of duds and malfunctions and fragments of artillery shells, and bomb or gas canisters with traces of mycotoxin.

· The delivery systems purportedly used by the Soviets and their allies (plastic bags that opened above the target, rockets and shells emitting not yellow but red and green clouds, tanks and planes spraying yellow liquids) fit no known type of chemical or biological attack system.

· The government claimed that the mycotoxins in its leaf samples were not naturally found in Southeast Asia, but studies showed that fungi capable of producing them have at one time or another contaminated foods throughout much of the world, including Asia. Furthermore, samples from a Brazilian shrub found amounts that were several times higher than those in the government's samples, so the latter actually may have contained normal levels.

· The State Department claimed to find "significant quantities" of T-2 (the trichothecene-based mycotoxin found in Indochina) in the blood samples of "victims" taken eighteen days after a yellow rain attack. But T-2 always disappears rapidly from the bloodstream of laboratory animals and is believed unlikely to be detectable after a maximum ninety-six hours.

· Mycotoxins are hard substances that cannot penetrate the lungs and skin. For respiratory poisoning they must be fragmented to the size of smoke particles. But smoke from a flying plane dissipates at the altitude of the flight and does not reach the ground.

· The descriptions of victims vomiting great quantities of blood after contact with yellow rain are implausible insofar as no vom-

iting of blood has ever been found in decades of laboratory
experiments with animals.

· The delivery of doses lethal to humans would require gigantic
quantities of yellow rain saturating an area in mycotoxin con-
centrations approaching one million parts per million instead of
fifty or one hundred parts per million found in the State Department samples. Actual CBW mycotoxins are hundreds of times
stronger than T-2. Most mycotoxin scientists agree that it would
not make sense to use T-2 as a chemical weapon. More than
3,000 *tons* of yellow rain would be required to attack a single
village, requiring 20,000 to 30,000 shells—some two hours of
fire from a full Soviet artillery division—or a minimum of 8,000
tons of bombs dropped from the air. There are quicker, more
conventional means of obliterating small villages.[17]

These rebuttals won almost no press coverage. In creating a climate of opinion, the facts of the matter may count for less than which
side has access to the mass media. In February 1984, responding to the
media-created opinion climate, the U.S. Senate voted unanimously to
condemn the Soviets for waging chemical war in Southeast Asia.

The press's handling of the government's propaganda campaign
resembled its treatment of Senator Joseph McCarthy's nefarious doings years before. First, the government releases sensational charges,
referring to "conclusive evidence" it possesses but doesn't make public. The press obligingly reports the charges, making no demand to see
the evidence and gives lesser play—if any at all—to the rebuttals. The
critics who demolish the government's case are largely confined to
scientific journals, a few low-circulation dissident and liberal magazines, and some foreign publications, none of which reaches a large
American public. The government then can ignore its critics and repeat its claims, knowing that the media will dutifully report the
charges, embellishing them with headlines, photographs, and "expert
testimony" from eager conservatives. Through the process of repetition, and aided by other propaganda campaigns about the Soviet
threat, these charges gain an undeserved plausibility.

On the infrequent occasions when a critical word does appear in
the press, the government is more likely to be chided for its mistaken
notions than attacked for its deliberate lies. Thus *New York Times*
editorials scolded the administration for being "too quick" with its
yellow rain charges, and for drawing upon "scientific advice" that was
"evidently insufficient," adding that "the failure to notice that yellow
rain is yellow because of its pollen content was a ludicrous over-
sight. . . ."[18] Here the *Times* was referring to the findings by two

American scientists that yellow rain in Southeast Asia was nothing more than the excretion of masses of wild honeybees, a story that was given wide play in the media, probably because of its novelty.[19]

In an interview on National Public Radio (March 30, 1984), one of the scientists, Matthew Meselson, maintained that the government was guilty of nothing more than "sloppy research" and "honest error." He did not explain how he came to that conclusion. In the one strong critical piece to appear in the *Washington Post*, former director of CBW for the U.S. army, Saul Hormats, exposed many of the implausible aspects of the government's case, only to conclude that "the State Department's allegations appear to be based on imaginative responses to naïve and gullible interrogators."[20]

By characterizing the administration's charges as nothing more than the product of innocent mistakes due to haste, sloppy research, honest error, naïveté, and gullibility, the media and the scientists quoted in the media were overlooking a great deal of evidence suggesting that the U.S. government was involved in deliberate fabrications as part of a protracted disinformation campaign extending over the better part of a decade.

On April 13, 1984, the *Washington Post* finally ran an article that attempted to summarize a few of the arguments made by critics, along with ones made by the government. The *Post* concluded that "there are eminent scientists on both sides of the issue," a statement that implied there was a serious split in the scientific community when actually just about all the independent scientists who addressed themselves to the issue, along with some within the government itself, judged the government's case to be severely deficient.

The reason why the U.S. government persisted in this campaign might be found buried in the sixteenth paragraph of an earlier *Post* story, which read, "Administration supporters have used the 'yellow rain' charges to bolster support for a Pentagon proposal to create a new generation of U.S. chemical weapons."[21] Both the story and its headline "SOVIET CHEMICAL WARFARE REPORTED LOWER IN 1983" uncritically accepted the government's claim that the Soviets were engaged in chemical warfare.

The national media continued to go along with the Reagan administration's CBW propaganda campaign. Thus when the White House suddenly proposed an on-site inspection treaty to ban the production, storage, and use of all chemical weapons, NBC evening news reported it was "because of their use in Southeast Asia, Afghanistan, and most recently by Iraq against Iran"[22]—without even so much as a hint to its viewers that there was little evidence to support the charges made against the Soviets in Afghanistan and Southeast Asia.

THE STRANGE FLIGHT OF KAL 007

On September 1, 1983, a South Korean 747 airliner, Flight 007, was shot down by Soviet interceptor planes after intruding deeply inside Soviet airspace over Kamchatka Peninsula and Sakhalin Island. The plane plunged into the Japan Sea and all 269 persons aboard perished. U.S. press reaction was instantaneous and unrestrained. CBS anchorperson Dan Rather talked of "the barbaric act" committed by the Soviet Union. Other news commentators referred to the Soviets' "inherent viciousness," "malice," "savagery," and "inhuman brutality." *New York Times* columnist Leslie Gelb wrote, "The Soviet Union is different—call it tougher, more brutal or even uncivilized—than the rest of the world." And *Washington Post* editor Meg Greenfield characterized the USSR as "an uncivilized and barbaric nation."[23] Members of Congress and government officials rushed forth with condemnatory statements that were eagerly picked up by the media. President Reagan talked of "an act of barbarism, born of a society that wantonly disregards individual rights and the value of human life."[24] By unanimous vote Congress adopted a motion accusing the USSR of "one of the most infamous and reprehensible acts in history," thereby demonstrating yet again how Congress can be stampeded by a government-media hype.

In the days following the incident, the government and the press treated as established facts the claims that the Soviets had cold-bloodedly shot down a plane they knew to be a civilian passenger airliner, that U.S. spy stations and aircraft had made no contact with KAL 007, and that the airliner had innocently "strayed" and "drifted" as much as three hundred miles over the most militarily sensitive area of the USSR for two-and-a-half hours in an oddly circuitous flight pattern through space conspicuously marked on all navigational maps as dangerous.

In successive television appearances, President Reagan and U.S. Ambassador to the United Nations Jeane Kirkpatrick produced monitored voice recordings that ostensibly demonstrated that Soviet pilots had made no attempt to contact the airliner by radio and had fired no warning shots. The official U.S. version of the events gained worldwide publicity. But the way the story fell apart received much less attention. Several weeks after the incident an analysis of the tapes showed that the Soviet fighters did have the necessary international radio frequencies to contact 007 and had used them frequently. The correct and undoctored transcript revealed that the pilot reported he was "locking off his missiles," indicating he had fired warning shots before releasing the cannon burst that downed the plane. No explanation was offered by Kirkpatrick or Reagan for the distortions and deletions in their version of the transcript. *No explanation was asked for by the major media, the commentators, and columnists who had been so outraged by the incident just a few weeks earlier.*

Here are some other sensational revelations mostly ignored by a press not noted for its indifference to sensational revelations:

- Ten minutes after its takeoff KAL 007 was already off course, according to radar data from the air traffic controllers in Anchorage who supposedly were monitoring the flight. Why was the plane not warned? Why has the United States refused to reveal its two-hour radio transcripts of Flight 007?
- KAL 007 was flying across Kamchatka at the very time a new Soviet PL5 missile was scheduled to be tested and—as was published in *Parade* magazine eight months later—"where an American spy plane was watching."[25] Upon spotting the intruder, the Soviets canceled the test. The United States has yet to explain why the American spy plane did not put 007 back on course.
- The West German magazine *Der Spiegal* reported that the United States maintained an "armada" of four hundred spy planes and a hundred ships to spy on Soviet territory. Surveillance experts considered it unthinkable for U.S. radar and interceptor specialists not to have tracked 007's flight path as it penetrated Soviet airspace, nor to have heard Soviet air defense go on alert, nor to have witnessed Soviet interceptor planes scrambling toward the airliner's path. Two former intelligence specialists, Eskelson and Bernard, who had flown aboard Okinawa-based RC-135s, revealed in the *Denver Post* that such spy planes reconnoiter the Sakhalin-Kamchatka areas twenty-four hours a day. They concluded that "the entire sweep of events . . . was meticulously monitored and analyzed instantaneously by U.S. intelligence." Their revelation was distributed by the Washington Post-Los Angeles Times News Service *but was carried by neither paper, nor picked up by any of the other major media.*[26]
- Designers of the elaborate computer system and radar system for the Boeing 747 jetliner claimed it was impossible for the 007 pilot to have made a navigational error of that magnitude even if some of the systems had failed. Captain Thomas Ashwood, vice-president of the Airline Pilots Association, called the chances of such an error "astronomical."
- When KAL 007 was hit and began to lose altitude, its pilot at

last broke radio silence to report he was going down—confirming Soviet suspicions that his radio worked and that U.S. and Japanese ground control stations could have contacted the plane.

· Upon closer analysis, the tapes verify the Soviet claim that KAL 007 had turned off its automatic identification system, even while its radio was still working. Why would it do so, except to remain evasive and avoid identification by the Soviet planes?

· The national security editor of *Defense Science* magazine noted that "Korean airlines regularly overfly Russian airspace to gather military intelligence," and KAL cockpit crews "are active members of the South Korean military." National Public Radio (September 25, 1983) reported that Korean CIA agents were on "just about every KAL flight."

· Since the early 1950s U.S. electronic surveillance aircraft have repeatedly penetrated Soviet airspace to gather intelligence and test Soviet tracking and interceptor response capabilities. It has been one of the most hazardous occupations in the espionage field. More than 25 of these spy places have been shot down and more than 120 Americans killed, including the 10 lost when a Navy reconnaissance bomber was attacked off Siberia by Soviet aircraft in 1951, the 17 aboard an RC-130 spy plane hit over Soviet Armenia in 1958, and the 31 crewmembers of an EC-121 spy plane downed over North Korea in 1969. None of this background information on U.S. aerial-spying was publicized by the media during the Korean airliner incident.

· Airliners are ideal vehicles for spying and are frequently so used. Spy planes get shot down if they penetrate too deeply and satellites pass over only at fixed and predictable times. Airliners can make reliable sensor readings and take high resolution photographs using infrared photography at night—and usually get away with it.

· The KAL Flight 007 was closely coordinated with the orbits of a U.S. Ferret spy satellite, entering over Kamchatka space exactly as the satellite passed overhead and could listen in on Soviet radar installations responding to the intruder. The Ferret satellite's next orbit coincided precisely with 007's flight over Sakhalin, again allowing the satellite to record the intensified radar activities of the Soviet defense system.

· The Soviets claimed their ground stations repeatedly tried to contact the plane by radio; and their pilot fired 120 tracer shells in front of the plane, dipped his wings, and tried other measures to direct the plane to land. The Soviets also claimed that 007's captain shut off his navigational lights and repeatedly took evasive action, indicating he knew he was being intercepted and was refusing to be escorted down. The U.S. government admitted two weeks after the incident that 007 relayed information to the ground via another KAL 747 jet that was fourteen minutes behind it.

The above information was culled from radical newspapers, specialized journals, and foreign publications, none of which reached an American mass audience. Some of these items were buried away in the mainstream press, appearing weeks or even months after the initial denunciatory deluge.[27] The U.S. government's version of the story immediately inundated the media, while information to the contrary belatedly peeked through here and there. For instance, not until five weeks later did U.S. intelligence experts admit there was no evidence that Soviet air defense personnel knew KAL 007 was carrying civilian passengers on a commercial flight and had probably mistaken it for an American RC-135 spy plane.[28] By then, however, the KAL 007 incident had proved a bonanza for the Reagan administration, creating a climate of outrage that had muted opposition to the deployment of the Pershing and cruise missiles. In the aftermath of the incident the Senate agreed to Reagan's plans for nerve gas and chemical warfare, overturning an earlier vote; a Congress that had previously resisted the MX missile now approved the program and also passed a record $187.5 billion defense bill authorizing a whole new series of weapons; and to top it all, the president dispatched some 14,000 U.S. troops to the Middle East without a murmur of protest from Congress.

The belated revelations demolishing the official version of the incident never undid the cascade of disinformation and manipulated outrage that had initially inundated the public. By the time the real facts began to surface, the government and the media had moved on to other matters.

Most Americans never heard the arguments that refuted the U.S. government's contentions about the airliner. Of those who did hear, relatively few would remember the particular refutations. What many did remember, however, is that the Soviets shot down a civilian airliner with a great loss of innocent lives. (Many never realized it was a *Korean* airliner and referred to it as "one of our planes.") Long after the specifics of a case are forgotten, or never learned, long after the case itself has been discarded by the cold war propagandists or demolished by opponents, there remains a residue of negative feeling and visceral impact that makes the next mobilization of bias that much more plausible sounding. As in any effective propaganda campaign,

SOMETIMES IT'S OKAY TO SHOOT DOWN A CIVILIAN AIRLINER

I doubt that any story has ever received the coverage of the downing of KAL 007 last fall [1983], sure proof that the Russians are the most barbaric devils since Attila the Hun so that we must place Pershing missiles in Germany and step up the war against Nicaragua. The densely printed *New York Times* index devotes 7 full pages to the atrocity in September 1982 alone. In the midst of the furor, UNITA, the "freedom fighters" supported by the US and South Africa, took credit for downing an Angolan jet with 126 killed. There was no ambiguity; the plane was not off course flying over sensitive installations. . . . It was simply premeditated murder. The incident received 100 words in the *NY Times* and no comment anywhere in the media.

This is not the only such case. In October 1976, a Cuban airliner was bombed by CIA-backed terrorists, killing 73 civilians. In 1973 Israel downed a civilian plane lost in a sandstorm over the Suez canal with 110 killed. There was no protest, only editorial comments about how "No useful purpose is served by an acrimonious debate over the assignment of blame" (*New York Times*). Four days later, Prime Minister Golda Meir visited the US where she was troubled with no embarrassing questions and returned with new gifts of military aircraft. Contrary to recent falsehoods, Israel refused to pay compensation or to accept any responsibility. . . . In 1955, an Air India plane carrying the Chinese delegation to the Bandung conference was blown up in the air in what the Hong Kong police called a "carefully planned mass murder." An American defector later claimed that it was he who planted the bomb in the service of the CIA. None of these incidents demonstrate "barbarism"; all have been quickly forgotten.

Noam Chomsky, "1984: Orwell's and Ours," The Thoreau Quarterly, volume 16.

the appeal is to well-established emotive impressions and conditioned responses rather than to specific facts and actualities. One opinion poll showed that a majority of Americans thought the government had not told the whole story about the KAL tragedy. This finding reveals the limits of propaganda. But the fact that most Americans did not unquestioningly swallow the whole story does not mean they were unaffected by it and by the daily ideological pounding of which it was a part. Not everybody bought the story, but millions did, and few could offer a coherent refutation—given what was provided by the news media.

THE CASE OF THE BULGARIAN POPE KILLERS

In 1979 a young man named Mehmet Ali Agca was arrested in Turkey and convicted of assassinating a prominent liberal newspaper editor. An investigation showed that Agca was a lifelong associate of Turkey's anticommunist terror group, the Grey Wolves, an affiliate of the fascist National Action Party (NAP), notorious for its massacres and assaults on labor, student, and community groups. Shortly after his conviction Agca escaped from prison with the assistance of guards and soldiers who were members of the Grey Wolves. A few days later in a letter to a Turkish newspaper, at the time of Pope John Paul II's visit to Turkey, Agca announced his intention to kill the pope. He denounced the pontiff for serving in the "West's campaign" to thwart a new Turkish and Arabic "political and military power in the Middle East." (The Grey Wolves and the NAP believed that Jews, Christians, democracy, and Communism were all corrupters of the Turkish people.) Financed by the Grey Wolves, Agca then traveled widely throughout Western Europe, visiting twelve countries, apparently undetected by the police, and linking up with NAP fascist groups that circulated among the two million Turkish migrant workers in Europe.[29]

On May 13, 1981, Mahmet Agca shot and wounded Pope John Paul II in St. Peter's Square. Placed at the scene of the crime with Agca, was Omar Ay, a lifelong friend and member of the Grey Wolves. The gun used by Agca, according to Italian Police, was supplied by Omar Bagci, another Grey Wolf. Agca's false passport was signed by a Turkish police official who also was with the Grey Wolves.[30]

Most of the media reported but downplayed Agca's fascist affiliations and ascribed his act to murky motives arising either from his "Islamic fanaticism" or his personal psychopathology or both. At the trial Agca claimed to have acted alone and was sentenced to life imprisonment. So it remained until a year later when, after visits by Italian secret police and intelligence agents who reportedly promised Agca a parole in ten years if he cooperated, the imprisoned gunman changed his story and now claimed he had been part of a conspiracy involving at least three agents of the Bulgarian secret service in Rome. Italian police arrested Sergei Antonov, the Rome representative of the Bulgarian national airline. Two Bulgarian embassy officials, also charged with being accomplices, had departed for Bulgaria in November 1982, some eighteen months after the shooting.

From the beginning, Agca's confession had the appearance of a coached, fabricated story. For instance, he said he had met Sergei Antonov, along with his wife and daughter in Antonov's apartment. But Antonov's lawyers were able to produce a passport, visa stamps, and a hotel registration authenticated by the Yugoslavian government, showing that his wife was in Yugoslavia en route to Bulgaria at the time of the alleged meeting; and Antonov's daughter was not in Rome at all during that school year but in Sofia.

Agca described Antonov as having a beard and (as he does now) a moustache, but photographic evidence and the testimony of witnesses established that the Bulgarian was cleanshaven at the time of the shooting.

After almost a year of solitary confinement, Agca supposedly was able to produce from his memory and repeat to the Italian police a half dozen telephone numbers, including those of the Bulgarian embassy and consulate switchboards. But if he knew the Bulgarians only by code names, as he claimed, the embassy and consulate numbers would have been useless in trying to contact them.

There remained a number of puzzling questions: Why would Bulgarian Communists recruit a lifelong fascist assassin who was fanatically antagonistic toward Communism? Why would he agree to work for them? Why would the Bulgarians pick Omar Bagci, a Grey Wolf (arrested in Switzerland two months after the shooting), as the person to provide the gun? How were the Bulgarians able to so thoroughly penetrate an organization like the Grey Wolves and manipulate so many of its members into cooperating in Agca's escape from prison, his travels in Europe, and the assassination attempt? Why would the Bulgarian secret police allow Agca to meet with his alleged conspirators in Antonov's apartment in a building owned by the Bulgarian embassy and thought by the Bulgarians to be under constant surveillance by the Italian police? Being the professional police operatives they allegedly were, why didn't Sergei Antonov and the other Bulgarians leave Italy immediately before or after the assassination attempt, instead of sticking around, living relatively normal lives in full view of the police and everyone else for another eighteen months or so—even after the Italian news media were openly speculating about a "Bulgarian connection"?[31]

The theory was that the Bulgarians were acting for the Soviets who wanted to eliminate the pope's influence within Poland. But is it credible that the Soviets thought they could solve the problems in Poland by shooting the pope, or that they could reap such significant benefit that it would be worth all the political risks and bad publicity?

Undaunted by these many improbabilities, sectors of the U.S. news media took up the cry against the would-be Bulgarian pope killers.[32] The story first appeared in the September 1982 *Reader's Digest*, written by the ubiquitous Claire Sterling who once again built her case on references to anonymous "western intelligence sources." Sterling dismissed Agca's links to Turkish rightists as just a "cover," and accepted at face value his "confession" of conspiring with the Bulgarians. And the Bulgarians, Sterling concluded, could be working for no one but the Soviets and the KGB. The "western intelligence sources" Sterling alluded to must have represented, at best, a very small portion of the Western intelligence community. The CIA and the Israeli and West German secret police were all skeptical about a Bulgarian connection. Even the head of the Italian special antiterrorist police, Anzuini Andreassi, rejected the "Bulgarian scenario" as "absolutely false."[33] Sterling took no note of all this.

Much of the subsequent press commentary was in the Sterling mode. For instance, in his widely syndicated column, Jack Anderson claimed that "the evidence has been mounting" that "Agca was working with the Bulgarian secret police," who in turn were surrogates of the Soviet KGB. But Anderson did not say what the evidence was. Instead he, too, referred to anonymous "western intelligence sources" who "say that the new Soviet dictator, Yuri V. Andropov, was at least a knowing accomplice in the pope's shooting, if he didn't actually orchestrate the whole thing when he headed the KGB."[34]

Following Antonov's arrest, the media escalated their reports on the "Bulgarian connection" even though there was not much to report. The *New York Times*, for instance, carried thirty-two news articles between November 1, 1982, and January 31, 1983, most of which contained no news content, being reports of somebody's opinion or speculation or reports about persons who refused to speculate about the case. Of the more direct news items carried by the *Times*, only one dealt with a really solid news fact—the arrest of Antonov in Rome.[35]

In March, the *New York Times* made quite a leap into the disinformation extravaganza with a long front-page article by Nicholas Gage, headlined "THE ATTACK ON THE POPE: NEW LINKS TO BULGARIANS."[36] The article focused on one Jordan Mantarov, identified as "a Bulgarian official" who defected in France in 1981. So secret was his defection that French intelligence "only recently told the United States Central Intelligence Agency about it." Mantarov claimed to have had a conversation in 1979 with a high-ranking Bulgarian intelligence officer who told him that Moscow had assigned the Bulgarian secret police to "eliminate" the pope because the pontiff had become a destabilizing element in Poland. The *Times* did not question why Mantarov had waited two years after his defection, and almost two years after the pope was shot, to alert the West to this sinister mission. Nor did the

Times question why a top Bulgarian intelligence officer would disclose the whole plot to a minor official like Mantarov who admitted to having no connection to police work. The article rested its case on the assertions of a Bulgarian defector who, like the right-wing witnesses of the McCarthyite era, suddenly surfaced years after the events with made-to-order recall and I-knew-it-all-along testimony.

Some three weeks later, the *Times* ran a brief story quoting a Bulgarian spokesman, Boyan Traikov, who said that Mantarov had never been a commercial attaché with the Bulgarian embassy in Paris, as he had claimed, but was a maintenance mechanic.[37] Craig Whitney, foreign editor of the *Times* admitted that Mantarov was not even listed on the Bulgarian embassy roster, which as a commercial attaché he definitely would have been.[38]

For the most egregious propaganda produced about the Bulgarian-KGB connection, the award must go to Marvin Kalb of NBC who ran not one but two television specials (January 25, 1983, and September 21, 1983). Kalb simply ignored the many facts and unanswered questions that did not fit his case and instead resorted to wild speculations and outright falsehoods, all wrapped in matter-of-fact intonements. For instance, he explained away Agca's fascist links by saying he was friendly with Grey Wolves "but never a member. He remained aloof." To label an organizational relationship that involved political murder, prison escape, underground travel throughout Europe, and other longtime personal and conspiratorial ties as "aloof," is a gross distortion.

Kalb called Agca "a terrorist without an ideology," thus minimizing his fascist commitments (in order to make a Bulgarian connection more believable), but it was not true. Agca's brother, interviewed by NBC on the same show, stressed the gunman's ideological dedication and said he was "a crusader, not a terrorist." Agca himself left a noticeable record of fervent statements and awful deeds on behalf of his fascist devotions—all of which NBC ignored.

Taking a page from Claire Sterling, Kalb declared that Lenin once said, "The purpose of terror is to terrorize." Thus Kalb falsely suggested that Lenin advocated rather than opposed terrorism—and such alleged advocacy, in Marvin Kalb's mind, apparently was another Soviet-Bulgarian link in the plot to kill the pope. The Bulgarian secret police must have been recruiting Agca in Sofia "without his even being aware of their possible plans for him," imagined Kalb, forgetting NBC's own earlier claim that Agca had been recruited by the KGB in Turkey. That all of Agca's contacts were Turkish Grey Wolves, ex-Nazis, and a few gangsters was proof to Kalb of a KGB connection! "These sophisticated layers of contacts," he fantasized, "[are] said to be typical of the highly professional operation of the Soviet KGB."

The KGB uses "remote proxies" so "there is never any evidence." Thus the absence of evidence itself was treated as evidence of a "sophisticated," "professional" KGB operation.

"A Soviet connection is strongly suggested but cannot be proved," Kalb said. Strongly suggested by Kalb. Then in a *fortissimo* finale, he exclaimed, "The evidence now is even more persuasive," yet the U.S. government is "etching no profile in courage" by "leaving Italy to stand alone before the pressures of the Soviet onslaught."

According to Kalb and NBC, the Soviets wanted to kill the pope because he had written a letter to Moscow in the summer of 1980 threatening to lay down his crown and join the Polish resistance should the Soviets invade Poland. NBC never explained why the pope would make such a threat before the Gdansk shipyard strike had even started and before the question of a Soviet invasion had become an issue. Kalb never mentioned that Agca threatened to kill the pope during the pontiff's visit to Turkey in 1979, *almost a year before the disturbances in Poland.* He also ignored the Vatican sources, quoted in an earlier ABC report on the case, who said John Paul II never wrote such a letter and that it would be unthinkable for him to resign and return to Poland.[39]

NBC said nothing about alternate theories. The *Washington Post,* however, did report that many Italian observers and political leaders thought the Italian social democratic government was using the alleged plot to win favor among Catholics, discredit Communist rivals, and gain support from conservative business leaders who were drifting back to the Christian Democrats.[40]

Not all the media propagandized the Bulgarian story. CBS remained somewhat noncommittal in its reporting and ABC did a special report (May 13, 1983) that actually cast doubt on the whole plot, pointing out some of the discrepancies noted above. But the major impact was still on the side of the Sterling-Kalb fabricators. The *Wall Street Journal* continued to run editorials on the case, charging the Soviets with terrorism; and even liberal columnists like Carl Rowan wrote of the Soviet-Bulgarian "attempt to kill Pope John Paul II" as "terrorism at its lowest."[41]

The story was once more given prominent play in June 1984 when the *New York Times* ran a long front page article by none other than Claire Sterling, again presented to the reading public as a reputable journalist.[42] The article rehashed the same old wild conjecture about the Bulgarian-KGB connection and delved into the Italian state prosecutor's "still-secret 78-page report," (conveniently leaked to Sterling) which she treated as the last word on the case. Sterling noted that the Italian authorities thought Agca's testimony should be believed "despite his earlier lies."

A few days later, the *Washington Post* ran a long story of its own with a banner headline across the front page: "ITALIAN PROBE CLAIMS BULGARIANS BEHIND ATTACK ON POPE."[43] Written by Michael Dobbs, the story was caught between its sympathy for the prosecutor's case and the lack of evidence to support that case. It made much of the prosecutor's allegation that a sealed Bulgarian embassy truck left Rome shortly after the shooting (as such trucks carrying diplomatic materials regularly did) and treated this as "circumstantial evidence" that one of the alleged Turkish accomplices might have been hiding inside it—an imaginative idea. The *Post* did note that "the Italian state prosecutor acknowledges that some of the evidence is contradictory and that his case is dependent on the credibility of Mehmet Ali Agca. . . ." The prosecutor also admitted that Agca had lied about a number of things and that there was a "clear contradiction" between his testimony "and that of all the other defendants in the case who have been interviewed by the Italian magistrates." Buried at the end of this unusually long story (almost a hundred column inches and nine photographs) were some of the rebuttals posed by the defense—which was more than was offered by Claire Sterling in the *Times* piece of the previous week.

An unwary, casual reader of the *Times* and *Post* stories (probably most readers) might easily have come away with the impression that there was a strong case against the Bulgarians. The critical reader who brushed aside the larded and rehashed paragraphs and the eye-catching, mind-stopping headlines, photographs and blurbs would be more likely to wonder why these two newspapers had devoted so much splash and spread to such a skimpy prosecutor's report.

Five months later the *Washington Post* ran a long—and redeeming article by Michael Dobbs entitled "A COMMUNIST PLOT TO KILL THE POPE—OR A LIAR'S FANTASY," which—while treating the nonexistent case of the prosecutor with much supportive care—also made a strong presentation of the defense and concluded that the case "depends entirely on information provided by a liar."[44] In confirmation of this, when Agca went on trial in June 1985, he declared himself on the witness stand to be none other than Jesus Christ incarnate.

BEYOND FACTS

As we have seen in earlier chapters, Red Menace scare campaigns have been going on for a long time, with various ebbs and flows. These government-media affairs are not the product of mass hysteria, although their intention is to create hysteria or at least mass support of official policy. The American people did not anxiously clamor for more and more news about terrorism, yellow rain, or the Bulgarian connection—but they were fed it all the same.

The distortions found in these cases did not result from poor and hasty journalistic preparation, inadequate space, faulty interpretation, or errors in emphasis, judgment, and clarity—to mention some of the usual chidings the press occasionally delivers upon itself. These cases give every appearance of being the products of a deliberate dissemination of outright lies circulated by high-placed officials, with the ready compliance of the news media. The absence of supporting evidence, the incredible charges, the obvious propaganda uses to which they were put, the suppression of contrary evidence all suggest that these were disinformation campaigns designed to create a climate of threat and alarm in order to justify policies of military spending, intervention, and domestic repression.

The disinformation campaigns presented above do not exhaust the supply. The media were also filled with reports about KGB infiltration of U.S. society (discussed in chapter 6), reports about a Cuban-directed campaign to flood the United States with narcotics (when in fact Cuba had taken stern measures against drug traffickers and had offered to cooperate with the United States in anti-narcotic measures), reports about Bulgarian drug smugglers (a subplot to bolster the pope killer image), reports of the Soviets using "slave labor," including Vietnamese, to build the gas pipeline (with an offering of evidence even skimpier than the few twigs presented in the yellow rain campaign), and reports of the Soviets' manipulating and controlling the Nicaraguan Sandinista government and the insurgency in El Salvador (see chapter 11). All these various government-media campaigns were related to each other. As part of a continual barrage, they gained credibility by sheer repetition and volume.

The media do not merely report what is fed them; they make choices regarding treatment, placement, tone, and prominence. The media flesh out and dramatize the official charges. They avoid questions that might prove too troublesome and embarrassing for ruling interests, and they clutter the communication universe with an outpouring of the accepted version of things.

These cases show that an absolute opinion-information monopoly is not necessary to maintain an ideologically conformist press. A near monopoly will do. We observed that the major media occasionally run something that tries to set the record straight; for instance, ABC's special report and the *Washington Post* article calling into question the Bulgarian-KGB plot; a *New York Times* editorial questioning the yellow rain story. But in each scare campaign these alternate views were lost in the volume of propaganda that went the other way. Submerged in the great disinformation tides, these brief dissents might win the attention and hold the memory of only the most critically alert media consumer.

No single one of these scare campaigns has a durable political presence, but taken together they help create a political climate conducive to domestic and cold war conservatism. Sometimes the campaigns are not all that persuasive; many people were skeptical of, or indifferent to stories of Bulgarian plotters and yellow rain (many also believed what they heard). But more important, *most of the press is energetically receptive.* And it is the press that creates *opinion visibility* in the public arena, if not always opinion conviction among the public itself. This opinion visibility, the visible images and audible opinions circulating in the media and among political leaders, lay the groundwork for specific domestic and foreign policies.

Even if a particular scare story does not generate much public response, its overall goal may be largely achieved. Even if the public is not completely persuaded by the message, it is "softened up" somewhat, thus making the next mobilization of bias that much easier and more credible. The story is never fully refuted in the mainstream press. The occasional debunking report that might surface as the issue dies down never quite eradicates the effects of the original sensationalist headlines—because it is not given the same sensationalistic play (more on that later). Factual refutations do not cancel out the residual feelings of alien threat and sinister menace. As we painstakingly try to show that these stories have little basis in reality, we find ourselves playing by a more restricted, rational set of rules than are utilized by the government-media propagandists. In these scare campaigns, evidential truth is only a secondary consideration, if that. The importance of these cases lies in their emotive impact, the evocation of imposing images, the repetitive psychological pounding, and the atmosphere created in the arena of public discourse—if public discourse it can be called.

As Senator McCarthy discovered, if the press is cooperative enough, the charges don't have to be true, no more than the claims made in a Geritol or Pepsi advertisement. Factual rebuttals mean less than we would suppose because facts are not really what are being treated. The specific facts of the matter are less important than the cumulative, residual effects that remain long after the specifics are forgotten or never learned. The refutations offered on these pages are important for an understanding of what the press is doing, but they do not deal with the experience of the disinformation campaign itself. The important thing is not factual conviction but the image impact of the Red Plot fantasies, the alarms and threats that fill the public communication space, emboldening conservative pressure groups to clamor for sterner measures, giving a momentum to the anticommunist cold warriors, and reducing many of us to an uneasy silence, as a nervous Congress rallies round the flag and joins in the next wave of domestic repression, human services cutbacks, military spending, and Third World counterinsurgency.

During the McCarthy era the press demonstrated that it could give "both sides" of a story but in a highly uneven way. Sensational charges repeatedly filled the air, while the refutations never cleared the air because they were accorded a lesser, belated exposure. This phenomenon has since come to be treated as some kind of unavoidable law of communication: the rebuttals never catch up with the original charge because they are not as sensational, nor as timely, hence, not as newsworthy. But is that really so? There actually is no objective reason the rebuttals cannot be given equal exposure and treated with the same urgency and importance as the original charges. *The refutation of a conspiracy is often no less sensational than the original conspiracy itself.* The charge for instance, that the Bulgarians killed the pope is sensational and newsworthy, but so is a refutation that suggests the whole thing is an enormous, audacious, deliberate, disinformation hoax. It is not that the other side's views are less interesting and less sensational, but that they are just treated in a less interesting and less sensational way.

What could have been more threadbare and tediously predictable than a report by the Italian prosecutor mouthing what his superiors in the interior ministry had been saying for almost two years, that Agca was guilty of conspiring with Bulgarian communists to shoot the pope? Yet this report, lacking in any new (or old) evidence, was treated by the *New York Times* and *Washington Post* as if it contained startling revelations. Similarly, what could have been more sensational than the revelation that KAL 007 was indeed a spy plane? Yet evidence to that effect from a study in the *Nation* was suppressed by the U.S. mainstream media.

Nor is it simply that the stories grow "old." The press will treat an old anticommunist rerun as if it were an exclusive premier. A war against "Soviet-sponsored terrorism" was declared by the Reagan administration when it first took office in January 1981 to be the government's top priority. The war was declared again in 1983 when the American embassy and the marine barracks in Beirut were bombed. Then for the third time, in April 1984, President Reagan revived the issue, calling for "anti-terrorist" legislation that would permit the government to designate "factions" or "groups" likely to commit terrorism and subject them to surveillance, infiltration, incarceration, and dispersal by deadly force if necessary. And in June 1984, Secretary of State Shultz called for sweeping "preemptive" measures against what he said was a Soviet-led "League of Terrorism" (with Syria, Iran, Libya, and North Korea as members), which uses "indiscriminate murder" to "undermine world stability."[45]

So in less than four years the Reagan administration declared war on "Soviet terrorism" four times, and on each occasion the press excitedly treated the story as fresh front-page, headline news, as a new revelation instead of a stale revival, never questioning why the danger had receded and why it had suddenly reemerged, presenting it as something actual rather than something that failed to correspond to any verifiable reality.

In contrast, the critical questions raised about such stories, the rebuttals against the calumnious disinformation campaigns, are downplayed or suppressed entirely. But if news from the other side is accorded minimal treatment, it is not because it is less revealing, for often it is just as newsworthy (if not more so) but because it is from the other side.

As we saw in chapter 7, there was no inevitable, objective journalistic condition that gave Senator McCarthy such leverage over his victims, although some observers believed there was. McCarthy had no immutable advantage in timing, position, and exposure built into the nature of his attacks—*none that was not given him by the press itself and swiftly taken from him by the press when he began to attack conservatives in his own party.* So today there is no inherent law dictating that the *New York Times* assign a disinformationist like Claire Sterling the story about the Bulgarian connection rather than, say, Edward Herman or Frank Brodhead who would have written an entirely different and more revealing and informative account—and had already done so for several smaller-circulation publications.

If the truth never catches up with the lie, it is not because of some natural law of communication but because of the way truth and lies are communicated. It is that persons who work hard for anticommunist disinformation campaigns are given direct access to, or sympathetic coverage by, the major media while those who would present evidence and arguments casting serious doubt on such fabrications are consigned to the periphery of the information universe.

Notes

1. *Washington Post,* January 27–30, 1981.
2. *Washington Post,* January 27, 1981.
3. *Wall Street Journal,* October 23, 1981.

4. *New York Times Magazine*, March 1, 1981; *Washington Post Magazine*, March 15, 1981. The *Post* also ran an article in the same issue by Blaine Hardin that raised serious questions about Sterling's reporting. However, it was the Sterling article that received front-cover exposure.

5. *New York Times Magazine*, March 1, 1981.

6. Ibid.

7. Blaine Hardin, "Terrorism," *Washington Post Magazine*, March 15, 1981.

8. V. I. Lenin, "The Autocracy and the Proletariat," in *Collected Works*, English ed. (Moscow: Profress Publishers, 1964), vol. 8, p. 22.

9. *Washington Post*, April 20, 1981; *Newsweek*, May 4, 1981: see also ex-CIA director Stanfield Turner's remarks, *Washington Post*, February 12, 1984.

10. *Washinton Post*, December 30, 1981.

11. *Washington Post*, January 20, 1984.

12. *New York Daily News*, April 5, 1980.

13. *New York Times*, September 14, 1981.

14. See Lee Ullian, "Haig Poisons Facts in New Anti-Soviet Blast," *Daily World*, September 18, 1981.

15. See for instance, "Blood Tests Prove Weapons Biological, State Department Says," *Washington Post*, January 30, 1982.

16. *Parade*, June 26, 1983.

17. The criticisms presented above are based on statements and reports by such leading mycotoxin specialists as Dr. James Bamburg of Colorado State University, Dr. Chester Mirocha of the University of Minnesota, Dr. Daniel Cullen of the University of Wisconsin, and Dr. Matthew Meselson of Harvard University. Their criticisms can be found in two articles by Nicholas Wade in *Science*, the authoritative journal of the American Association for the Advancement of Science, October 2, 1981, and November 27, 1981; see also the articles by Constance Holden in *Science*, April 9, 1982; and by Eliot Marshall in *Science*, May 30, 1980. See also correspondence in *Science*, August 22, 1982; and the report by Meselson in *Science*, October 23, 1981. Much of the evidence and arguments made against the State Department charges are summarized in an excellent piece by Alfred Kutzik, "Chemical War or Disinformation?" *New World Review*, March–April 1983. See also Nikolai Antonov, " 'Yellow Rain'—Weapon of Disinformation," *Political Affairs*, August 1982. The prestigious *Chemical and Engineering News* ran a critique of the yellow rain thesis summarized in the *Progressive*, March 1984. Saul Hormats, a leading authority on CBW, published a criticism in the *Washington Post*, February 26, 1984. A very useful book on the subject is Grant Evans, *The Yellow Rainmakers* (London: Verso, 1983) distributed in the U.S. by Schocken Books.

18. *New York Times* editorials, November 17, 1981, and June 3, 1983.

19. See the front-page story in the *Washington Post*, March 29, 1984; the three network evening news shows also carried the "bees feces thesis."

20. *Washington Post*, February 26, 1984.

21. *Washington Post*, February 22, 1984.

22. NBC, April 18, 1984.

23. See the major electronic and print media from September 2 to September 28, 1983.

24. R. W. Johnson, "KAL 007: Unanswered Questions," *World Press Review*, March 1984, pp. 23–26, originally published in the *Guardian* (England).

25. Anthony Sampson, "What Happened to Flight 007?" *Parade*, April 22, 1984, pp. 12–13.

26. Six months later the two specialists were contacted by the FBI and informed that their statements had violated U.S. espionage laws. The *Washington Post* did run this story, February 3, 1984.

27. See for instance, Johnson, "KAL 007: Unanswered Questions"; Bamford, "The

Last Flight . . ."; Jack Smith, "U.S. Story Going Further and Further Off Course," *Guardian*, September 28, 1983; John Wojcik, "More Questions about Flight 007," *Daily World*, September 14, 1983; *New York Times*, September 25, 1983; *Far Eastern Economic Review*, September 22, 1983; Tim Wheeler, "U.S. Flyers: Reagan's Not Telling All," *Daily World*, September 17, 1983. Some eight months after the fatal incident, *Parade* magazine published an article (Sampson, "What Happened to Flight 007?"), indicating that U.S. intelligence could have alerted 007 and that the failure to do so "has given fuel to the conspiracy theories." The article does not deal with the evidence that might support these "conspiracy theories" but instead repeatedly states that the 007 incident "increased the Soviets' paranoia." Apparently the ultimate culprit was Soviet paranoia not U.S. espionage. An excellent treatment is David Pearson, "KAL 007: What the U.S. Knew and When We Knew It," *Nation*, August 18, 1984, pp. 18–25.

28. This admission was carried in the *New York Times*, October 7, 1983.

29. Frank Brodhead and Edward S. Herman, "The KGB Plot to Assassinate the Pope: A Cast Study in Free World Disinformation," *CovertAction*, Spring–Summer 1983, pp. 13–24.

30. Ibid.; see also Diana Johnstone, "Tale of Intrigue and Political Diversion," *In These Times*, January 12–18, 1983; and "The Pope Plot," *Counterspy*, June–August 1983.

31. For a discussion of these kinds of critical questions see Brodhead and Herman, "The KGB Plot . . ."; also Victor Perlo, "Why Slander Bulgaria?" *Daily World*, May 28, 1983.

32. For instance see *Time*, *Newsweek*, and the *Wall Street Journal* in December 1982 and early January 1983.

33. *New York Times*, December 18, 1982; Associated Press report, December 17, 1982.

34. *Washington Post*, January 19, 1983.

35. Brodhead and Herman, "The KGB Plot . . .," p. 23.

36. *New York Times*, March 23, 1983.

37. *New York Times*, April 8, 1983.

38. Brodhead and Herman, "The KGB Plot . . .," p. 23.

39. ABC special report, May 13, 1983.

40. *Washington Post*, January 6, 1983.

41. See *Wall Street Journal*, December 21, 1983; and Rowan's column in the *Washington Post*, April 29, 1983.

42. *New York Times*, June 10, 1984.

43. *Washington Post*, June 18, 1984.

44. *Washington Post*, November 18, 1984.

45. *New York Times*, June 25, 1984.

10

Doing the Third World

Despite a vast diversity of cultures, languages, ethnicity, and geography, the nations of Latin America, Africa, and Asia, with few exceptions, show some striking similarities in the economic and political realities they endure. Lumped together under the designation of the "Third World," these countries are characterized by (1) concentrated ownership of land, labor, capital, natural resources, and technology in the hands of rich persons and giant multinational corporations; (2) autocratic police states with military forces financed, trained, equipped, and assisted by the United States—the function of these forces being not to protect the populace from foreign invasion but to protect the small wealthy owning class and foreign investors from the populace; (3) the population, aside from a small middle class, enduring impoverishment, high illiteracy rates, malnutrition, wretched housing, and nonexistent health services, a peasantry indebted, indentured, or displaced from the land; and a working class underemployed and grossly underpaid. Because of this widespread poverty, these nations have been mistakenly designated as "underdeveloped" and "poor" when in fact they are overexploited and the source of great wealth, their resources and cheap labor serving to enrich investors. Only their people remain poor.

For the better part of a century now, successive administrations in the United States have talked about bringing democracy and economic advancement to the "less-developed" peoples of the Third World, when in fact, the overriding goal of U.S. policy toward these countries has been to prevent alternate noncapitalist social orders from arising, ones that would use the economy for purposes of social development and for the needs of the populace, rather than for the capital accumulation process. The purpose of U.S. policy has been not to defend democracy, in fact, democracies—as in Iran (1953), Guatemala (1954), Indonesia (1965), and Chile (1973)—are regularly overthrown if they attempt to initiate serious economic reforms that tamper with the existing class structure. The U.S. goal is to make the world safe for multinational corporate exploitation, to keep things as they are even while talking about the need for change and reform.[1]

173

In all this, the U.S. corporate-owned news media have been, intentionally or not, actively complicit. As one critic of the press observed, "It is a truism that in U.S. foreign reporting the State Department often makes the story"[2]—to which we might add: and when not the State Department, the CIA, the Pentagon, or the White House itself. Consider how the Vietnam War was covered.

THE VIETNAM APOLOGY

The U.S. press, expecially television news, is credited with bringing the Vietnam War home to millions of Americans, thereby inciting their impassioned opposition. Certainly daily media exposure to the fact that the war existed served as a continual reminder of the seemingly endless and senseless nature of the conflict. But in fact most of the really damaging news about the cruelties and costs of the Vietnam War reached Americans through alternative popular channels such as campus teach-ins; student, church, and labor groups; peace organizations; the radical press; and the underground press. What the business-owned media left unreported was far more spectacular than what it reported.

From 1945 to 1954 the United States spent several billion dollars supporting a ruthless French colonialism in Vietnam, but the American public was never informed of this. In the following decade Washington assumed full responsibility for the maintenance of the South Vietnamese right-wing dictatorship, but the public neither read nor heard a word of debate in the media about this major policy commitment. In 1965 the U.S. government began a massive buildup of ground forces in Vietnam, but Americans were told that the troops were merely a small support force. The *New York Times* and other major news agencies knew the real nature of the escalation but felt it was in the "national interest" to keep this information from the public.[3] Reporters who covered the Vietnam War were expected to "get on the team"—to share the military's view of the war and its progress—and most of them did. The press, with some exceptional instances, censored the worst of the war, saying almost nothing about the massive saturation bombings of Vietnam, Cambodia, and Laos, the "free-fire zones," U.S.-sponsored torture, the Phoenix death squad program, the massive destruction of Indochinese rural life, the indiscriminate killing of the civilian population, and the dumping of 12 million tons of Agent Orange and other toxic chemicals on the countryside—the effects of which are still being felt in Vietnam in the form of premature deaths, deformed births, and abnormally high cancer rates.

Throughout the Vietnam War, the insurgent forces were described as the "enemy," although it was never explained why they deserved to be so considered, it being assumed that the "Communist" label was sufficient explanation. Reporters who prided themselves on their objectivity saw cities "fall" to the "enemy" when they could have as easily viewed them as "liberated," or merely changing political hands.[4] Communists "nibbled" and "gobbled" territory and engaged in "terror" attacks, but the war of terror waged by the U.S. military, was never labeled as such. Stories describing how American soldiers slaughtered hundreds of defenseless women, children, and old people in the village of My Lai were turned down by the major wire services, several magazines and newsweeklies, one network, and major newspapers in New York and Boston. The My Lai story was not broken until more than a year and a half after it happened and by a small news outfit, the Dispatch News Service.[5] When finally picked up by the mainstream press, the story was treated as an isolated incident not representative of U.S. conduct in the war. In fact, the systematic obliteration of villages, described as "pacification," was a commonplace occurrence and a conscious U.S. counterinsurgency goal.

The opinions proffered by broadcast commentators and newspaper editorial writers were generally supportive of the U.S. effort in Indochina until the very last years of the war. A 1968 survey by the *Boston Globe* of thirty-nine leading American newspapers with a total circulation of 22 million showed that, while several had become more critical of the U.S. military escalation and others more "hawkish," not one newspaper advocated withdrawal from Vietnam, despite the opposition of millions of people in the United States and in other nations.[6] As the war dragged on, many major newspapers, including the *Washington Post* and the *New York Times,* began to shift toward a more critical editorial opinion, yet they also supported, almost to the last days, additional military aid to the tottering Saigon regime.[7]

Much of the opposition to the war itself was couched in terms that implicitly assumed the United States was acting with good intentions but that the effort was not working. A few national figures like Senator J. William Fulbright (D.-Ark.) noted the profoundly immoral effects of our Indochina policy on the Indochinese, but most political leaders and news media refrained from questioning the legitimacy of the war, asking only: Will our efforts succeed? Are we overcommitted? Have we seen the light at the end of the tunnel? Are we relying too heavily on military means? Throughout this kind of debate, the implication was that if the United States could have won, then the intervention and all its dreadful devastation would have been justified.

After the war, the U.S. media strove to put the best face on U.S. involvement. American intervention in Vietnam, declared Richard Stout in the *New Republic*, "was not wickedness; it was stupidity . . . one of the greatest blunders of our history."[8] James Reston in the *New York Times* chided President Ford for leaving the impression in a comment of his that "somehow the United States was responsible for the carnage in Southeast Asia."[9] Even the *Times's* most outspoken critic of the war, columnist Anthony Lewis, concluded that "the early American decision on Indochina can be regarded as blundering efforts to do good. But . . . no amount of arms or dollars or blood" would have enabled the United States to build "a nation on the American model in South Vietnam."[10] The U.S. media, assisted by academics and officials, rewrote the shameful history of the Vietnam War, asserting that the United States had selflessly intervened to try to install a Western-style democracy.[11] Left out of this view was any thought that the United States had waged a horrific war in support of a dictatorship and against a largely civilian population to prevent a popularly supported but noncapitalist alternative social order from gaining power.

After the war, the news about Vietnam, in keeping with the media's treatment of socialist societies everywhere, was all bad. Vietnam was reportedly impoverished because of "economic failure" and not because of the massive destruction of capital resources inflicted by U.S. forces. Little if anything appeared in the major media about the tens of thousands of *Vietnamese* victims of Agent Orange, the tens of thousands of Vietnamese amputees and others permanently crippled and disabled by U.S. firepower, the 100,000 Vietnamese drug addicts hooked by the same suppliers who serviced the invading troops, and the hundreds of thousands of Vietnamese prostitutes, petty criminals, mentally disturbed persons, and other social victims of the war. Or if attention *was* given to them, nothing was said about U.S. responsibility in their creation. Nor did the American press give much attention to the educational, health, housing, and agrarian development programs of the revolutionary Vietnamese government. Relying on the establishment news media, one came away with the impression that the U.S. *defeat* in Vietnam, rather than the murderous intervention, was the only thing Americans needed to regret.

MURDER IN CHILE

In 1970, when a socialist candidate, Salvador Allende, was elected president of Chile and began initiating reforms, that country suddenly became the hottest news story in Latin America. From the beginning the U.S. press saw the democratically elected government as an ominous threat to democracy. ABC's Howard K. Smith observed that the new "Marxist" government had "outright Communist internal policies." Both the New York Times and the Washington Post pondered whether Chile's "free institutions" could survive what the Times termed a "sharp turn to the left." And a Los Angeles Times editorial claimed to discern "totalitarian inclinations" in Chile.[12]

The truth was that for almost three years President Allende presided over a country whose citizens enjoyed a wide range of civil liberties, the absence of the death penalty, and freedom for all political organizations including ultra-rightist ones. One government-owned television station supported Allende's policies but the other television stations and some two-thirds of the country's radio stations were controlled by the opposition, as were all the privately-owned newspapers.[13] The U.S. media suppressed these facts.

The U.S. press questioned the legitimacy of Allende's mandate by repeatedly reminding its audience that he was a "minority president," having won only a 37 percent plurality. The press never mentioned that a conservative predecessor, Jorge Alessandri, had also been a minority president, not an unusual occurrence in Chilean (or many other Latin American) multiparty politics, nor for that matter in American politics; Abraham Lincoln, Woodrow Wilson, Harry S. Truman, John F. Kennedy, Richard M. Nixon had all been elected with less than a majority of the popular vote. Reports also appeared asserting that the popularity of Allende's ruling Popular Unity coalition was waning, when actually the vote for Popular Unity candidates rose to 43.4 percent in the 1973 municipal elections.

What exactly was Allende doing to deserve such a bad press? He was moving toward an egalitarian socialized society, having begun by nationalizing the copper mines owned by U.S. multinational corporations. And, under a statute passed in 1967 by a conservative Chilean Congress but left largely unimplemented, his government was taking unused land from big estates and distributing it to landless peasants. Through a variety of government programs, agricultural production showed a dramatic upsurge, the inflation rate dropped by half, construction was up 9 percent and unemployment down to less than 5 percent, the lowest in a decade. Beef and bread consumption increased by 15 percent in the 1971–1972 period. A government program sought to provide every Chilean child with a half-liter of milk daily. During Allende's first year, the economy enjoyed an 8.5 percent growth in GNP, the second highest in Latin America. Generally, Allende pursued policies that threatened the prerogatives of the rich, cut into profits while increasing wages, and brought a modest redistribution of goods and services in favor of the poorer strata. These were the nefarious "totalitarian inclinations" of the Popular Unity government.[14]

In response, the Chilean business class withheld investments, hoarded supplies and destroyed livestock. The United States eagerly assisted in this campaign to "make the economy scream" (President Nixon's phrase) by cutting off food aid, denying Chile any new loans, and cutting exports to Chile by some 40 percent and imports from that country almost by half. Only the Chilean military flourished, being the recipient of a sumptuous $47 million in U.S. aid.

The U.S. news media chose to ignore the fact that the Chilean economy was under assault from within and without and nevertheless had been performing more democratically than under previous administrations. Instead the press ran alarming reports of impending economic collapse.[15] By 1973 acts of economic sabotage and political violence by rightists had become a daily occurrence. Pro-Allende radio and television transmitters were blown up, and military personnel sympathetic to the existing constitutional government were purged, arrested and in some cases tortured and executed.[16] Such things were not dealt with in U.S. press reports, which continued to describe the Popular Unity government as infected with extremist and undemocratic tendencies, lacking a popular mandate, isolated from the people and destroying the economy with its own excesses and incompetence.

The democratic government was overthrown in September 1973, in a violent coup led by right-wing generals who abolished the constitution, suppressed all political parties, closed all newspapers except two right-wing dailies, outlawed all independent trade unions, and arrested, tortured, and executed thousands of persons. Editorial opinion in the United States was remarkably mild, considering the press's seemingly arduous concern for the survival of Chilean democracy during Allende's tenure. The *New York Times* observed, "Dr. Allende and his Popular Unity Coalition dominated by socialist and Communist parties attempted to socialize Chile. The Government met stiff opposition from the upper and middle classes, and the armed forces, traditionally nonpolitical, finally sided with the regime's opponents."[17]

These few sentences carry a bundle of deceptions. The Socialist and Communist parties who supposedly "dominated" the government were duly elected by the Chilean people and adhered strictly to constitutional procedures. They attempted to "socialize Chile," but the *Times* did not explain what that phrase meant, what the government actually did, what programs it started for the people. Instead, "socializing Chile" was presumed to have been something reprehensible. The *Times* said the government met "stiff opposition from the upper and middle classes." In fact, it met political violence and economic sabotage. Nor did the armed forces "finally" side with the regime's opponents after much scrupulous neutrality; far from being "nonpolitical," they plotted and conspired from the first months Allende took power, purging their ranks, aiding the efforts of right-wing terrorists, and disarming the few on the left who had guns.

For the destruction of Chilean democracy and the murder of President Allende and thousands of his followers, the U.S. press tended to blame the victims themselves. Thus in an editorial immediately after the coup, the *New York Times* noted, "No Chilean party or faction can escape some responsibility for the disaster, but a heavy share must be assigned to the unfortunate Dr. Allende himself. Even when the dangers of polarization had become unmistakenly evident, he persisted in pushing a program of pervasive socialism for which he had no popular mandate."[18]

The last to be blamed by the U.S. press for the military takeover was the military itself. Also free of blame was the U.S. government, which financed, equipped, trained, advised, and assisted the Chilean military before, during, and after the takeover. The leading U.S. newspapers took pains to report there was no evidence of U.S. involvement in the destruction of Chilean democracy. On the day after the coup, the *New York Times* could report as part of a "news" story: "The United States Government—which had a record of interfering in Chilean politics, principally with money before Dr. Allende came to power in 1970—has maintained the position of a disinterested bystander since then, except for protests against his expropriation policy."[19] The *Times* did not explain why the U.S. government's claim to neutrality should have been accepted as true when Washington's economic war to destabilize the Allende government was a known fact as was the CIA funding of opposition right-wing political parties and media in Chile.[20]

When Allende was in office, and long after his death, he was inevitably described as a "Marxist" by the U.S. press, which he was, and his government was often called "Marxist," which it was not, being a loose coalition of left-leaning political groups some of which were reformists and decidedly non-Marxist. In contrast, neither General Augusto Pinochet nor his government were ever described as "fascist"—which they were—by any of the establishment news organizations in the United States.[21] Allende's democratically-elected government was always "the Allende regime" while Pinochet's dictatorship was more respectfully described as "the Chilean government" in the years immediately following the coup.

The day after he was murdered by the generals, Allende was portrayed unsympathetically in the *New York Times* as "a man of the privileged class turned radical politician," known for his "dandy" ways and "stylish dress."[22] And a few days later: "Allende was very much a political animal, a small stocky, quick-moving man with gray moustache, ruddy face, thick, heavily rimmed spectacles."[23] In contrast, the *Times* described Allende's executioner, General Pinochet, as "a powerfully built six-footer," "energetic and very disciplined and until recently he never talked politics."[24] (At least not in public.) He was also "quiet and business-like" and though "tough" he had a "sense of humor." Certainly here was a mass murderer we could all warm up to.

It was Pinochet's unmentionable fascism rather than his vaunted "sense of humor" that had the upper hand in his regime's treatment of political prisoners arrested after the coup. The tortures delivered upon Pinochet's victims included application of electric shock to different parts of the body, particularly the genitals; forcing victims to witness the torture of friends and relatives; raping women in the presence of other family members; burning sex organs with acid or scalding water; placing infected rats into the vagina; mutilating, puncturing, and cutting off various parts of the body, including genitalia, eyes, and tongue; injection of air into women's breasts and into veins (causing slow, painful death); shoving bayonets and clubs into the vagina or anus, causing rupture and death.[25]

Occasionally the news media mentioned that things were not going well in Pinochet's Chile, that some people were being treated harshly, but reports of actual atrocities by the Chilean military and police seldom, if ever, found their way into the mainstream media. In time, Chile was out of the headlines, being treated with the same benign neglect accorded any other U.S.-sponsored dictatorship.

On the tenth anniversary of the military coup, the *Washington Post* ran an opinion piece by Nathanial Davis, U.S. ambassador to Chile during the time of the coup, which asserted that the United States had absolutely nothing to do with the overthrow of the Chilean democracy, and that Allende had caused his own downfall by collaborating with leftist extremists and thereby "alienating people." Davis did not mention that it was not "people" who overthrew Allende but the U.S.-trained and U.S.-financed Chilean military.[26]

In 1984, eleven years after the coup, the *New York Times* was still cooing over General Pinochet, describing him in one news story as "the Chilean President," and "Chile's Leader" (never as "Chile's Dictator") who "seemed relaxed and expansive as he sat down to breakfast in a splendid but simply decorated conference room in Moneda Palace." The Moneda's previous occupant, "Salvador Allende Gossens, a Marxist, died inside." (Allende was murdered by Pinochet's forces.) The *Times* continued with its cozy framing of Pinochet: "The general's 68 years are belied by his boxer's physique, matched by a trim gray moustache. . . . He eats frugally—tea and toast for breakfast—hardly drinks" and exercises regularly.[27] Pinochet, the *Times* reported, said he is "a lover of liberty, a right to which all men are born." But he had no confidence "in orthodox democracy. It was too easy to infiltrate and destroy." (He knew of what he spoke.) So he favored "a protected democracy" with a strong political role for the military. "He has managed to stay in power," the *Times* reported, "through what even his opponents recognize is political acumen . . ." (not terror, torture, and death squads.)[28] Not a word in this news story would have displeased General Pinochet.

A couple of days later, a *Times* editorial chided Pinochet for "his excesses" and for comparing himself to the "best Roman Emperors." The editorial then offered a misleadingly favorable account of Pinochet's eleven years in office: "After a period of turmoil, General Pinochet brought order to street and factory and renewed economic growth." In fact, Pinochet's policies brought runaway inflation, a drastic drop in real wages, an upward redistribution of income, a sharp growth in unemployment, a huge increase in the foreign debt, and a fall in savings and investments to below the late 1960s level.[29] The *Times* editorial also maintained that "the poor were consoled with record levels of social spending."

In fact, there were heartless cutbacks. The milk program for Chilean children was abolished almost immediately after the generals came to power, and health, sanitation, housing, and community services were subjected to drastic cuts. The public sector was sharply reduced in a massive, bargain-priced sell-off to private business.[30] "A 1980 plebiscite," the *Times* continued, "even allowing for the repressive conditions of the vote, must be said to have given the general's authoritarian Constitution the endorsement he sought." One must ponder the meaning of this sentence. How does a plebiscite voted under admittedly repressive conditions for an admittedly authoritarian constitution amount to a popular endorsement? For all its professed dedication to democracy, the *Times* and other major media have been less critical of democracy's mortal enemies in Chile than of capitalism's democratic opponents in that country.

STOMPING ON GRENADA

In 1983, when the U.S. government invaded the tiny and relatively defenseless sovereign nation of Grenada (population 110,000), in an unprovoked assault and in blatant violation of international law, killing scores of the island's occupants and defenders—the American press pretty much went along with it. To be sure, there were editorials in important newspapers like the *Boston Globe*, the *Washington Post*, and the *New York Times* denouncing the invasion. (The *Post* eventually flip-flopped and came out in support of the aggression.)[31] And there was a long article in the *Times* that, while not criticizing the invasion itself, raised questions about the Reagan administration's "deliberate distortions and knowingly false statements" in regard to the military action.[32] The press did strongly criticize the barring of reporters and the censoring of information from Grenada during the first two days of the invasion.

The overall media thrust, however, was to accept the U.S. action as a kind of natural happening. The first question reporters asked President Reagan during the press conference at which he announced the invasion was "Is it true that two of our helicopters were shot down?" an inquiry that implicitly accepted the legitimacy of the attack, focusing on *how* we were doing and not on *what* we were doing. From the beginning, the press evidenced that same pattern of complicity observed throughout most of the Vietnam War, raising no questions about international law or moral propriety. Correspondents like Jack Smith of ABC news and commentators like Bill Moyers of CBS, positively aligned themselves with the aggression, seeing it as a necessary "mission" to restore democracy.[33]

Most of the press went along with the White House claim that the invasion was a rescue operation on behalf of American students at the St. George medical school. *Time* magazine headlined its cover story: "Rescue in Grenada."[34] The networks and newspapers ran pictures and accounts of "rescued" students kissing U.S. soil, telling how happy they were to be safely home. Ignored were the medical students who testified that they were never threatened by the Grenadians nor by Cubans, nor prevented from leaving the island. (The *New York Times* did mention these latter students a week later—in the thirty-eighth paragraph of an article on Grenada.[35])

The press accorded generous exposure to the official view that Grenada was a Cuban military bastion. Grenada's "defenders were Cuban—and extremely well armed," reported *Newsweek*.[36] *Time* described them as "well-armed professionally trained soldiers."[37] They were reported to number as many as "1,000 to 1,500 Cuban troops."[38] In fact, only 784 Cubans were found on Grenada by U.S. forces, exactly the number Castro said there were. Only a handful were military personnel, the rest being construction workers, medical personnel, and diplomatic personnel with their children and other relatives.[39]

On the second day of the operation, when the Reagan administration announced that the invasion was not merely a rescue operation for the students but for the entire Caribbean, the U.S. press went along with the revised and expanded version. The administration claimed it had discovered enormous warehouses full of "deadly armaments" and "secret documents" that purportedly showed Grenada was, in President Reagan's words, "a Soviet-Cuban colony being readied as a major military bastion to export terror and undermine democracy." The government produced footage of seized arms caches supposedly representing a "massive arsenal" sufficient to arm "8,000 to 10,000 terrorists." The footage and the charges were given top play by the three major networks, the newsweeklies, and most newspapers. "American military sources say they were staggered by the depth and strength of the Cuban military presence," reported ABC.[40]

Eventually when journalists were allowed to visit the island, some sent back reports indicating that the arms cache actually consisted of defensive small arms, obsolete rifles, and some artillery and vehicles, enough to equip an army of about two thousand and a militia of twice that size, hardly the stuff to terrorize and dominate the entire Caribbean.[41] And, contrary to what the State Department claimed, the "secret documents" contained "no evidence that a terrorist training base existed or that Cubans had planned to take over Grenada," the *New York Times* belatedly and inconspicuously reported.[42] The major media gave these corrective reports nowhere near the prominent play accorded the government's original charges.

All three networks accepted Reagan's view that Grenada was of enormous military and strategic value to Cuba and the Soviet Union without explaining why, except to transmit unquestioningly the Pentagon's fantasy that a revolutionary Grenada would allow Havana and Moscow to control crucial oil tanker lanes that came from the Atlantic through the Caribbean. The news media also transmitted the official fabrication that the Cubans had directed the killing of Grenadian leader Maurice Bishop by a left faction just before the U.S. invasion. In fact, Castro had a personal friendship with Bishop and had issued a strong denunciation of the "ultraleftists" responsible for the killing.[43] A CBS correspondent argued the U.S. government's case this way:

> The Grenadians said their new all-weather night-and-day airport, with its 10,000 foot runway built by Cubans was for jumbo jets carrying tourists. Washington said, "Nonsense." The Grenadians said the new port facilities under construction were for banana boats. Washington said, "No way." Washington believed this tiniest Caribbean country was being redesigned from a tourist haven to a Communist airbase and a way station, a stopping-off point for Cuban soldiers on their way to Africa, for East Bloc supplies on their way to Nicaragua . . .[44]

And what Washington believed was what the press told us. The State Department offered no evidence, nor did the press demand any, to support the assertion that the airport was for military purposes. Anyone familiar with the special requirements of military airports, including their underground storage and special defense facilities, would know that the Grenadian airport was indeed as the Grenadians had contended, a civilian one—and was being built not only with Cuban help but with investments from a number of Western capitalist countries, including Great Britain.[45]

The experiments in grassroots economic democracy and social justice, which were the hallmark of the New Jewel government, constituted a side to the Grenada story that the press left entirely untouched. Under the New Jewel, grade school and secondary education were free for everyone for the first time. Free health clinics were opened in the countryside (thanks mostly to Cuban assistance). Unemployment dropped dramatically from 49 to 14 percent in three years. Free milk and other foodstuffs were being distributed to the needy, as were materials for home improvement. Cultural and sports programs were set up for young people. Measures were taken in support of equal pay and equal legal status for women. The government leased unused land to establish farm cooperatives, and sought to turn agriculture away from cash-crop exports and toward self-sufficient food production.[46] *None of these developments was reported in the U.S. media, neither while they were happening nor as background material during the invasion.*

While the Reagan administration and the press never tired of pointing out that the New Jewel revolutionary government had not held the elections promised in 1979, they failed to mention that the revolution did institute experiments in a local town-meeting type of direct democracy that proved popular, and that in 1983 a team of lawyers in Grenada had begun work on a new constitution that was to be submitted to the public for approval, after which elections would be held under its provisions.[47]

All in all, assisted by the media, the Reagan administration was able to leave the impression it had acted with good cause to thwart a Cuban-Soviet military buildup in the Caribbean that threatened the security of the entire region. U.S. marines and the 82nd Airborne Division were portrayed as rescuers and helpers, while Cuban teachers, doctors, and construction workers were seen as agents of terrorism. Here was an inversion of reality equal to any Orwellian doublethink.

To the above cases we could add studies of how the media have treated—or mistreated—Cuba, Nicaragua, Zaire, Guatemala, Indonesia, East Timor, Portugal, Ethiopia, Cambodia, Turkey, the Dominican Republic, the entire Arab World, and most other Third World nations and regions, an undertaking that would fill many volumes.[48] What becomes apparent in the cases already presented are the patterns of omission and distortion, specifically (1) the way the media consistently suppress descriptions of the *content* of Third World struggles for national independence, economic justice, and revolutionary reform; (2) the way the media ignore U.S. sponsorship of reactionary repression and underplay the repression itself; (3) the way the media reduce Third World struggles to an encounter between U.S. virtue and Communist evil. In the next chapter I will deal with these and other patterns in more detail.

Notes

1. See Michael Parenti, ed. *Trends and Tragedies in American Foreign Policy* (Boston: Little, Brown, 1971); Eduardo Galeano, *Open Veins of Latin America* (New York: Monthly Review Press, 1973); Noam Chomsky and Edward S. Herman, *The Washington Connection and Third World Fascism* (Boston: South End Press, 1979).
2. Julia Preston, "Killing Off the News in Guatemala," *Columbia Journalism Review*, January/February 1982, p. 35.
3. Robert Cirino, *Power to Persuade* (New York: Bantam, 1984), p. 63.
4. Andrew Kopkind, "The Press at War," *Ramparts*, August/September 1975, p. 37.
5. Cirino, *Power to Persuade*, pp. 61–62.
6. James Aronson, *The Press and the Cold War* (Boston: Beacon Press, 1973).
7. Kopkind, "The Press at War."
8. TRB column, *New Republic*, April 25, 1975.
9. James Reston column, *New York Times*, April 4, 1975.
10. *New York Times*, April 21, 1975; see also Anthony Lewis's columns of April 24, 1975, and May 1, 1975; and Noam Chomsky, "The Remaking of History," *Ramparts*, August/September 1975, pp. 30–35, 49–53.
11. Quoted in Chomsky, "The Remaking of History."
12. All the quotes in the above paragraph are from Roger Morris, Shelly Mueller, and William Jelin, "Through the Looking Glass in Chile: Coverage of Allende's Regime," *Columbia Journalism Review*, November/December 1974, pp. 16–17. Some of the citations that follow are from the systematic and excellent study by John Leggett et al., *Allende, His Exit and Our "Times,"* (New Brunswick, N.J.: New Brunswick Cooperative Press, 1978).
13. Morris et al., "Through the Looking Glass . . ." p. 18.
14. James Petras and Morris Morely, *The United States and Chile: Imperialism and the Overthrow of the Allende Government* (New York: Monthly Review Press, 1975); also statistics provided by John Pollock and cited in Morris et al., "Through the Looking Glass . . ."
15. *New York Times*, August 31, 1973; also Leggett et al., *Allende, His Exit and our "Times."*
16. Petras and Morely, *The United States and Chile . . .*
17. *New York Times*, September 15, 1973.

18. *New York Times,* September 12, 1973.
19. Ibid.
20. Ten years later, Nathanial Davis, who had been U.S. ambassador to Chile during the coup, admitted that such assistance to opposition parties was given but insisted the United States had nothing to do with overthrowing Allende. *Washington Post,* September 11, 1983.
21. Legget et al., *Allende, His Exit and Our "Times," p. 65.*
22. *New York Times,* September 12, 1973.
23. *New York Times,* September 16, 1973.
24. Ibid.
25. Jose Yglesias, *Chile's Days of Terror: Eye-Witness Accounts of the Military Coup* (New York: Pathfinder Press, 1974).
26. *Washington Post,* September 11, 1983.
27. *New York Times,* August 8, 1984.
28. Ibid.
29. Edward S. Herman, *The Real Terror Network* (Boston: South End Press, 1982), p. 189; also James Petras, "Chile and Latin America," *Monthly Review,* February 1977, pp. 13–24.
30. Herman, *The Real Terror Network,* p. 190; Cynthia Brown, "The High Cost of Monetarism In Chile," *Nation,* September 27, 1980, pp. 271–75.
31. *Washington Post,* November 9, 1983.
32. *New York Times,* November 6, 1983.
33. ABC and CBS evening news reports, both October 26, 1983.
34. *Time,* November 7, 1983.
35. *New York Times,* November 6, 1983; also Alexander Cockburn in the *Village Voice,* November 8, 1983.
36. *Newsweek,* November 7, 1983.
37. *Time,* November 7, 1983.
38. Network television reports, October 27, 1983.
39. *New York Times,* November 6, 1983; see the speech by Fidel Castro printed in full as a paid advertisement in the *New York Times,* November 20, 1983.
40. ABC evening news, October 27, 1983.
41. John Judis, "Grenadian Documents Do Not Show What Reagan Claims,"; and Daniel Lazare, "Reagan's Seven Big Lies About Grenada" both in *In These Times,* November 16, 1983.
42. *New York Times,* November 6, 1983.
43. Ibid.; also Castro's statement *loc. cit.*
44. Quoted in Cockburn *loc. cit.*
45. Christopher Hitchens, "The Case of the Menacing Runway," *Nation,* May 29, 1982, pp. 649–51.
46. "A Tottering Structure of Lies," *Sojourner,* December 1983, pp. 4–5; also Michael Massing, "Grenada Before and After," *Atlantic Monthly,* February 1984, pp. 79–80.
47. "A Tottering Structure of Lies," p. 5.
48. Other writers have criticized the media's treatment of the Third World: see Noam Chomsky and Edward S. Herman, *After the Cataclysm* (Boston: South End Press, 1979) on media distortion of Indochina events and U.S. policies; Herman, *The Real Terror Network* on Latin America; Edward Said, *Orientalism* (New York: Pantheon, 1978) and Said's *Covering Islam* (New York: Pantheon, 1971) on the Arab and Muslim worlds; David Paletz and Robert Entman, *Media Power Politics* (New York: Free Press, 1981) on Zaire and the press; and my "Portugal and the Press," *Progressive,* December 1975, pp. 43–45.

11

Variations on a Theme for Counterrevolution

The news media have little to say about how socialism improves the lives of people in impoverished lands and how capitalism causes or aggravates their impoverishment. When reporting on the Third World, as when reporting on most other things that have an economic content, the corporate-owned press transforms brutal autocrats into "tough leaders" and popular insurgencies into diabolic, Moscow-directed aggressions. What follows are some of the major thematic distortions and omissions in the U.S. media's coverage of the Third World.

AMERICAN POLICY AS VIRTUOUS

The press sometimes will criticize U.S. policy in the Third World as "ill-defined," or "overextended," but never as lacking in virtuous intent. For example, we saw how the news media presented the Vietnam War as a valiant but quixotic attempt to bring Western democracy to an Asian people. To maintain this image, the news media say little about the U.S. role in financing, equipping, training, advising, and directing the vast repressive apparatus of military and paramilitary forces in right-wing U.S. client states around the world.[1] For instance, in 1983 when House and Senate committees approved $100 million in "security assistance" to Guatemalan dictator Rios Montt to tide him over for two more years of butchering his country's rural population, neither the *New York Times* nor the *Washington Post* deemed the event worthy of mention.[2]

The brutality does not go entirely unnoticed. But press reports are usually sparse in content, rarely doing justice to the endemic nature of the repression. Nor is much said about how repression is linked to the class interests within Third World states, how it functions to protect the few rich from the many poor. Nor is any link likely to be made

187

between the repression and U.S. policy. Thus when *Time* magazine devoted a full-page story to torture throughout the world, the U.S. came out looking like Snow White.[3]

Following the official line, the major media will readily deny that the United States harbors aggressive intentions against socialist or other left-leaning governments, and will dismiss such charges by them as just so much "anti-American" propaganda and as evidence of *their* hostility toward *us*. Or the media will condone the aggressive actions as necessary for our national security or implicitly accept them as a given reality needing no justification.

For instance, in 1961 Cuban right-wing emigrés, trained and financed by the CIA, invaded Cuba, in the words of one of their leaders, to overthrow Castro and set up "a provisional government" that "will restore all properties to the rightful owners."[4] Reports of the impending invasion circulated widely through Central America. In the United States, however, where there reputedly existed the freest press in the world, few people were informed.[5] The mounting evidence of an impending invasion was suppressed by the Associated Press and United Press International and by all the major newspapers and newsweeklies, seventy-five of which—in an impressively unanimous act of self-censorship—rejected a story offered by the editors of the *Nation* in 1960 detailing U.S. preparations for the invasion.[6] Fidel Castro's accusations that the United States was planning to invade Cuba were dismissed by the *New York Times* as "shrill . . . anti-American propaganda," and by *Time* magazine as Castro's "continued tawdry little melodrama of invasion."[7] When Washington broke diplomatic relations with Cuba in January 1961, the *New York Times* explained, "What snapped U.S. patience was a new propaganda offensive from Havana charging that the U.S. was plotting an 'imminent invasion' of Cuba. . . ."[8]

Yet, after the Bay of Pigs invasion proved to be something more than a figment of Castro's anti-Americanism, there was almost a total lack of media criticism regarding its moral and legal impropriety.[9] Instead, editorial commentary referred to the disappointing "fiasco" and "disastrous attempt" and the need to free Cuba from the "Communist yoke" (an endeavor assumed to be laudable even though the Cuban people themselves had failed to rise up and join the invaders, as the latter had anticipated).

Revelations about the full extent of U.S. involvement in the Bay of Pigs, including the CIA training camp in Guatemala began to appear during the post-invasion period in the same press that earlier had denied such things existed and had accused Castro of anti-Americanism for saying they did. These retrospective admissions of U.S. involvement were reported unapologetically as news and as background for further moves against Cuba.[10]

A more recent case is Nicaragua. Despite the fact that the United States had already invaded Nicaragua three times in this century, had mined Nicaragua's harbors, blown up her oil depots, and was openly supporting a "contra" war of terror, while U.S. fleets stood at the ready off both Nicaraguan coasts and U.S. planes regularly invaded Nicaraguan air space, and despite the fact that the U.S. secretary of state was promising to "cast out" the Sandinistas from "our hemisphere" and the secretary of defense was invoking the Monroe Doctrine to justify future actions against that country, Nicaraguan charges in 1984 that the United States was planning an invasion were dismissed by ABC news as "the Sandinista paranoia" and by the *Washington Post* as "Nicaraguan paranoia."[11] Even if the United States never actually sends American troops into Nicaragua, the unrelenting economic, diplomatic, and military aggression perpetrated by Washington seemingly would make it difficult to dismiss the alarm felt by Managua as "paranoia." (The paranoia charge was inadvertently put to rest in June 1985 by none other than President Reagan and Secretary of State Shultz who both announced that the United States might have to invade Nicaragua before too long.)

THE NONEXISTENCE OF IMPERIALISM

While Washington policymakers argue that U.S. overseas intervention is necessary to protect "U.S. interests," the press seldom asks for any explanation of what are "U.S. interests" and who is served by them. Nothing is said about the class interests involved or about how our taxes and sons are used to shore up and defend the overseas investments of the big corporations.

In tiny El Salvador alone, U.S. Steel, Texas Instruments, Alcoa, Westinghouse, Phelps-Dodge, American Standard, Pillsbury, United Brands, Standard Fruit, Del Monte, Cargill, Procter and Gamble, Chase Manhattan, Bank of America, First National Bank, Standard Oil of New Jersey, Texaco, and at least twenty-five other major companies have "vital interests," reaping big profits by paying Salvadoran workers subsistence wages to produce everything from aluminum products and baking powder to transformers, computers, and steel pipes— almost all for export markets and all done without minimum wage laws, occupational safety rules, environmental controls, and other such costly hindrances to the process of capital accumulation.[13] Of many hundreds of reports in the major broadcast and printed media appearing in recent years, I found none that discussed these facts. Nor does the press say much about El Salvador's internal class structure, in which a small number of immensely rich families, numbering a few thousand people, own 60 percent of the farmland and receive 50 percent of the nation's income.[14]

In Nicaragua before the Sandinista revolution, capital investment and U.S. military aid helped produce an impoverished people and a rich ruling class: 5 percent of the population owned 58 percent of the arable land; the Somoza family alone owned 23 percent. Sixty percent of the people were unemployed and 50 percent had a yearly income of $90. Half the children of Nicaragua suffered from malnutrition and almost half died before the age of four. Eighty percent of the population was illiterate.[15] If mention *is* made of such things, they are seldom linked to the larger system of multinational exploitation. *What capitalism as a transnational system does to impoverish people throughout the world is simply not a fit subject for the U.S. news media.*[16]

The U.S. press never heard of U.S. imperialism. Instead, poverty is treated as its own cause. We are to believe Third World people are poor because that has long been their condition; they live in countries that are overpopulated, or there is something about their land, culture, or temperament that makes them unable to cope. Occasionally, corrupt rulers are blamed, as when the *New York Times* reported that President Marcos of the Philippines was a practitioner of "crony capitalism," concentrating wealth in the hands of a few favored friends and relatives, passing over more qualified persons and freezing out competitors.[17] The press made the same complaint about the Somoza family of Nicaragua in the last days of its rule. But these critical observations fall short of any indictment of imperialism itself, concentrating instead on the "abuses" and "excesses" committed by a corrupt coterie that has violated capitalist norms of competence and competition.

"MODERATE AUTHORITARIAN" REGIMES

Nations like Guatemala, South Korea, South Africa, Indonesia, Chile, Turkey, Pakistan, Zaire, and El Salvador are not just military dictatorships, they are client states of the United States; that is, their economies serve the needs of Western, especially American, capitalism, providing natural resources, cheap labor, and profitable investment markets in exchange for millions of dollars in aid that go to the client-states' wealthy ruling elites and military chieftains (often one and the same). As already noted, the everyday acts of repression, torture, and assassination perpetrated by these regimes with the aid and assistance of U.S. counterinsurgency agencies, are usually ignored. The press responds quite differently if the political repression takes place in a Communist country. The imposition of martial law in Poland in December 1981, resulting in the arrest of hundreds of Polish Solidarity leaders and the death of several protesters, was given elaborate and condemnatory exposure in both the broadcast and print media for many weeks. At that same time a massive political repression was continuing in Turkey, involving the incarceration of over 100,000 persons, and the torture and execution of about 5,000, including several hundred leaders of the Turkish labor movement. Labor unions and peasant cooperatives numbering several million in membership were banned; all leftist political parties were outlawed. Collective bargaining was abolished, wages held down, and benefits severely cut. Thousands of teachers were among those imprisoned along with even larger numbers of students. Turkey's entire educational system was put into the hands of the military and the press was muzzled. The suppression of Turkish democratic forces received but passing attention in the U.S. media even though it was of a magnitude many times greater than anything going on in Poland.[18] The news out of Turkey in 1981 was of Secretary of State Alexander Haig and Secretary of Defense Caspar Weinberger visiting the Turkish generals, pledging assistance and praising them for having restored "stability" in their country.

The scale and savagery of political repression is less a factor in commanding the media's attention than the politics of victim and victimizer. If the left is suppressing the right, as with the treatment of small numbers of dissidents in the USSR, then the American public is treated to a protracted and unremitting press campaign. But if the repression is by the right against the left, even if of much greater scope and ferocity, the news is suppressed or downplayed and given none of the detailed repetition and strong editorial commentary needed to create a climate of opinion on the issue.

One study shows that from 1976 to 1981 the New York Times made only 64 mentions of 15 clergymen, student leaders, labor leaders, poets, and journalists who had played leading political roles and had been imprisoned, tortured, or murdered by the governments of various right-wing client states (36 of these references were to the Salvadoran Archbishop Oscar Romero alone). In contrast, during this same period, the Times mentioned four Soviet dissidents 499 times and accorded them far more elaborately detailed coverage.[19] Americans knew of Andrei Sakharov, living in forced internal exile in the Soviet Union, but few ever heard of the Uruguayan dissident Zelmar Michelini, who was tortured and murdered, or his daughter, who "disappeared." Thanks to our news media, the American public knew in 1982 and 1983 almost as much about the daily moves of Lech Walesa as did the Polish police. But few Americans would recognize the name of Enrique Alvarez Cordova, a leftist leader in El Salvador who was tortured, mutilated, and murdered by government forces; neither would they recognize Suleyman Kirteke, the labor union official who awaited death in a Turkish prison with legs, hands, and eyes swollen black from torture—during the very days Lech Walesa was fishing and giving press conferences to admiring throngs of Western correspondents in Gdansk.

Along with downplaying the repression and atrocities, the press describes U.S. client states as "friendly to U.S. interests," again with no precise explanation as to what that might mean. The press also regularly describes client state leaders as purveyors of order and stability. Popular agitation is assumed to be an undesirable thing while the absence of such agitation, even if achieved with police repression is taken as beneficial.

Terms like "the country's strongman," "tough," "severe," "firm," "no-nonsense," and "clampdown" give a noncriminal, disciplinary framing to the coups and massacres perpetrated by the Chilean, Indonesian, Argentinian, Uruguayan, Turkish, Bolivian, and Brazilian militaries, all of whom were supposedly obliged to take firm action against the prevailing chaos. Thus the *Washington Post* could describe the bloody repression in Turkey as "a military clampdown that rescued the country from the brink of civil war"; and the *New York Times* noted how Pinochet "took power" in Chile "amid social chaos."[20]

Often the "military clampdown" is portrayed as an evenhanded one, equally repressive of left and right extremists. Thus press stories about Guatemala long have propagated the fiction of a besieged centrist government trying to end a "terrorist war that has been raging for years between leftist and rightist groups."[21] But reports by Amnesty International indicated that the "large-scale extrajudicial executions of noncombatant civilians," numbering many thousands in Guatemala had been perpetrated by government troops, and paramilitary death squads.[22]

By portraying the military autocrats as striking a course between the violent extremes of left and right, the press is able with one stroke to exonerate them from any complicity in the government-sponsored mass terror and transform them into a middle-of-the-road peaceable leadership that is potentially, if not actually, democratic. Thus, in all apparent seriousness, NBC news in 1980 could describe the government of El Salvador, which had been terrorizing and murdering peasants and workers for several decades, as "moderate."[23] And the *Chris-*

tian Science Monitor exonerated the Salvadoran military government of any guilt: "The country's buffeted junta, weathering almost daily disorders and vicious verbal attacks from both the left and the right, faces its most serious tempest to date.[24] The image is touching: the "buffeted" generals steering the ship of state through disorderly waters, enduring "vicious verbal attacks" from left and right, with nothing to help them through their travails except their troops, death squads, artillery, jet bombers, helicopter gunships, and the CIA, Pentagon, and U.S. State Department.

The *New York Times* repeated the State Department line that the "moderate" Salvadoran government was implementing "the most sweeping land reform—and fastest—ever carried out in Latin America"[25]—so fast as to soon become indiscernible. Other junta activities received less fanfare: Within a two-year period, according to the legal aid office of the Archdiocese of San Salvador, some 32,000 people, mostly noncombatants, were killed by the military's "search and destroy" missions. By 1981, some 800,000 refugees, or one out of every five Salvadorans, had fled the country, the military's moderation having proven too much for them.[26]

POWER-HUNGRY LEFTISTS WHO DO NO GOOD

The accomplishments of revolutionary governments and movements in advancing the well-being of their people remain one of the more thoroughly suppressed stories in the American press. "You never read anything about the good that Allende was doing," admitted one former attaché to the U.S. embassy in Chile.[27] We noted how the press squelched news about the economic advances of the Allende government, the New Jewel in Grenada, and the postwar Vietnamese government.[28] Consider now revolutionary Nicaragua: By 1984, after five years of Sandinista rule, infant mortality dropped to the lowest in Central America; unemployment declined from 60 to 16 percent, while inflation was reduced from 84 to 27 percent. The percent of the national budget spent on health increased 600 percent. Staple foods consumption increased 30 percent. Rural clinics, free hospitals, and vaccination campaigns produced a 50 percent drop in malaria and dramatic declines in children's diseases. Land was distributed to more than 40,000 families and to cooperatives. Over 85 percent of the population was now able to read and write to at least a third-grade level.[29] Of these accomplishments, the U.S. press reported only the literacy campaign.

Countries going through progressive transformations *that limit the prerogatives of private capital* are characterized in the U.S. news as taking the "totalitarian road."[30] The U.S. press charges the leftists with intent to destroy individual freedom and democracy—in countries where no · freedom and democracy had existed under the previous regimes. Thus the *Washington Post* described Nicaragua as "swaying on the edge of repression" and tending "toward Cuban-style totalitarianism."[31] Such charges came at a time when eight independent radio stations in Nicaragua regularly carried the pronouncements of opposition parties—even as the country was under daily attack from the contras. (Radio is the principal means of communication in many poor countries.) According to Peter Marchetti, an American Jesuit priest in Nicaragua:

> These radio stations are much more critical of the Nicaraguan government than radio stations in the United States are critical of our government. "All Things Considered" would seem like a controlled press compared to the ideological pounding the government receives from the radio stations in Managua.[32]

In addition, the American news media have said little about the grass roots organizations formed in Nicaragua and other revolutionary countries to represent peasants, workers, womens groups, store owners, professionals, artisans, and whole communities. And little has been said about the liberating effects of no longer having to worry about the brutalities of the national guard, massive unemployment, and hunger.

Ten years after the military coup in Chile, CBS news stated that the Chilean army now felt "change would not bring democracy but a return to Marxism."[33] CBS never explained why this was a bad thing. Similarly when the Sandinistas embarked upon a program of socialist reconstruction, the American press saw the emergence of a "Marxist" regime—again with no explanation as to why this was so terrible.[34] Nor need the press offer any explanation. After almost a century of propaganda, designations like "Marxist," "Communist," "leftist," or "leftist guerrillas" create their own automatic negative framing. Thus, in regard to the invasion of Grenada in 1983, a *New York Times* editorial decided that the fear was "real" that Grenada could "infect the [Caribbean] region with militant leftism."[35] But the *Times* offered not a word about the actual programmatic content of Grenadian "militant leftism." In such instances the media do not publicize the mainstream capitalist ideology as such, they just assume it.

In actuality, the distinguishing characteristic of "Marxists" or "leftists" as opposed to "rightists" is a commitment to the kind of social and economic change that benefits the less favored mass of peasants and workers at the expense of the wealthy classes of the Third World and Western financial interests. The revolutionary and Marxist left is committed to using a country's resources and labor for the purpose of eliminating poverty and illiteracy and serving the social needs of the populace rather than the profit needs of rich investors. These are not only the theoretical goals of socialism but the actual accomplishments of revolutionaries in power.

From the U.S. news media one learns that "Communists" are not persons motivated by longings for justice, equality, and a decent life, but conspirators who "take advantage" of such longings. Discussing the struggles in Guatemala and El Salvador, *Washington Post* editor and columnist (and former CIA agent) Philip Geyelin referred to "communist exploitation of grievances," and "the communist contribution to instability."[36] We learn that leftists try to "gain strength," "create chaos," "take advantage of turmoil," "destabilize," and "grab power," subverting whole countries in the doing.[37]

What moves them to such perilous undertakings? As the press would have it, Marxists and other leftist revolutionaries will risk and sacrifice their lives because of nothing more than a nihilistic pursuit of power. Supposedly they do not seek the power to end misery and

195

hunger; they simply hunger miserably for power. If they initiate land reform, health campaigns, and other good things, it is only to win popular support and further secure their power base. So wanting in virtue are they that even their seemingly good acts can be dismissed as venally motivated. The press does not explain why—if revolutionaries are driven only by a hunger for power—do they identify themselves with the oppressed and powerless rather than with the powerful oppressors. Why do they take such a dangerous and painfully circuitous road to power when they might more advantageously apply their talents and energies to winning the rewards of rank, celebrity, and influence by serving the existing system in the manner of countless political climbers in both rich and poor countries?

The stereotype of the Communists as demon aggressors predominates in the U.S. news media even when they make friendly overtures toward the U.S. government. In 1984 the *New York Times* ran a "news analysis" headlined "WHAT'S BEHIND CASTRO'S SOFTER TONE." The headline itself suggested that Castro was up to something. The opening sentence read, "Once again Fidel Castro is talking as if he wants to improve relations with the United States" ("as if," not "actually"). Castro, explained the *Times,* was interested in "taking advantage" of American trade, technology, and tourism and would "prefer not to be spending so much time and energy on national defense." Here seemed to be a promising basis for improved relations. Cuba's own self-interest, Castro was saying, rested on closer economic ties with Washington and cuts in Cuban defense spending and not, as the United States was saying, on military buildups and aggressive confrontations. Nevertheless, the *Times* analysis made nothing of Castro's stated desire to ease tensions and instead presented the rest of the story from the U.S. government's perspective. It noted that "most Reagan Administration officials seem skeptical. . . . The Administration continues to believe that the best way to deal with the Cuban leader is with unyielding firmness. . . . Administration officials see little advantage in wavering."[38] The article did not explain what justified the "skeptical" stance, nor why a negative response to Castro should be described as "unyielding firmness" rather than, say, "hostile rigidity"; nor did it say why a willingness to respond seriously to his overture must be labeled "wavering." The *Times* left the impression that power hungry Castro was out to get something from us but our leaders weren't about to be taken in by his "professed" desire for improved relations and his "softer tones." There was no mention in the article—either from the U.S. government or from the *Times* itself—of what the United States had to lose if it entered friendlier relations with Cuba.

ECONOMIC "FAILURES"

Along with suppressing good news, the U.S. press exaggerates and even fabricates bad news about leftist countries, blaming their conditions of want on socialist "mismanagement" and Marxist "tampering" with what is misleadingly assumed to have been a previously healthy prerevolutionary economy.

In Nicaragua the war of attrition conducted by Somoza's national guard in the last year of his dictatorship destroyed one-third of the farmlands, hundreds of factories and smaller workplaces, utility plants, and thousands of homes; 50,000 people were killed; 160,000 were wounded or maimed; 40,000 children were orphaned—out of a population of 2 million.[39] After the revolution, wealthy persons smuggled money out of the country, the United States cut off aid and trade, and the CIA-financed contras carried on a war of attrition from Honduras. The Sandinista revolution inherited a grim legacy of hunger, sickness, unemployment, foreign debt, and continued military and economic aggression from abroad. Ignoring all these adverse factors and the gains made by the Sandinistas in the face of them, the *Washington Post* could editorialize that the Nicaraguan "economy is in a calamitous condition, in good measure because of arbitrary interference by an untutored, Marxist-oriented government."[40]

The press treatment of Grenada offers another case in point. After the New Jewel Movement overthrew the corrupt and undemocratic Gairy government and began instituting economic reforms, the United States withdrew all aid and suspended all credits to the tiny island. In 1982, despite recession and a sharp drop in tourism (much of it due to U.S. propaganda against the revolution), Grenada's gross national product grew by 5.5 percent with an inflation rate of only 7 percent.[41] Yet soon after the U.S. invasion, the *Washington Post,* without offering any supporting information, transmitted the White House view that "the economy of Grenada was left 'bankrupt' by its former Marxist rulers."[42]

In a rare reference to the economic, rather than the political side of the shortlived leftist military takeover in Portugal in 1974, the *New York Times* reported in 1975 that the Portuguese military was pushing an economic program that threatened to "dismantle the economy and cause an even deeper economic crisis" than the one already created by the left.[43] It is difficult to imagine what a dismantled economy would look like or why the officers would pursue such a goal.[44] The *Times* offered not a word of evidence to support this fanciful conclusion nor any actual information about the economic program itself—which consisted of drastic cuts in military spending and increases in social programs.

The press views any attempt to alter the capitalist economy as an attempt to dismantle all economic arragnements. What might be harmful to capitalist class interests is treated as harmful to all of society itself. Likewise, any attempt to transform the *capitalist* social order is portrayed as an attack on *all* social order and an invitation to chaos.

To better create an impression of economic failure and widespread disaffection, the news manufacturers concentrate on the discontent of "middle-class" persons—without mentioning that in Third World countries the "middle class" numbers not more than 5 to 20 percent of the population and is usually a markedly privileged group. These privileged "middle-class" persons—farm owners, lawyers, business people, managers of small companies, and opposition political leaders—are the ones most likely to get quoted in the *New York Times, Washington Post, Time,* and *Newsweek* and to have their opinions treated as the accurate view of reality. "I cannot say I interviewed many peasants, and nobody else did either." admitted one reporter, referring to his experience in Chile—but he could have been talking about almost any other Third World country.[45]

What wins the attention of the U.S. press is not the distribution of bread and powdered milk, the development of clean drinking water, or the creation of jobs in government-sponsored projects out in the impoverished countryside; rather it is the "empty shops" in posh "middle-class" neighborhoods, which can be treated as evidence of the revolutionary government's economic failure.

DEMOCRACY IS IN THE EYES OF THE BEHOLDER

When a client state holds an election, U.S. officials and the American press see democracy blooming, but these same opinion makers dismiss elections in revolutionary countries as a "sham." Compare how the media treated the elections held in reactionary El Salvador and revolutionary Nicaragua in 1984.

In El Salvador the military had repeatedly terrorized religious, peasant, and labor organizations critical of the government. The university was occupied and closed down by the army. All opposition newspapers were driven out of existence by 1981. Whole villages suspected of supporting the revolutionaries were massacred by the army or hit by napalm and fragmentation bombs. By 1980, a broad left-center coalition of radicals, Communists, social democrats, and some Christian Democrats formed a revolutionary front, joining together in a popular insurgency against the military regime whose support came principally from large investors, big landowners, the U.S. government, and crypto-fascist organizations.[46]

It was against this backdrop that the 1984 Salvadoran presidential election was conducted. Guided and financially assisted by the U.S. government, the contest pitted José Napolean Duarte, a right-wing Christian Democrat and long-time apologist for the reign of terror, against Roberto d'Aubuisson, a death-squad leader and long-time practitioner of terror. Upon being elected president, the "moderate" Duarte, who had been the favorite of the State Department and the U.S. press, appointed Colonel Lopez Nuila, death-squad leader, as deputy minister for public security, and José Francisco Guerrero, a leader of the far-right ARENA (d'Aubuisson's party), as attorney general.[47]

Rather than dismissing the election as a meaningless charade, the *New York Times* called it "laudable" and "a step toward democracy."[48] And the *Washington Post* hailed Duarte as "El Salvador's first president with an authentic democratic mandate."[49] The absence of the major opposition on the ballot was dismissed by the *Times* as a "boycott" by left-wing parties.[50] Similarly, ABC news reported that "the left was invited by the government to participate but refused." ABC failed to mention that the invitation contained a suicidal precondition: the guerrillas were to lay down their arms and campaign under the guns of the very state that had recently eradicated hundreds of their leaders and tens of thousands of their supporters.[51]

At election time in El Salvador, the U.S. press was filled with stories of polling places crowded with people eager to cast a ballot for Duarte or d'Aubuisson, but never was it mentioned that voting was obligatory and that the failure to vote—as detected by the absence of a stamp on one's identification card—could lead to arrest. The press also did not mention that ballots were numbered and the numbers recorded on registration lists next to voters' names so officials could, if they wanted, find out how any person voted.

Of the twenty-eight articles run by the *New York Times* between February 1 and March 30 on the election, not one mentioned the lack of press freedom, freedom of organizations to function openly, and the limits placed on candidates to qualify and campaign freely.[52] As Edward Herman noted, the media's swift and magical transformation of a deranged, murderous military regime into an incipient democracy remains one of the great propaganda achievements of recent times. It certainly helped convince Congress to vote for increased military aid to El Salvador less than a fortnight after the election.[53]

None of the uncritical generosity extended by the U.S. press to-

ward the Salvadoran contest was evidenced in its treatment that same
year of the Nicaraguan election for president and National Assembly.
Electoral standards in Nicaragua were far from perfect. Opposition
candidates could not hold open air meetings in certain areas, and were
harassed by crowds of Sandinista sympathizers on about a half-dozen
occasions. Yet the election cannot be dismissed as a sham. The campaign period was twelve weeks long, longer than in some Western
European countries. The government allocated 9 million cordobas
($321,000) to each opposition party, and the more affluent conserva-
tive candidates also drew on funds of their own and imported any
campaign materials they wanted. Opposition parties were alloted free
time each day on national television and national radio (something
minority parties in the United States do not receive). The one opposition daily newspaper, La Prensa, which had been frequently censored,
was left unhampered throughout the election period. In addition, the
opposition parties had their own newspapers, all of which were guaranteed freedom of the press except on military matters. The amount of
press censorship in Nicaragua was less than what Tory Americans
endured during the American Revolution and what all Americans experienced during World War II. The six opposition parties on the
ballot, ranging from left to procapitalist rightist, offered a more ideologically varied and pluralistic choice than anything in the El Salvadoran election. Most of the above facts were suppressed by the U.S. news
media.[54]

The same American press that had nary a word to say about
restrictions on speech, press, and organizational freedom in El Salvador seemed preoccupied with the subject in regard to Nicaragua. Thus
freedom of the press was raised in 75 percent, and organizational
freedom in 50 percent, of the New York Times articles on the Nicaraguan campaign—the same newspaper that did not once mention these
issues in regard to El Salvador.[55] Time magazine reported that "the
procedures under which the elections were held were unfair" but did
not specify how so.[56] Elaborate coverage was given to a coalition of
four conservative parties that boycotted the election ostensibly because
of (unspecified) restrictive campaign conditions. Unless one happened
to have read the Providence (R.I.) Evening Bulletin one may not have
known that U.S. embassy officials in Managua bribed non-Sandinista
opposition leaders to drop out of the campaign. The major U.S. media
had nothing to say about that.[57]

The American press generally gave far less coverage to the Nicaraguan elections than to the Salvadoran elections. Over a 7-day
period the three networks devoted 22 stories to the 1982 Salvadoran
election, for a total of some 95 minutes, but only about 18 minutes in

over three months to the Nicaraguan contest. Stories carried by the *New York Times* were typically headlined "CLEAR CHOICES IN SALVADOR, MURKY PLANS IN NICARAGUA", "SANDINISTAS MAY WIN BIG IN ELECTIONS, BUT AGAINST WHOM?", and "GOING THROUGH THE MOTIONS IN NICARAGUA."[58] The election day story carried by the *Los Angeles Times,* headlined "NICARAGUANS MUSTERED TO POLLING PLACES," noted that opposition leaders accused the Sandinistas of "unfairly using government resources and power to assure its candidates of a big victory, and important opposition parties are boycotting the vote." The only direct quote in the entire piece was from a 76-year old shopkeeper and nonvoter who reportedly said, "The majority of the people are voting because they were threatened; they were told that if they didn't vote, they were counterrevolutionaries. We don't have freedom—we are destroyed."[59] A *Washington Post* story, headlined "CONTROVERSIAL VOTE SET TODAY IN NICARAGUA," emphasized the "pervasive presence in the society" of Sandinista supporters, thereby treating Sandinista popularity as a sign of undemocratic political monopoly. The story did note that the opposition parties, while small, were outspoken in their criticisms of the government; but it drew no conclusion as to whether this indicated free campaign conditions.[60] Some days later in a brief report on the election outcome, the *Post* eagerly noted that the turnout "fell short of the 80 percent" the Sandinistas had hoped for. (It was 75.5 percent or almost 25 percent higher than the U.S. presidential election of that year.) Just as the press had seldom mentioned that the voting in El Salvador was compulsory, so did it rarely, if ever, mention that voting in Nicaragua was voluntary.

In sum, we witnessed a double standard in the press treatment of elections in reactionary El Salvador and revolutionary Nicaragua. The background of terror and repression that made free elections impossible in El Salvador was ignored by the press, which instead chose to treat a contest between two right-wing candidates as proof of democracy. The relative freedom to organize and campaign and the media access and public funds accorded opposition parties in Nicaragua also were ignored by the news media, which chose to treat the complaints of some nonparticipating conservative opposition leaders as evidence that the election was rigged. The overwhelming electoral strength of the Sandinistas was treated as an indication not of Sandinista popularity but of the lack of democracy. The press constructed a no-win image situation for the Sandinistas. A poor showing by the opposition parties (the Sandinistas won 67 percent of the vote) was interpreted to mean that the election was somehow unfairly rigged against them. By this logic, the stronger the opposition, the more democratic would the electoral process have been. However, a poor showing by the Sandinistas would have been seized upon by the press as proof of their lack of popular support. It seems that nothing short of a total Sandinista defeat (and a canceling of its revolutionary program) would have fully qualified Nicaragua as a democracy in the eyes of the business-owned U.S. press.

RED PUPPETS

To convince the U.S. public that small countries like Vietnam, Nicaragua, and Grenada are a threat to U.S. security, Washington portrays them as puppets of larger Communist powers, especially the Soviet Union. The Soviets, in turn, are said to be impelled by an implacable drive for world domination and a hostility toward the one great power, the United States, that stands as a bulwark of freedom against their expansionist appetite. As observed in chapter 8, the press has given uncritical and repeated rendition to this official scenario.

In 1981 Secretary of State Haig announced an intention to draw the line against "Soviet-Cuban aggression" in El Salvador. The news media were not long in taking up the cry. The *Baltimore Sun* carried a front-page story headlined "HAIG DESCRIBES SALVADOR INSURGENCY AS SOVIET ATTEMPT TO OVERTHROW JUNTA." The *Washington Post* and *Boston Globe* carried similar reports; the *New York Times* described the rebel opposition—which, as noted earlier, drew its support from a broad cross-section of the Salvadoran society—as a small extreme leftist group, armed by "the Soviet Union and Cuba."[61] NBC's ardent cold warrior, Marvin Kalb, reported "massive" Soviet interference, all "coordinated by Cuba" in what Kalb called "a systematic, well-financed, sophisticated effort to impose a Communist regime in El Salvador."[62]

What evidence was there of Soviet and Cuban intervention? The State Department published a White Paper on the "secret documents," supposedly captured from Salvadoran insurgents, which recorded Soviet and Cuban arms shipments. The government's charges were given prominent play in all the major broadcast and printed media. Few journalists read the White Paper, basing their stories on the State Department's summation appearing in its opening pages. No reporter or editor questioned why a guerrilla movement would keep written records of secret arms shipments as might a department store keep invoices. ABC correspondent Barrie Dunsmore announced, "The report contains documents, letters, and photographs captured in November and January, which firmly establishes the links between the leftist insurgents in El Salvador and Communist governments world-wide."[63] The report contained no such thing, according to Latin American specialist James Petras, one of the few knowledgeable persons who took the trouble to read it in its entirety. Marshaling evidence, much of it from official sources, Petras showed that the rebels were poorly armed and that most of their weapons were either made by them, captured from government forces, or bought on the flourishing black market. His article, published in the *Nation* (March 28, 1981), was ignored by all the major media.

The next month, however, the *Los Angeles Times* did run a short opinion piece by John Dinges who was the first American newsperson to comb through the documents themselves only to discover that they failed to support State Department claims regarding Soviet and Cuban shipments of two hundred tons of modern arms. "Reading the documents," observed Dinges, "it is impossible to determine where the numbers come from. The State Department has declined further elaboration on its conclusions, and has stopped providing copies of the original documents."[64]

Only in June, almost a half-year after the White Paper, the *Wall Street Journal* and the *Washington Post*—publications that previously had gone along with the State Department's propaganda campaign (the *Post* had refused to print Dinge's telling exposure of the documents even though he was a member of their staff)—ran critical reports finding that the White Paper contained "factual errors, misleading statements and unresolved ambiguities that raise questions about the administration's interpretation of participation by communist countries in the Salvadoran civil war."[65] But by then the White Paper had served its purpose of frightening Congress into voting a dramatic increase in military aid (from $5 million to $30 million) to the Salvadoran generals and allowing the administration to send U.S. military and counterinsurgency "advisers" to that country.

The *Wall Street Journal* and *Washington Post* stories might be taken as evidence of how the press can correct itself, even if belatedly. But in the face of long-standing propaganda about Red puppetry these two exposés hardly counted for very much. Not long after their appearance, commentaries reappeared, telling how the Salvadoran rebellion was orchestrated by foreign communist powers. Thus *Washington Post* columnist Stephen Rosenfeld could write that "the embers were glowing in El Salvador," but Cuba and Nicaragua "supplied the fuel and the bellows that turned them into fire—in the name of revolution."[66] And the *New York Times* could editorialize about the need to find effective ways of rallying "the hemisphere against meddling by Cuba and Nicaragua in other nations' conflicts."[67] In the communication universe, the truth breaks through like an occasional light. But when the light passes, the darkness takes over again and the cold war, interventionist, anticommunist lies are reiterated as if they had never been refuted.

"INFERIOR" PEOPLES AND THEIR "ANTI-AMERICANISM"

For centuries imperialists have justified their mistreatment of other peoples by portraying them as wanting in ethical, cultural, and political development. If there be turmoil in some part of the Third World, then the trouble supposedly rests with the people themselves and not with anything the intruders are doing to them. When the U.S.-supported coup overthrew Allende and led to the bloody repression of the Pinochet regime, "blaming the people" became the media's favorite explanation. Thus CBS commentator Eric Sevareid opined that the Chilean people brought it on themselves, another Latin American example of "an instability so chronic that the root causes have to lie in the nature and culture of the people."[68] By way of explaining why Chileans would support Allende and the Popular Unity government, Barnard Collier wrote in the New York Times Magazine, "The Chileans do not believe in facts, numbers or statistics with the earnest faith of an English-speaking people."[69]

While talking to a correspondent who had just reported on the rebellion and famine in Tigray, NBC anchorperson Tom Brokaw could only think of asking, "You're in London now, which is one of the most sophisticated and civilized cities in the world. Do you have much culture shock after being in that part of Africa?"[70] The riots that occurred in India in the wake of Prime Minister Indira Gandhi's assassination evoked this comment from a CBS news correspondent (November 1, 1984): "Things like that always happen in India. This is how things end in India—never. They simmer, then boil over, and explode again and again."

The negative and racist representations of Arabs and Islam in the American media are too numerous to record here and have already been thoroughly critiqued by Edward Said and others.[71] Perhaps one or two examples might suffice: A CBS correspondent in the Middle East ended his report by saying, "But of course sound argument has not always dictated Arab behavior."[72] In a series of articles about Islam, New York Times columnist Flora Lewis quoted "expert" opinion that Arabic poetry is "rhetorical and declamatory, not intimate and personal," thereby revealing her abysmal ignorance of Arab poetry and her readiness to embrace an anti-Arab stereotype. She also described "the Islamic mind" as unable to employ "step-by-step thinking," an assertion which, had it been applied to "the Christian mind" or "Hebrew mind," would likely have been denounced by the *Times* as nonsensical and bigoted.[73]

Not surprisingly, the Russians are another people who have been the target of stereotypic pronouncements from the press. One reads and hears that Russians are "unsmiling," "rude," and "unable to look you in the eye."[74] Robert Kaiser, former *Washington Post* correspondent, declared that "the Russians have a great urge for order. It is part of their personality."[75] And ABC commentator Barbara Walters talked about how the Russian people lack "a sense of responsibility because they are told what to do, when to do it."[76]

Conflicts that arise between the United States and oppressed peoples are explained away as manifestations of the latter's "anti-Americanism." During the 1979 Iranian hostage crisis, ABC asked an "expert" whether being a Shiite Muslim meant being "anti-American," he replied that it did.[77] Over film footage of Muslim crowds chanting "God is great," ABC commentator Frank Reynolds voiced what he supposed was their real meaning: "hatred of America." Similarly CBS's Walter Cronkite spoke of "Muslim hatred of this country."[78] When thousands marched in the Philippines against the abominated Marcos regime, the *New York Times* reported, "Anti-Marcos and anti-American slogans and banners were in abundance, with the most common being 'Down with the U.S.-Marcos Dictatorship!' "[79] A week later, the *Times* again described Filippino protests against U.S. support of the Marcos dictatorship as "anti-Americanism."[80]

Since the end of World War II, the press has regularly treated Soviet opposition to such specific U.S. policies as the rearming of West Germany, the escalation of nuclear arms, and U.S. intervention in Cuba, Southeast Asia, and elsewhere as manifestations of anti-American sentiment and hostility toward the United States. After noting that the Ethiopian revolution of 1974 "grew out of a general despair with prevailing conditions, without much ideology behind it," the *Washington Post* then claimed the revolution had an "anti-American thrust"[81]—when it might more accurately be called anti-capitalist and anti-imperialist.

Protests in Mexico, Argentina, Cuba, Nicaragua, and other Latin American nations against CIA counterinsurgency have all been reduced by the American press to expressions of anti-Americanism. The same with protests in West Germany, England, and other Western nations against the placement of U.S. cruise and Pershing missiles in Europe. In this way the press can ascribe the opposition directed against U.S. policies to some kind of nationalistic prejudice within the protesters and can ignore the substance of the protest. Thus the West Germans do not dislike us for putting missiles on their soil, rather they oppose the missiles because they dislike us. And as previously noted, they are anti-American, as John Vinocur, a *New York Times* editor claimed, because they suffer from a "malaise" and an "Angst" that come in part from a lack of sufficient authority.[82]

THE LIMITS OF ACTUALITY

Despite the faithful service it performs, the press is not always successful in producing news that is pleasing to corporate and governmental leaders. On infrequent occasions, either in response to the anti-interventionist sentiment found among large sectors of the public and within Congress, or because self-censorship does not operate with perfect effect, the press will run stories and commentaries that cast a critical light upon this or that policy. Recall, for instance, how the *New York Times* criticized the lies used by the State Department to justify the invasion of Grenada, or the unique CBS special, "Central America in Revolt," aired March 20, 1982, which informed the American public that the CIA overthrew "perhaps the only democratically elected president in Guatemalan history" and which actually talked about conditions of class oppression in Guatemala and interviewed guerrillas who described the evolution of their movement from political to armed struggle. Consider also the several guest opinion columns in the *Washington Post* and *New York Times* that have offererd a critical perspective of U.S. policy in Central America, including one in the *Post* by Miguel D'Escoto, foreign minister of Nicaragua, who wrote an informative defense of the Nicaraguan elections.[83]

Mainstream press reports that challenge the official view are relatively few in number, lacking the kind of repetition and follow-up needed to create a persuasive and enduring climate of opinion around them. They are particularistic offerings linked to no generalizable critique, floating past us in the great tide of establishment news and commentary. While iconoclastic views may on rare occasions make their way into the news, the general thrust is never out-of-step for too long with the procapitalist, antisocialist, cold war containment perspective propagated by the government. This establishment view with its massive omissions, background assumptions, preordained images, and coded vocabulary about U.S. virtue and Communist evil carries the day.

Political leaders, however, seldom appreciate the supportive function the media perform on their behalf. They see the press as merely doing its job when it pushes the official line, and as falling down on the job on those infrequent occasions it does anything less. Instances of relatively unfiltered information and critical commentary in an otherwise controlled (or self-controlled) information field are disturbing to policymakers, who treat anything short of unanimous support for their undertakings as evidence of irresponsible and harmful media behavior. Expecting the press corps to be a press chorus, the political leader, like any imperious maestro, reacts sharply to the occasionally discordant note.

However, these infrequent deviations are not the main cause of friction between officialdom and the press. There is a larger question of "responsibility." To be sure, the media know how to be "responsible," how to be as deaf, dumb, and blind as the government wants. For instance, members of the press knew the United States was flying U-2 planes over Soviet territory; they knew Washington was planning an invasion of Cuba at the Bay of Pigs; they knew there were facts about the Tonkin Bay incident in Vietnam that differed from the official version; they knew the United States was engaged in a massive, prolonged saturation bombing of Cambodia; they knew the United States was lending a helping hand in the mass slaughter of Indonesians, Guatemalans, and Salvadorans. But in each instance they chose to act "responsibly" by not informing the American public. Journalistic responsibility should mean the unearthing of true and significant information. But the "responsibility" demanded by government officials and often agreed to by the press means the opposite—the burying of information precisely because it is troublesomely true and significant.

Despite its best efforts, however, there are limits to how much the press can finesse reality. These are the limits of propaganda itself, as Dr. Goebbels discovered when trying to explain to the German public how invincible Nazi armies could win victory after victory while retreating on both fronts in 1944 and 1945. To maintain credibility and audience interest, the press must do more than issue supportive reports about official policy—even if that remains its main activity. While seeing the world pretty much through the same ideological lens as government elites, the media also find it necessary to say something about *some* of the inescapable realities that corporate-political elites would prefer to leave unnoticed.

Coverage of troublesome realities, even if essentially sympathetic to the policymaker—as it almost always is—can itself prove troublesome. News from Central America and the Third World, for instance, while heavily skewed to the dominant ideology, still contains images of violent involvement in a foreign land, an engagement that most Americans see as not in their interests. The sending of U.S. forces to Lebanon may be portrayed as a peace-keeping mission, but the slaughter of 261 marines is a reality that cannot be ignored and outweighs any positive framing the press might lend to the venture. Similarly, for years the press transmitted the official view of the Vietnam War but again the persistence of a costly conflict outweighed the upbeat predictions and anticommunist rationales manufactured by both the government and the media. The press could omit and distort what happened in Indochina but it could not totally ignore the awful *actuality* of the event itself.

This effort by the media to make some minimal response to reality, even while attempting to invent another reality, sometimes educates the public in ways unintended by the communicators and unwelcomed by the policymakers. Rather than responding only to the manifest content, filled with images and arguments about how the United States is fighting Communism and saving democracy, the public eventually picks up on the *latent* message: war, U.S. involvement, death, destruction, more taxes, and the draft. Thus despite the best efforts of the Reagan administration at news-managing the El Salvador story, and despite the active collaboration of the press, a majority of the public, according to most polls, still feared that El Salvador would become another Vietnam, opposed sending U.S. troops and U.S. aid, and said they would support young men who refused to be drafted to fight in Central America.[84]

Now if the public does not support a policy, the administration concludes it cannot be because of anything wanting in the policy but in the way the media packaged it. Leaders are often tempted to blame the press when things go wrong with their plans or when policies fall into public disfavor. If the press had not said this or that, had held its tongue or cast things in a more favorable light, then the leader presumably would have had less trouble managing the world, and certainly less trouble managing the U.S. public. The press, as shown in the preceding pages, faithfully serves the official viewpoint, but it cannot *always* do so in just the Alice-in-Wonderland way policymakers might want while still retaining its own credibility as an information conduit and its effectiveness as an opinion manager. By the very act of going after the news—however superficially and narrowly—the press sometimes encounters the limits of actuality and therefore introduces elements of reality that may activate public resistance. So every administration has complained, in effect, that the press either does not do its job (or does it too well). So President Reagan argued that the media should exercise "self-censorship" and should "trust us and put themselves in our hands," consulting with officials and holding back stories "that will result in harm to our nation."[85]

The press insists that it already does that very thing and that the government officials do not appreciate how cooperative it can and wants to be. Leading journalists like James Reston of the *New York Times* have complained that the government has refused to take newspeople into its confidence on important matters even though they have demonstrated their trustworthiness by holding back on stories.[86] While quick to proclaim its independence, the press is equally quick to remind leaders that it shares the same basic view of the world as do they and the same commitment to (and definition of) the national interest. But officials suspect that even a sympathetic and well-kept press can create headaches.

In relation to the state, the press remains like the adolescent who wants both more input into family decisions and more independence from them. As usual, the press sees no contradiction between its professed dedication to "objectivity" (telling it like it is and letting the chips fall where they may) and its professed dedication to "cooperation" and "responsibility" (suppressing troublesome stories). Political leaders, however, do see a contradiction and refuse to trust the press completely, even though they are willing to use it as much as possible. So the press remains the restive adolescent of a seemingly ungrateful parent—never totally independent nor totally trusted and denied both complete autonomy and full partnership.

Notes

1. Edward S. Herman, *The Real Terror Network* (Boston: South End Press, 1982).

2. For readings on Guatemala see John Fried, Marvin Gettleman, Deborah Levenson, and Nancy Pekenham, *Guatemala in Rebellion* (New York: Grove, 1983).

3. *Time*, April 16, 1984.

4. Manuel de Varona, quoted in the *New York Daily News*, January 8, 1961.

5. Victor Bernstein and Jesse Gordon, "The Press and the Bay of Pigs," Columbia University Forum reprint, Fall 1967.

6. Robert Cirino, *Power to Persuade* (New York: Bantam, 1974); also Bernstein and Gordon, "The Press and the Bay of Pigs."

7. *New York Times*, January 8, 1961; *Time*, January 13, 1961; for a fuller discussion see Bernstein and Gordon, "The Press and the Bay of Pigs."

8. *New York Times*, January 8, 1961.

9. Neal Houghton, "The Cuban Invasion of 1961 and the U.S. Press, in Retrospect," *Journalism Quarterly*, 42, Summer 1965, pp. 423–24.

10. Ibid.; see for instance Hanson Baldwin's column, *New York Times*, August 1, 1961, and Tad Szulc's article in *Look*, July 18, 1961.

11. ABC evening news, November 9, 1984; *Washington Post*, November 11, 1984; see also Kevin Kelley's discussion in the *Guardian*, November 21, 1984.

12. *New York Times* editorial, March 30, 1983.

13. See Marvin Gettleman et al., *El Salvador: Central America and the New Cold War* (New York: Grove, 1981).

14. Gettleman et al., *El Salvador: Central America and the New Cold War.*

15. Joseph Collins, *What Difference Could a Revolution Make?* (San Francisco: Institute for Food and Development Policy, 1982).

16. For a striking exception, see the excellent series of articles by A. Kent MacDougall in the *Los Angeles Times*, November 2–15, 1984, on the disparities between rich and poor in the Third World. While MacDougall does not indict capitalism as a system, he does show how "industrialization" and propertied classes in the Third World have done little for the mass of people and have actually increased poverty and the concentration of wealth.

17. *New York Times*, August 19, 1981.

18. Lincoln Smith, "Where's the Solidarity for Workers in Turkey?" *Daily World*, April 8, 1982. Smith cites findings from the World Federation of Trade Unions investigation of Turkey; see also Joyce Chediac, "Turkey: the Secret El Salvador," *Workers World*, February 19, 1982; and Mehmet Demir, "Turkey: Repression Tightens Grip as Rightwing Gathers Strength," *Guardian*, September 12, 1984.

19. Herman, *The Real Terror Network*, p. 197.

20. *Washington Post*, September 16, 1984; *New York Times*, August 26, 1984.

21. Associated Press report in *Philadelphia Inquirer*, October 29, 1981.

22. Amnesty International report, August 1982; and Amnesty International newsletter, January 1981; also Fried et al., *Guatemala in Rebellion.*

23. NBC evening news, February 19, 1980.

24. *Christian Science Monitor*, July 9, 1980.

25. *New York Times*, July 8, 1981.

26. Gettleman et al., *El Salvador: Central America and the New Cold War*; also Cynthia Arnson, "White Paper," *Nation*, May 9, 1981.

27. Roger Morris, Shelly Mueller and William Jelin, "Through the Looking Glass in Chile," *Columbia Journalism Review*, November/December 1974.

28. See the case studies in chapter 10. For a recent account of socialist reconstruction in Vietnam, see Kathleen Gough, *Ten Times More Beautiful: The Rebuilding of Vietnam* (New York: Monthly Review, 1978).

29. See Alexander Sukhostat, "Nicaragua—Defending the Revolution," *Political Affairs*, December 1981, pp. 28–35; Collins, *What Difference Could a Revolution Make?*

30. Fried et al., *Guatemala in Rebellion*; also Stephen Schlesinger and Stephen Kinzer, *Bitter Fruit* (Garden City, N.Y.: Anchor Press, 1983).

31. *Washington Post*, November 25, 1981; November 10, 1981; and editorial, March 28, 1984.

32. Peter Marchetti interviewed in *Monthly Review*, July/August 1982.

33. CBS evening news, October 12, 1983.

34. For instance, *Washington Post*, November 25, 1981.

35. *New York Times* editorial, October 26, 1983.

36. *Washington Post*, December 25, 1981.

37. See for instance the *New York Times* story on unrest in Argentina, December 20, 1982.

38. *New York Times*, August 5, 1984.

39. Sukhostat, "Nicaragua—Defending the Revolution."

Variations on a Theme for Counterrevolution 211

40. *Washington Post* editorial, November 10, 1981.
41. "A Tottering Structure of Lies," *Sojourner,* December 1983.
42. *Washington Post,* December 7, 1983.
43. *New York Times,* March 17, 1975.
44. See the discussion in Alex Keyssar, "Reporting the Revolution: Portugal and the American Press," *Nieman Reports,* Summer 1975, pp. 3–7; also my "Portugal and the Press," *Progressive,* December 1975, pp. 43–45.
45. Morris et al., "Through the Looking Glass . . ." p. 25.
46. William Leogrande and Carla Anne Robbins, "Oligarchs and Officers," *Foreign Affairs,* Summer 1980, pp. 1084–1103.
47. DC CISPIS report, August 1984 (Washington, D.C.: Committee in Solidarity with the People of El Salvador).
48. *New York Times* editorial, October 7, 1984.
49. *Washington Post* editorial, May 8, 1984. For an in-depth study of U.S.-staged elections in the Dominican Republic, Vietnam (during the U.S. occupation), and El Salvador, see Edward Herman and Frank Brodhead, *Demonstration Elections* (Boston: South End Press, 1984).
50. *New York Times* editorial, March 30, 1984.
51. ABC evening news, March 28, 1984.
52. Edward S. Herman, "The New York Times on the 1984 Salvadoran and Nicaraguan Elections," *CovertAction Information Bulletin* (Spring 1984), p. 10.
53. Ibid.
54. One of the few exceptions was the guest column by Miguel D'Escoto, Nicaraguan foreign minister, in the *Washington Post,* October 1, 1984.
55. Herman, "The New York Times on the 1984 . . ." p. 11.
56. *Time,* November 19, 1984.
57. See the report: "Nicaragua-Baiting," *Nation,* November 24, 1984.
58. *New York Times,* March 12, 1984; August 26, 1984; and November 4, 1984; respectively.
59. *Los Angeles Times,* November 5, 1984.
60. *Washington Post,* November 4, 1984.
61. *New York Times,* January 4, 1981.
62. NBC evening news, February 20, 1981; see the discussion in Jonathan Evan Maslow and Ana Arana, "Operation El Salvador," *Columbia Journalism Review,* May/June 1981, p. 55.
63. ABC evening news, February 23, 1981.
64. John Dinges, "White Paper or Blank Paper?" *Los Angeles Times,* March 17, 1981.
65. *Washington Post,* June 9, 1981; see also *Wall Street Journal,* June 8, 1981. The information on the Post's rejection of the Dinges article is from a conversation I had with Dinges in October 1984.
66. *Washington Post,* November 6, 1984.
67. *New York Times,* December 8, 1982.
68. CBS evening news, September 13, 1973.
69. *New York Times Magazine,* May 7, 1972.
70. NBC evening news, November 29, 1984.
71. Edward Said, *Orientalism* (New York: Pantheon, 1978); his *Covering Islam* (New York: Pantheon, 1981); and Laurence Michalak, *Cruel and Unusual: Negative Images of Arabs in Popular American Culture* (Washington, D.C.: American-Arab Antidiscrimination Committee, January 1984).
72. Robert Cirino, *The Power to Persuade* (New York: Pathfinder, 1974), p. 53.

73. *New York Times*, December 30, 1979.

74. For instance, Stephen Radchenko's report on a trip to the USSR in *City Paper*, Washington, D.C., July 13, 1984.

75. Kaiser appeared on *20/20*, an ABC program, November 22, 1984.

76. Walters was hosting *20/20* November 22, 1984.

77. ABC evening news, November 21, 1979. The interview was with Professor J.C. Hurewitz.

78. Said, *Covering Islam*.

79. *New York Times*, August 22, 1984.

80. *New York Times*, August 28, 1984.

81. *Washington Post*, September 13, 1984.

82. *New York Times Magazine*, November 15, 1981; and the discussion in chapter 6.

83. *Washington Post*, October 1, 1984.

84. CBS-Washington Post opinion polls in 1982; see Dan Hallen, "For Media, It's Not Another Vietman," *In These Times*, April 14, 1982.

85. Hallen, *op. cit.*, quoting from an interview of Reagan in *TV Guide*.

86. For Reston's (and the *New York Times's*) role in censoring the Bay of Pigs story, see Gay Talese, *The Kingdom and the Power* (New York: World Publishing, 1969).

12

Methods of Misrepresentation

No communication system can report everything that happens in public life. Some selectivity is inevitable, and, by its nature, selectivity is conducive to a measure of bias. But even if total objectivity is unattainable, we might still aspire to standards of fairness and accuracy in reporting and try to develop a critical analysis of how the news is distorted.[1] What follows is a discussion of some journalistic methods of misrepresentation. Much of the pertinent illustrative material has been presented in preceding chapters.

IS IT PROCESS OR PROPAGANDA?

We have noted the media's tendency to favor personality over issue, event over content, official positions over popular grievances, the atypical and sensational over the modal and systemic. Supposedly these biases inhere in the nature of the media themselves, specifically the routine newsgathering practices of reporters, the visual nature of the camera, the limitations of media budgets, the limitations of broadcast time and print space, poor journalistic preparation, the market need to accentuate the sensational and eye-catching, and the need to reduce a complex happening to a concise story. Certainly these are real factors. But news production is not a purely autonomous process, responsive only to its own internal imperatives. As we have seen, many distortions are of a more political nature and reveal a pattern of bias that favors the dominant class ideology. If the selective factor is merely a need to be entertaining and sensational, why are so many dreary news items (for example, visiting dignitaries at the White House, vacuous official announcements, heat waves and cold spells in Europe) given consistently generous coverage, while many interesting and even sensational things are regularly suppressed. What is the principle of selectivity involved?

213

Why is the Tylenol poisoning of several people by a deranged individual (or individuals) big news, but the death of many more persons from unsafe drugs marketed by supposedly reputable companies not news? Why is a plane crash killing forty-three people headline news, while the far more sensational story of the industrial brown-lung poisoning of thousands of factory workers remains a suppressed story for years? Why does the press rapturously report the pope's endless trips abroad while ignoring the involvement of his priests in the struggles of the world's poor—until the pope attacks them for such involvement? Why are unsubstantiated government charges about Soviet chemical warfare treated as top news while the telling refutations by scientists are suppressed or slighted? There is nothing in the inherent logic of media technology or in the nature of the newsgathering process that explains these disparities but there is much in the underlying structure of political and economic interest that does.

What is it about the dynamics of newsgathering and the foibles of reporters that obliges the press to treat capitalism as a benign system and socialism as a pernicious one? Not much. But there is plenty to explain that bias in the pattern of ownership and control, the vested class interests, the financial muscle of big advertisers, and the entire capitalist social and cultural order.

During the Watergate scandal, we heard a great deal about John Mitchell, H. R. Haldeman, John Dean, and John Erlichman; but Claude Wild, William Keeler, Orin Atkins, and some twenty other top business executives remained unknown to most of us even though they also were convicted of Watergate crimes. As top donors of dirty money, these businessmen were all given suspended sentences, light fines—and what amounts to media protection. The corporate financial underpinnings of Watergate, Andrew Kopkind noted, were never exposed by an American press that has seldom been ready to publicize big business influence over public policy.[2] Again, there was nothing in the nature of the media as such, but much in the nature of the politico-economic structure of which the media are an integral part that explains why one set of names in the Watergate cover-up was widely publicized while another set was hardly touched by the national media.

To continue: There is nothing in the limitations of time, space, and staff that oblige the media systematically to ignore third-party presidential candidates while assigning an army of journalists the agonizing task of having to file a "new" story every day of the campaign about major candidates who seldom say anything new. But there is something about progressive third-party candidates themselves, their attempts at raising questions about the desirability of the corporate capitalist system, that makes them politically unsafe for national media coverage.

The media's intermittent fascination with "international terrorism" might be seen by some as the press just doing its thing, seizing upon a sensational theme of political violence and villainy. But in fact, the press is doing the *government's* thing, reporting a "threat," then dropping it, then resuscitating it again as a sensational new story in perfect orchestration with official pronouncements. Terrorism may naturally lend itself to media hype, as some people would contend; but the U.S.-sponsored state terrorism of many despotic Third World regimes, having a scope and ferocity far exceeding what the U.S. press and government normally define as terrorism, receives relatively little notice and even when mentioned is seldom linked to U.S. policies.

An example of this might be the non-stories of Indonesia and East Timor. In 1965 the Indonesian army overthrew left-leaning President Achmed Sukarno and embarked upon a murderous campaign to eradicate the Indonesian Communist Party and the entire left; they slaughtered about a half million people (some estimates are as high as a million) in what was the greatest genocidal action since the Nazi Holocaust.[3] Here was a sensational story if ever there was one, but it was almost three months before it broke in the American press, in *Time* magazine, and a month after that before the *New York Times* carried a rather brief report.[4] This mass atrocity was treated, if at all, in a fatalistic tone, with a striking lack of indignation or critical editorial comment, as if the victims were just the unfortunate figures in some tragedy ordained by destiny.

Except for one or two passing and even congratulatory references, the press had nothing to say about the role of the CIA and the U.S. military in arming and assisting the Indonesian generals before, during, and after the bloody takeover. The press also had nothing of substance to say about the economic interests underlying the coup: the abolition of Sukarno's land reform program, the destruction of Communist Party libraries, clinics, cooperatives, and schools, the massive dispossession of peasants, the widening gap between village rich and poor, the post-coup influx of American, Dutch, and Japanese corporations, the power of the "Tokyo Club" of financiers who rescheduled Indonesia's debts in exchange for more exploitative investment terms, and the takeover of Indonesia's mineral resources by foreign firms.

The subsequent slaughter perpetrated by the Indonesian military in East Timor from 1976 onward is another sensational and terrible story suppressed or underplayed by the U.S. press. When East Timor, a Portuguese colony at the eastern edge of the Indonesian archipelago, was granted independence by Lisbon in 1975, a brief struggle ensued on the island between Timorese elites and a popular leftist organization called Fretilin, with the latter emerging triumphant. Soon after, the Indonesian military invaded East Timor, engaging in a murderous counterinsurgency campaign against the Timorese population which included the systematic destruction of whole villages, crop destruction and defoliation, and the creation of concentration camps in which tens of thousands of victims perished.[5] The Indonesian policy of extermination destroyed about half of the Timorese people. As of 1985 the destruction of East Timor continued and the U.S. media continued to treat this remarkable, sensational story as nonexistent.

It could be argued that places like Indonesia and East Timor are just too remote and obscure to win the attention of an American press noted for its generally deficient foreign news coverage. But during the days of Sukarno's realm, when Indonesia was taking an openly anti-imperialistic stance, it was regularly—and negatively—covered by the U.S. press. And as for East Timor, Noam Chomsky observed that the New York Times index gave six full columns of citations to remote Timor in 1975 when Fretilin was emerging the victor and the situation was of great concern to the State Department and the CIA. In 1977, however, as the Indonesian army's war of annihilation reached awesome proportions, the Times index gave Timor only five lines.[6] Politics rather than geography determined the amount of coverage.

For twenty years or more, successive famines in Ethiopia and other African nations were given only perfunctory media attention. The famine of 1984 and 1985, one of the severest, which gripped at least twelve nations in Africa was again afforded slight play, except for Ethiopia, which—now an avowedly Marxist-Leninist nation—became the focus of a news hype not seen since Polish Solidarity days. Here supposedly was a Communist regime that could not or would not feed its people, a favorite media theme. When famine can be turned into an anticommunist story, it becomes big news.

Favorable stories about socialist or emerging leftist revolutionary economies are not assigned by editors nor tolerated by media executives and owners. The suppression of positive news from socialist countries is so persistent and pervasive as to suggest that something more than insufficiencies in foreign coverage, lackadaisical journalists, and space limitations are at the heart of the matter. When we see that news selectivity is likely to be on the side of those who have power, position, and wealth, we move from a liberal complaint about the press's poor job to a radical analysis of how the press fulfills its system-supporting function.

Sometimes omissions and suppressions are not enough and the press lends itself to the dissemination of outright lies. One way to lie is to accept at face value what are known to be lies, passing them on to the public without adequate countervailing response. *Face-value framing* has characterized the press's performance from the McCarthy era down to more recent times, including most everything the government says about Nicaragua, the Soviets, yellow rain, Grenada, KGB "penetration," civil rights, labor disputes, or whatever. Without ever saying a particular story is true or not, but treating it at face value, the press engages in the propagation of misinformation—while maintaining it is being merely noncommittal and objective. When challenged on this, some reporters will argue that they cannot inject their own personal judgments into their reports, an argument that overlooks the fact that they are not being asked to—and, in any case, often already do so. My criticism is that they (or their editors and owners) fail to do what they claim they do, give us a range of information and views that might allow us to form opinions contrary to the ones that permeate their news reports. Referring to a speech President Reagan made in March 1984, one critic notes:

> The speech was filled with enough accusations of Communist subversion to make one wonder if the White House had hired Joe McCarthy's ghost as a speechwriter. It would seem important for Americans to realize that many of the things their president had just told them were at best unproved assertions or one-sided interpretations and at worst demonstrably false statements. Yet not one of the network commentators pointed this out in the post-speech summary, and neither did the next day's accounts in the *New York Times* or the *Washington Post*. To do so would have implied that the president was either a liar or a fool, hardly a politically neutral message. Instead objectivity prevailed over accuracy.[7]

More to the point, the *appearance* of objectivity, as achieved through face-value framing, prevailed over accuracy.

Untruths that are repeated again and again in every major national medium soon take on a life of their own, to be passed on sometimes with little conscious awareness that a fabrication has been disseminated. But along with the transformation of falsehood into unconscious "fact," there are still plenty of plain old deliberate lies. A report from Indonesia by Gerald Stone in the *London Times* (September 2, 1975) found that the Indonesian press was spreading false stories about widespread atrocities by the Timorese liberation force, Fretilin, as part of "a purposeful campaign to plant lies." But when *Newsweek* prepared Stone's story for an American audience, it had him reporting on the "devastation" and "bloodbath" caused by "the Marxist Fretilin party." *Newsweek* made it appear as if Stone had found the atrocity stories to be true when in fact he had found them to be lies.[8] This was more than a case of sloppy inaccuracy; it was an instance of conscious deliberate misrepresentation.

UNBALANCED TREATMENT

In accordance with the canons of good journalism, reporters are supposed to balance their stories, tapping competing sources to get both sides of a dispute. However, as we have seen, even when statements from both sides are presented, they often are not accorded equal space, positioning, and framing. Furthermore, the rule overlooks the fact that *both* sides may not be *all* sides, and that important but less visible interests, extending beyond the confines of the immediate issue, are habitually shut out of the news.

In any case, even this minimal rule of getting "both sides" often falls by the wayside, sometimes because of space limitations, the pressure of deadlines, careless reporting, and other such factors, but more often because of the political bias that dominates news production. Those who have power, position, and wealth are less likely to be slighted in news reports than those who have not. On the infrequent occasions when wealthy and powerful interests are attacked in the media, they are almost certain to be accorded adequate space to respond. But the media are less energetic in their search for a competing viewpoint if it must be elicited from labor leaders, student demonstrators, peace advocates, Black or Latino protesters, Communists, Third World insurgents, the poor, the oppressed, or other politically marginal and dissident interests (except dissidents from socialist countries who are accorded the kind of news coverage and favorable editorial comment that heads-of-state might envy). For example, observing press reports on Africa, one critic concludes: "Even when American newsmen take the trouble to visit Black Africa, they seem incapable of talking to ordinary people about what is happening to their country."[9] *Time* and *Newsweek* articles on the struggles in Namibia, for instance, concentrated on the concerns and efforts of South African military commanders and officials in Pretoria, Geneva, and Washington, but offered no statements from the Namibian revolutionaries or other Namibians.[10]

In an earlier chapter, I noted how the McCarthy model predominates. A high official, usually the president or a cabinet secretary, makes an outlandish charge about "Soviet terrorism" or "KGB penetration" and the press dutifully runs the story—again and again—without presenting an alternative view. Twice in three minutes, NBC news reported President Reagan's charge that the airport being built by revolutionary Grenada was for "Soviet and Cuban military purposes."[11] Not once did NBC ask the president to explain how he knew the airport was intended for military purposes rather than for tourism as the Grenadians maintained. Not once did NBC allow a Grenadian representative or American critic of the president's policy to offer evidence to the contrary.[12]

Regarding the Geneva arms talks of 1985, President Reagan described himself as optimistic because "this is the first time [the Soviets] have ever publicly stated a desire to reduce the number of their weapons."[13] CBS carried this incredible comment without bothering to point out that the Soviets have made repeated overtures to reduce nuclear weapons, including the previous year's unilateral offer to decrease their intermediate range missiles in Europe from 800 to 162. When dealing with the Soviets or other Communists, the press feels no need for balance.

What the press lacks in balance, it sometimes makes up for in *false* balancing, as when it tries to create an impression of evenhandedness by placing equal blame on parties that are not equally culpable. Thus, for years the news media ascribed the killings in Guatemala and El Salvador to "extremists of both the left and right" when in fact almost all the killings were done by rightist death squads linked to the military. The false balancing created a false impression: A massive state terrorism against popular organizations was reduced to a gang war between leftist and rightist outlaws. False balancing also allows journalists to adopt a condemnatory view of all sides, both those who are fighting for and those fighting against, social justice. In this way the press manages to keep an equal distance from both falsehood and the truth.

Another way to stack the deck with false balancing is to employ a double standard in interviews. For instance, Ted Koppel, friend and admirer of conservatives like George Will and Henry Kissinger (and who in 1984 earned $750,000 as host of ABC's *Nightline*), has gained a reputation for asking probing inquiries. Indeed he does, except that he challenges viewpoints that veer somewhat leftward far more vigorously than those that stay snugly mainstream. Hostile probes can sometimes give a respondent the opportunity to offer clarifying arguments, assuming the person is up to the task and is allowed enough time. But the overall impression left by an antagonistic interview is that there is something highly questionable about the interviewee. Conversely, the effect of a friendly interview is to send a cue to the audience that the respondent is to be trusted and believed.

FRAMING

The most effective propaganda is that which relies on framing rather than on falsehood. By bending the truth rather than breaking it, using emphasis, nuance, innuendo, and peripheral embellishments, communicators can create a desired impression without resorting to explicit advocacy and without departing too far from the appearance of objectivity. Framing is achieved in the way the news is packaged, the amount of exposure, the placement (front page or back, lead story or last), the tone of presentation (sympathetic or slighting), the accompanying headlines and visual effects, and the labeling and vocabulary. Just short of lying, the media can mislead us in a variety of ways, telling us what to think about a story before we have had a chance to think about it for ourselves.

One common framing method is to select labels and other vocabulary designed to convey politically loaded images. These labels and phrases, like the masks in a Greek drama, convey positive or negative cues regarding events and persona, often without benefit of—and usually as a substitute for—supportive information. Thus, on CBS television news Dan Rather referred retrospectively to the Black civil rights movement and student antiwar movement as "the civil disturbances of the sixties." How different an impression would have been created had he labeled them "movements for peace and justice," or "movements against military intervention and for racial equality."[14] Other examples of labeling:

· A news story in the *Los Angeles Times* described Nicaraguan leader Daniel Ortega's denunciation of U.S. policy as being "as strident as ever," implying that Ortega was given to excessive and unjustified attacks.[15] The report said nothing about U.S. policy itself or about the content of Ortega's criticism—which readers might not have found "strident."
· A report in the *Washington Post* described a province in El Salvador as "guerrilla-infested," rather than "guerrilla-controlled" or "prorevolutionary," thereby reducing the insurgent populace to a kind of lice.[16]
· In a *Washington Post* story filed from Paris, we read that "many French political commentators, as well as the Kremlin's propagandists" were complaining about the course of French foreign policy. The French have "commentators," the Soviets have "propagandists."[17]
· Throughout the 1984 press coverage of the Lebanon crisis, the press incessantly referred to the "Soviet-made" antiaircraft mis-

siles and other arms possessed by the Syrians and Lebanese. But at no time were the Israeli arms described as "U.S.-made"— which they were. The impression left was that the Soviets were somehow the instigators in what was actually an Israeli invasion of Lebanon.

· During the Geneva arms negotiations of 1982 and 1983, the news media repeatedly referred to "offers" made by the United States regarding the deployment of its intermediate range missiles, and "demands" made by the Soviets. Thus a headline in the *Washington Post* read, "SOVIET DEMANDS SEEN IMPERILING TALKS IN GENEVA,"[18] (seen by U.S. officials, that is).

· On CBS evening news, Dan Rather framed a Soviet proposal as follows: "The Soviet Union today made another propaganda peace pitch designed to enhance its image in Western Europe," calling for the "mutual nonuse of military force" in Europe. Rather's only other comment was that "the West rejected" the suggestion as "not negotiable."[19] No lie was uttered here. The Soviets indeed did make the proposal, and the United States did reject it. But by labeling the Soviet move as "another propaganda peace pitch," Rather let us know that the U.S. rejection was the only sensible move—without giving us an explanation as to why this was so.

· CBS television news, on another occasion, referred to the U.S. cruise and Pershing missiles being placed in Europe as "necessary" for the defense of Western Europe. But CBS did not say a word about their strategic first strike capacity and their destabilizing effect in reducing the U.S. attack time to a few minutes, which minimizes or even obliterates the Soviet capacity for deterrence.[20] Soviet intermediate range missiles, however, were described by CBS as "growing in numbers" and "an increasing menace to Western Europe." By labeling Soviet intermediate missiles (which in fact were not destabilizing—having no strategic capacity to reach U.S. strategic missiles) as a threat, and U.S. missiles as purely defensive, CBS and the other national media could present a simple but misleading picture, in accordance with the Reagan administration's nuclear arms policy.

· At one time or another, President Reagan labeled the Soviets as "those monsters," "our adversaries," and "the enemy."[21] Taking such terms at face value the press gave them wide circulation and unchallenged credibility. The endless negative stereotypes, unburdened by any factual particulars, *assume* that we and the Soviets are locked in some inexorable adversarial relation against which all other policy considerations must be measured.

"Disinformation" may not always be the right word for this kind of media message, for disinformation implies that false and fabricated evidence has been disseminated. But in such instances, *no evidence of any kind,* no matter how false, has been offered. Given the anti-Soviet orthodoxy of the U.S. press, there is no need even for the appearance of evidence. One can pass off the most blatant and sweeping assertions as incontrovertible fact.

THE GREYING OF REALITY

Much news media framing is designed not to excite or incite but to neutralize. While we think of the press as geared to crisis and sensationalism, often its task is just the opposite, dedicated to the greying of reality, blurring popular grievances and social inequities. In this muted media reality, those who raise their voices too strongly against social and class injustices can be made to sound quite shrill.

Instead of neutralizing themselves as observers, reporters and editors are more likely to neutralize their subject matter, giving it an innocence it may not deserve. One way to do this is by applying gloss-over euphemisms and passive phrases. We have already noted how the *New York Times*—years after the fact—reported that President Salvador Allende of Chile "died" in the Moneda Palace when actually he had been murdered there by the military.[22] The *Times* demonstrated how it could turn the 1973 Chilean coup—in which tens of thousands were victimized—into a neutral event by using muted phrases like "the armed forces took power,"[23] and telling us the "chaos" caused by the Communists "brought in the military."[24]

When men, women, and children in the villages of Morazan province were massacred by the El Salvadoran army, the *Times* described it as "a military operation in which some 500 civilians reportedly died in El Mozote."[25] The *Washington Post* treated the Morazan massacre with sentences like "[A survivor] broke down only when speaking of what she said were the deaths of her children" and "Like so much else in the civil war that is wracking this tiny country, these conflicting accounts are impossible to verify."[26] The *Christian Science Monitor* wrote, "Death and destruction still loom high in the saddle in El Salvador," a metaphor that conveniently avoided telling us who the homicidal horsemen really were.[27]

The acts of repression in Turkey by a fascist military regime, involving mass imprisonment, murder, torture, and the destruction of trade unions and other popular organizations, were described in the *Washington Post* as "controversial measures," and as a "drive to restrict political dissent." We learn that General Kenan Evren, the military despot of Turkey, has a "down-to-earth approach" and involves himself in "the rough and tumble of everyday politics," and that his "current crackdown" leading to the imprisonment of "29,940 men" has "all but stamped out terrorism" as if all these victims were terrorists and the Evren regime itself was not engaging in massive terrorism.[28]

Faced with a genocide in East Timor perpetrated by the Indonesian military, complete with widespread burning of crops and intensive aerial bombings of the countryside to starve out and destroy the population that supports the guerrillas, the *Washington Post* could neutralize as follows: "More than 100,000 islanders—one sixth of the population—died in the famine and disease brought on by the hostilities."[29] And "the warfare between the Indonesians and Fretilin forces further disrupted the fragile agrarian economy and caused heavy casualties."[30] Again, the Indonesians did not starve out and massacre multitudes; the Timorese just "died," when the "warfare" impersonally "caused heavy casualties."

Another way to neutralize the news is by scanting its content. We noted how the media are able to reduce political campaigns to a string of issueless, trivial pseudo-events, and feed us stories about labor-management conflicts, political protests, and revolutionary and socialist countries without ever telling us much about their substance, about the interests and goals motivating the event makers. When political struggles are deprived of their content, as for instance when positions taken by the Soviets in opposition to U.S. policy are never explained in their substance, we are left with the presumption that the conflict is caused by an innately hostile adversary. By slighting content and dwelling on surface details, the media are able to neutralize the truth while giving an appearance of having thoroughly treated the subject.

AUXILIARY EMBELLISHMENTS

Through the use of various peripheral framing devices, a story can be packaged so as to influence our perception of its content. The most common accoutrement in the print media is, of course, the headline. Not only can headlines mislead anyone who skims a page without reading the story, they can create the dominant slant on a story, establishing a mind-set that influences how we do read the story's text. Thus, it takes a careful reading of a front-page *Washington Post* report, headlined "U.S. SEEKS NICARAGUAN SOLUTION," before one realizes that the "solution" sought is not a peaceful settlement of hostilities but a way of continuing military aid to the contras and expanding ecomonic sanctions against Nicaragua in the face of congressional opposition.[31] The headline editorializes the story, inviting us to see Reagan's policies toward Nicaragua the same way Reagan does, as a search for a solution rather than as a cause of the problem.

Political cartoons and caricatures also are common embellishments, time-honored forms of editorial comment and readily recognized as such. Less easily detected might be the illustrations that appear in the news and commentary sections. The hammer and sickle symbol has been so frequently used as a sinister embellishment (sometimes adorning a menacing bear) in newspaper illustrations and as a visual backdrop in television news reports that it now evokes a feeling of distaste and alarm in many Americans—even as it remains a symbol of hope and betterment to millions of others in various parts of the world.

Photographs play a similar role, sending us a cue about what to think of a story before we get a chance to read it. Acts of violence during antiwar protests or labor disputes are more certain to get photographed and appear in the news than less damning shots showing large disciplined crowds making their point. Individual demonstrators who convey a kooky appearance will more likely catch the camera's eye than those of more conventional deportment, the purpose of such photographs being not only to highlight the unusual but to delegitimate the protesters, making *them* the issue rather than the thing they are protesting.

Photographs of political leaders can be very political. The president of the United States enjoys almost daily favorable pictorial treatment in the major print and electronic media and is only rarely pictured unsympathetically. However, favorable photoplay is less likely to be accorded heads of state who have been defined as adversaries.

A long *New York Times Magazine* article by David Shipler, entitled "Russia, A People Without Heroes," was accompanied by no less than ten photographs all of which were unusually muted, grainy, and gray, with thick ragged black borders and with captions like "Russians have become so amorphous, so dispersed, because there are no roots, no foundations . . ." (accompanying a picture of Russians going down an escalator). The photographs accompanying this article conveyed an impression of glumness, oppression, and joylessness, and were clearly meant to do so.[32]

A *60 Minutes* report (August 1, 1982) on U.S. intelligence work during World War II turned into a cold war message and a plug for government secrecy. As Harry Reasoner announced, "Today as we rush to disclose everything . . . we must remember that some secrets are worth keeping secret—not to make war but to keep the peace," the screen showed Nazi troops marching past Hitler, then a quick cut to Soviet troops marching past a large image of Lenin in Red Square. Thus the camera invited us to equate the Soviet Union with Hitlerian world conquest. Whether one agreed with the equation or not, the point is, it was made quite effectively and evocatively through a visual effect that evaded rather than encouraged the viewer's conscious judgment.

As anyone who has sat through a Hollywood romance or adventure film might know, music is another evocative media embellishment that can play on our feelings. Television news reports on the Soviet Union are often accompanied with tunes that are either mournful or menacing. In the spring of 1984, National Public Radio's "All Things Considered" did a report on the kinds of music it used as background to its news (spritely tunes for amusing stories, serious ones for serious reports, wry ones for satirical purposes, and so forth). An especially dirgelike theme was identified by Noah Adams as used for "sad stories, especially from Eastern Europe." That Adams saw nothing politically manipulative about using music in this way testifies to the unexamined and unchallenged nature of the political orthodoxy so fostered. Such use of thematic background music is designed to "set the mood," eliciting receptive feelings and deterring resistant thoughts.

Newscasters use themselves as auxiliary embellishments. They cultivate a smooth delivery, have trained voices and restrained demeanors, and try to convey an impression of objective detachment that places them above the rough and tumble of their subject matter. Newscasters and, in a different way, newspaper editorialists and columnists affect a knowing, authoritative style and tone designed to foster credibility and an aura of certitude. One recalls A. J. Liebling's caustic observation, "The reluctance to admit ignorance . . . is with most of the press as strong as the refusal to accept reality." So what we sometimes end up with is *authoritative ignorance* as emphatically expressed in remarks like, "How will this situation end? No one can say for sure." Or, "Only time will tell." Or, "That remains to be seen." (better translated as, "I don't know and if *I* don't, then no one else does because I am the most knowing.") Sometimes the aura of credibility is preserved by palming off trite truisms as penetrating truths. So newspeople learn to fashion sentences like "Unless the strike is settled soon, the two sides will be in for a long and bitter struggle." And "The space launching will take place as scheduled if no unexpected problems arise." And "Because of heightened voter interest, election-day turnout is expected to be heavy." And "Unless Congress acts soon, this bill is not likely to go anywhere."

In sum, as highly skilled specialists, news manufacturers are more than merely conduits for official and moneyed interests. They help create, embellish, and give life to the news, with an array of stereotyped, often misleading, but well-executed images, tones, evasions, nuances, suppressions, and fabrications that lend confirmation to the ruling class viewpoint in a process that is not immediately recognized as being the propaganda it is. Their authoritative voices on radio and television, their decisive wrap-ups and reassuring appearances before the camera, and their endless columns of system-sustaining stories and commentaries help make us believe "that's the way it is." At the same time, this media message preempts the public agenda and crowds out genuine public discourse on what the world might really be like and how we might want to change it.

Notes

1. Robert Holsworth and J. Harry Wray, *American Politics and Everyday Life* (New York: Wiley, 1982), p. 83.
2. Andrew Kopkind, "The Unwritten Watergate Story," *More*, November 1974, and Holsworth and Wray, *American Politics . . .*, p. 82.
3. Noam Chomsky and Edward Herman, *The Washington Connection and Third World Fascism* (Boston: South End Press, 1979), pp. 205–17; Diedre Griswold, *Indonesia, The Second Greatest Crime of the Century* (New York: World View, 1970).
4. See *Time*, December 17, 1965. A year after the massacre, an article appeared by Seth King in the *New York Times Magazine*, May 8, 1966, which provided one of the few instances of informative coverage.
5. For a thorough treatment of East Timor, see Chomsky and Herman, *The Washington Connection . . .* pp. 132–204; also Pat Flanagan, "East Timor: the Final Solution," *Monthly Review*, May 1980, pp. 41–46.
6. Noam Chomsky, "East Timor: The Press Cover-Up," *Inquiry*, February 19, 1979.
7. Mark Hertsgaard, "How Reagan Seduced Us," *Village Voice*, September 18, 1984, p. 42.
8. *Newsweek*, September 15, 1975.
9. David Spurr, "Writing off Third World Issues," *In These Times*, April 14–20, 1982.
10. Ibid.
11. NBC evening news, October 20, 1983.
12. Christopher Hitchens, "The Case of the Menacing Runway," *Nation*, May 29, 1982, pp. 649–51.
13. CBS evening news, January 23, 1985.
14. Todd Gitlin, "Spotlights and Shadow: Television and the Culture of Politics," *College English*, 38, April 1977, p. 792.
15. *Los Angeles Times*, October 6, 1984.
16. *Washington Post*, October 25, 1984.
17. *Washington Post*, April 22, 1983.

18. *Washington Post,* May 6, 1983.
19. CBS Evening News, January 29, 1985.
20. CBS Evening News, January 8, 1985.
21. *New York Times,* September 2, 1983, and February 3, 1985.
22. *New York Times,* August 8, 1984, and the discussion in chapter 10.
23. *New York Times,* February 28, 1980.
24. *New York Times,* August 12, 1984.
25. *New York Times,* August 26, 1984.
26. These *Post* examples are provided by John Dinges in "El Salvador's New Year," City Paper (Washington, D.C.), February 3, 1984.
27. *Christian Science Monitor,* July 9, 1980.
28. *Washington Post,* April 23, 1983.
29. *Washington Post,* January 16, 1983.
30. *Washington Post,* November 25, 1982.
31. *Washington Post,* January 28, 1985.
32. *New York Times Magazine,* October 16, 1983.

13

Control, Resistance, and Culture

Along with owners and advertisers, political rulers exercise a substantial influence over what becomes news. We have seen how shifts in official policy are faithfully reflected in media coverage and editorial opinion. How is such a confluence achieved between a supposedly democratic government and a pluralistic press that is neither formally owned nor officially censored by the state?

GOVERNMENT MANIPULATION AND COERCION

Common class interests often make for common political perspectives. When it comes to "meeting the challenge of Communism," for instance, media owners are eager allies rather than independent critics of the nation's political leaders, sharing the same view about the desirability of the existing economic system at home and abroad and the pernicious nature of those who might want to change it through agitation and class struggle.

Aside from the coincidence of ideological perspectives, newspeople generally are attracted to power, finding it more comfortable to stand with than against it. Those who wield words are often intoxicated by the thought that they might also wield state power, or at least exercise a determining influence over those who do. The late publisher of the *Washington Post*, Philip Graham, made much of his close association with President John Kennedy and believed he had a crucial influence in shaping White House policies. "The reality was of course very different," writes Deborah Davis. "Apart from theoretical discussions which the publisher regularly translated into pro-Kennedy editorials and features, such as the spread he printed on Kennedy's opinions of Khrushchev (all negative), there was little presidential interest in him."[1] A former member of the *Post* editorial staff records, "Washington journalists are just like other people. Many of us are suckers for people who have fame and power."[2]

Aware that newspeople are ready to be seduced, rulers are not above playing the seducer, enticing publishers, editors, and journalists with invitations into the charmed circles of power. Under the Reagan administration, the White House conducted what its deputy social secretary described as "a series of small receptions for groups of 8 to 10 journalists," informal get-togethers with the president himself— with no tape recorders or note taking allowed.[3] Such off-the-record sessions amount to a mind massage, an attempt to get journalists to feel positive toward the illustrious personage, leaving them flattered by his attentions and more appreciative of his burdens and viewpoints.

In addition to the cozy receptions are the grand occasions, the gala events at the White House featuring—along with the usual array of business bigwigs, diplomats, members of Congress, and sports and entertainment celebrities—a selection of journalists, editors, and publishers. The White House state dinner for the grand duke and duchess of Luxembourg in 1984, for instance, had a guest list that included Ted Koppel, ABC *Nightline* host, and his wife; Bryant Gumbel, cohost of NBC's *Today* show, and his wife; Gene Roberts, senior vice-president and executive editor of the *Philadelphia Inquirer*; Nicholas Thimmesch, resident journalist at the American Enterprise Institute; and Mortimer Zuckerman, publisher of *U.S. News and World Report*.[4]

The government exercises a more substantial influence over news organizations by providing them with vast quantities of the product they market: information (and misinformation). News manufacturers find it in their interest to cooperate as much as possible with important suppliers. A daily assembly line of proposals, tips, press releases, documents, and interviews rolls out of the White House and the various federal departments. In a matter of hours, the networks, wire services, and major dailies are telling the public what the government wants them to hear. During the Nixon administration, the Pentagon alone spent $80 million a year disseminating information that fit into its view of the world; it employed a public relations staff of over three thousand people, many of whom could supply news nuggets to cooperative reporters—and nothing at all to uncooperative ones.[5]

Every morning the White House senior staff meet to decide, as one participant put it, "What do we want the press to cover today, and how?" Within minutes after the decisions are made, the "line of the day" is sent out via computer to all senior adminstration officials and to thousands of government public relations people and press secretaries throughout the bureaucracy, covering agencies that deal with both domestic and foreign affairs. As a follow-up, high-level

Washington officials call each network fifteen minutes before the evening news telecast to check on what will appear.[6]

The president obtains prime-time exposure to address the nation almost anytime he desires and exercises a daily built-in control over journalists. "You're locked into this little press room," lamented *Washington Post* reporter Austin Scott, "with only a telephone connecting you to the rest of the White House, and they have the option of taking your calls or not. All you get is staged events—press conferences, briefings, photo opportunities."[7] Reporters who refuse to go along with the controlled information flow, may find themselves left with nothing to report. As ABC correspondent Sam Donaldson put it, "[White House officials] serve up what they want, and also deny us the opportunity to do anything else. So our options are, do nothing or do it their way."[8]

Top administrators, including the president himself, will telephone news executives to convey strongly worded "suggestions" and complain about particular stories and reporters. Dan Rather of CBS revealed that Reagan administration officials frequently went over his head to top CBS executives to complain about his reporting. The White House was especially displeased with CBS coverage of the unemployment situation and criticisms of the barring of reporters from the Grenada invasion. (CBS did not criticize the invasion itself.) Rather asked, "Why are they doing it so often and at such a high level? Because they are trying to change the coverage." As to whether such pressure has an effect, he concluded, "I don't care how good you are, how tough you are; in some way, on some days it is bound to work on your subconscious."[9]

Sometimes media heads try to act as buffers between state and journalist, but more often they seem quite ready to comply. "It is not uncommon for stories to be discreetly killed or softened" at White House request, reports one media critic.[10] After meeting with the three network chiefs, in his capacity as White House aide, Charles Colson concluded, "The networks badly want to have these kinds of discussions which they said they had with other administrations but never with ours. They told me anytime we had a complaint about slanted coverage for me to call them directly. [CBS Board Chairman William] Paley said that he would like to come down to Washington and spend time with me anytime I wanted. . . .He also went out of his way to say how much he supports the president, and how popular the president is."[11]

Besides just complaining about press treatment, the White House has ways of retaliating (which is one reason its grievances are given such quick attention by media executives). Officials can deny interviews, withhold access to information, give scoops to favored reporters and misleading information to disfavored ones, and award prestigious government positions to especially cooperative newspeople. After publishing an article in *Newsday* (a large-circulation Long Island, New York, daily) critical of the shady dealings of President Nixon's close associate Bebe Rebozo, reporter Martin Schramm was denied access to White House communication director Ron Ziegler, and *Newsday* was excluded from the press corps that accompanied Nixon on his historic trip to China.[12] When the *Washington Post* went after Nixon in the Watergate scandal, the White House prepared to retaliate by "taking an obstructionist position toward the *Washington Post* Company's television licenses when they came up for renewal around the country."[13]

When dealing with the media, rulers are not above utilizing the police powers of the state. On a number of occasions, the FBI has harassed newspersons who persisted in writing troublesome stories.[14] The Justice Department won a Supreme Court decision[15] requiring reporters to disclose their sources to grand juries, in an attempt to reduce the press to an investigative arm of the courts and prosecution. Dozens of reporters have since been jailed or threatened with prison terms on the basis of that decision. On repeated occasions the government has subpoenaed documents, tapes, and other materials used by news organizations. Such interference imposes a "chilling effect" on the press, encouraging self-censorship. Thus CBS offered to cooperate more closely on news stories about the White House in return for government assistance in quashing a congressional contempt citation against the network for its mildly critical documentary about the Pentagon.[16]

Government repression was quite blatant when directed against the New Left "underground" newspapers that sprang up across the nation during the late sixties. These publications were harassed and attacked by police, FBI, CIA, and rightist vigilantes. News offices were broken into, ransacked, and even bombed; files and typewriters were stolen; telephones were tapped; and staffs were infiltrated by undercover agents or arrested on trumped-up drug or obscenity charges, causing suspension of publication and prohibitive legal costs. Underground newspaper street vendors were repeatedly threatened and arrested by police in a number of cities and mail distribution was sometimes interrupted. After visits from the FBI, printers were persuaded to discontinue their services; newsstands were persuaded not to handle underground papers; landlords suddenly doubled the office rent, forcing publications to move; and the Internal Revenue Service sought lists of backers and contributors of radical publications for possible tax violations.[17]

The government's campaign against the left extends into the mainstream press also. The Federal Communications Commission (FCC) is required by law to provide response time for various interests that are attacked or offended by statements in the broadcast media. For Americans who are too far left, however, this "fairness doctrine" has never applied; the FCC stated it has no intention "to make time available to Communists or to the Communist viewpoints."[18] The FCC did not specify what were "Communist viewpoints" but apparently there are more than one and they are all excluded from fair treatment.[19]

WORKING FOR BIG BROTHER

Government agencies that are supposedly dedicated to intelligence gathering and national defense are just as often involved in propagandizing the American public. According to released government documents, in the late sixties the FBI planted stories in "friendly news media" designed "to discredit the New Left."[20] The Pentagon sends out hundreds of stories and canned editorials each week that are picked up by newspapers and broadcast stations across the country and presented to the public as trustworthy products of independent journalism.[21] According to officials at the United States Information Service (USIS), the government has teams of propagandists in Washington who crank out stories that are wired daily to USIS's 206 offices in 127 countries.[22] Many of these news plants appear in the foreign press then return as "blowback," that is, they are picked up by U.S. correspondents abroad and transmitted to an unsuspecting American public.

One of the most active news-manipulating agencies is the CIA, which turns journalists into paid agents and plants CIA agents in news organizations in order to disseminate stories that support the policies of the national security state. In his book, *Deadly Deceits,* ex-CIA agent Ralph McGehee shows that "the American people are the primary target audience of [CIA] lies."[23] In the early 1950s some 400 to 600 journalists were in the pay of the CIA. The Copley Press alone had at least 23 intelligence agents masquerading as "reporters" on its payroll. Many of the press's paid agents have been media executives and editors.[24] A reporter "may receive an assignment from an editor, who is on the CIA payroll, and never suspect for whom he is working."[25]

At least twenty-five news organizations have served the CIA, including the *Washington Post,* the *New York Times,* CBS, ABC, NBC,

Time, Newsweek, the Associated Press, United Press International, the Hearst newspapers, the Scripps-Howard newspapers, *U.S. News and World Report,* and the *Wall Street Journal.* Among the prominent news executives who knowingly have cooperated with the CIA are William Paley, chairman of the board of CBS; Henry Luce, late owner of Time Inc.; Arthur Hays Sulzberger, late publisher of the *New York Times;* Robert Myers, publisher of the *New Republic;* James Copley, owner of the Copley News Service; Barry Bingham Sr., publisher of the *Louisville Courier-Journal* and Norman E. Isaacs, its executive editor; Richard Salant, president of CBS News; and on the *Washington Post* alone, the following executives or senior editors: John S. Hayes, Alfred Friendly, Benjamin Bradlee, Chalmers Roberts, James Wiggins, and Philip Geyelin.[26]

The CIA runs the biggest news service in the world with a budget larger than those of all the major wire services put together. In 1975 a Senate intelligence committee found that the CIA owned outright "more than 200 wire services, newspapers, magazines, and book publishing complexes" and subsidized many more. A *New York Times* investigation revealed another fifty media outlets run by the CIA in the United States and abroad, and at least twelve publishing houses, which marketed over 1,200 books secretly commissioned by the CIA, including some 250 in English. As the *Times* explained it, these figures were far from the whole story.[27] The CIA subsidized books on China, the Soviet Union, and Third World struggles which were then reviewed by CIA agents in various U.S. media, including the *New York Times.*[28]

CIA operatives have planted stories of Soviet nuclear tests that never took place and fabricated "diaries" and "confessions" of defectors from socialist countries. In the early 1950s a news story claiming that China was sending troops to Vietnam to help insurgents fight against the French proved to be a CIA fabrication.[29] The agency induced the *New York Times* to remove a reporter, Sidney Gruson, from a story about the CIA-inspired overthrow of a democratic government in Guatemala because he was getting too close to uncovering the U.S. plot.[30] Stories about Cuban soldiers killing babies and raping women in Angola, concocted by the CIA, were planted abroad, then picked up by AP and UPI stringers for "blowback" runs in the U.S.[31]

In his stories to the *New York Times* about the overthrow of the constitutional government of Muhammad Mussadegh in Iran in 1953, correspondent Kenneth Love made no mention of the crucial role played by the CIA, not because he didn't know about it but because he knew too much, being himself a CIA agent, and by his own admission playing an active role in the coup.[32]

Supposedly such practices ceased after the CIA penetrations of cultural and news organizations were exposed in the 1970s. In fact, there is reason to believe they continue. Thus as late as 1984 it was revealed that the CIA subsidized travel to El Salvador by eleven European and Latin American journalists who were fed the agency's view of things in that country.[33] And the CIA furnishes information to ultra-right groups like Accuracy in the Media, which these groups in turn run in their newsletters and feed to politically sympathetic newspapers.[34]

THE LIMITS OF POWER

If economic and political elites control the press, why are they often distrustful of, and irritated by, what appears in it? And why do they find it necessary to exert repressive measures against their own media? As mentioned in earlier chapters, there are a number of things that make the press less than absolutely compliant, introducing an element of indeterminacy and resistance.

1. One reason deviancy occasionally peeks through an otherwise controlled press is because ideological control is not formal, overt, and ubiquitous, but informal, covert, and implicit. Therefore it will work with imperfect effect. Dissenting information will sometimes slip through. For example, one evening in January 1985, on the NBC evening news, anchorperson Tom Brokaw noted quickly, almost furtively, that corporations are today paying a substantially smaller portion of the nation's income tax than five years ago. No elaboration, no pie charts, just a two-line news item that seemed to have been slipped in. Similarly the print media sometimes carry revealing items, buried in otherwise standard stories, exceptional things that are likely to go unnoticed—except to the closely critical reader—because of their poor placement and lack of projective framing. The presence of such nuggets scattered here and there in the mountains of dross is what enables critics of capitalism occasionally to draw damaging information from the capitalist media itself. When detected as deviancies, these items are quickly suppressed. A staff member of a local early morning radio news program in Washington, D.C., pointed out to me, "Sometimes the seven o'clock morning edition will carry an item or two that has some real zip. These run because the station manager hasn't arrived yet. They're cut out of the eight o'clock edition because by then he's at his post. . . . I wouldn't say it's a regular occurrence, but it happens once in awhile."

2. Sometimes editors run stories because they are unable to foresee their troublesome implications and unintended spin-offs. While the

"blame-the-journalist" critics argue that distortions are caused by inadequate information and hasty preparation, I am suggesting there are times when haste and low information levels lead to greater revelations than would normally be allowed were reporters and editors better apprised of a story's potentially discordant ideological effects. Even the best-informed newspeople cannot always anticipate the effects of their stories. A report on how a particular corporation is taking care of a toxic spill may be intended to show the firm's socially responsible behavior and reassure the public, whereas it actually has the unintended but more accurate effect of revealing how big companies are poisoning the environment. Early news reports (1980–1981) about the growing effectiveness of guerrilla forces in El Salvador, while intending to alert the public to the emergence of a new Communist menace, had the unintended effect of activating an anti-interventionist peace movement in the United States, causing officials in the Reagan administration to request that the press not give so much attention to El Salvador. Today reports about El Salvador usually tell us of the U.S.-supported "democracy" and of a Salvadoran military that is better-trained and ever more effective in containing the rebels.

   3. Serious differences sometimes arise among politico-economic elites on how best to advance their common class interests. These differences will be reflected in the news media. Thus while remaining generally supportive of the president's adversarial approach to the Soviets, the press gave space and time to such elite critics as Cyrus Vance and Robert McNamara, who called for a return to a policy of mutual deterrence and détente. To the extent such differences among elites are played out in the media, they add to the appearance—and substance—of diversity, if not on fundamental questions then on tactical ones.

   4. When the press has a direct and enduring interest in an issue, it is likely to be less compliant than usual—as with the question of protecting the confidentiality of its sources. If reporters are unable to guarantee confidentiality, they run the risk of having their sources dry up. Another area of conflict between state and press arises when reporters are victimized by state violence. Reports of widespread brutality by police, army, and federal marshals against antiwar participants in the 1960s were so thoroughly suppressed by the major news organizations that on one occasion protesters had to buy a page in the *New York Times,* which they filled with eyewitness accounts of violent mistreatment by authorities.[35] But the police riot against antiwar demonstrators in Chicago during the 1968 Democratic National Convention did make the news in a big way—mostly because of the deliberate acts of police violence against members of the press.

Likewise, the mass execution of young males by Somoza's national guard during the last days of his rule received little, if any, notice in the U.S. media until ABC's Bill Stewart was executed by guardsmen while covering the Nicaragua uprising. In the days that followed, the film of Stewart's execution (taken by an American cameraperson standing a distance away) was played repeatedly on network news, and for the first time the American press also began mentioning that young Nicaraguans were being systematically murdered by the guard. The killing of foreign newspeople, as opposed to American journalists, is less likely to be accorded elaborate treatment. From 1980 to 1982 at least twenty-six print and broadcast journalists were murdered or "disappeared" in Guatemala, and over thirty were killed in El Salvador; but since almost all of these were Guatemalan and Salvadoran nationals, there was no discernible outcry in the American press.[36]

5. Journalists who believe they are autonomous professionals expect to be able to report things as they see them. If the appearance of journalistic independence is violated too often and too blatantly by superiors, this can have a demoralizing and demystifying effect, reminding the staff that they are not working in a democratic institution but one controlled from the top with no regard for professional standards as they understand them. As noted, publishers and network bosses regularly oversee the news production process and frequently intervene with suggestions and direct commands. But to avoid being criticized as censors and intrusive autocrats, they sometimes grant their news organizations some modicum of independence, relying on hiring, firing, and promotional policies and more indirect controls. They might show themselves willing to make an occasional concession so as to minimize the amount of overt intrusion.

The idea of a free press is more a myth than a reality, but myths can have an effect on things and can serve as a resource of power. The power of a legitimating myth rests on its ability to be believed and not exposed as a sham. So at times superiors will hesitate to violate the professional prerogatives of subordinates and will make concessions. To offer an instance: at the time of the death of Adam Clayton Powell, Jr., the *Washington Post*'s only Black editorialist, Roger Wilkins, decided to write a favorable editorial about him. The White-owned, mainstream media had long portrayed Powell as an uppity, high-living Black Congressman who played fast and loose with House expense accounts; but Blacks saw him as one of the first public figures who fought against federal funding of segregated services and for numerous measures benefiting poor people. Wilkins's boss, Philip Geyelin, thought the condemnation of Powell should have been much stronger than the criticism Wilkins   had included in his editorial. Wilkins resisted.

> Phil and I stared at each other for a tense moment and then he said, "Okay let's see if we can work out some language that we both can agree on." So he wrote a sentence and I softened it and then he stiffened it a little and then I softened it a little and then we let it go, both dissatisfied. The piece ran and I had to admit that it wasn't too horrible, though not exactly what I would have wanted. Phil had to admit about the same thing. . . . I took solace in . . . the fact that our editorial was wiser and more human by far than the crabbed and ugly denunciation of Adam that ran on the *New York Times* editorial page.[37]

Another incident should suffice: after a year of unremittingly hostile reports about the leftist armed forces movement in Portugal, the *New York Times* agreed to run a guest opinion column by me that offered a more sympathetic view of the struggle in that country. The day before the column was to appear, however, managing editor Abe Rosenthal intervened to suppress it. My repeated inquiries brought only evasive responses from the opinion-page editors who had accepted the piece. Only after three months of badgering telephone calls from me, reminding the *Times* editors that they were under an obligation to give their readers a glimpse of the other side, and after two updated rewrites by me, did the *Times* print it—the only 800 words the newspaper ever ran that contradicted the thousands of column inches that echoed the White House line. Somehow I had prevailed upon the opinion-page editor who had prevailed upon Rosenthal. Even then, the piece appeared only after Portugal had dropped from the news and was once more safely in the Western capitalist camp. And lest *Times* readers be unduly swayed, my guest column was accompanied by a hostile editorial denouncing the left in Portugal and calling for support of conservative "pluralistic" forces. So, on infrequent occasions, in limited, lopsided ways, the legitimating myth of "allowing both sides a hearing" can be used by dissenters to drive a wedge into a monopoly press that finds it difficult to practice within its own ranks the pluralism it so vigorously preaches to the world.

6. The press is not totally immune to the pressures of those who struggle for a more egalitarian and peaceable world. It must make some adjustment to democratic forces as when the emergence of independent nations in Africa and Asia induces it to discard *some* of its more blatant colonialist, racist stereotypes. The emergence of the civil rights movement in the United States, which won the sympathy and support of large sectors of the public, brought dramatic shifts in media coverage of the struggle for racial equality and of Black people in

general—although it hardly ended racist reporting and stereotyping. Similarly, as opinion turned with increasing militancy against the Vietnam War, the press began to entertain criticisms about the feasibility (but not the morality) of the war. "As the ruling media brass and their advertisers began to realize that no amount of lying or propaganda could turn defeat into victory," writes Mike Zagarell, and as they witnessed how the Vietnam conflict was causing a crisis within the United States, "media coverage began to shift, giving more prominence to those who called for a saner outlook."[38]

The greater the opposition is believed to be toward a leader or a policy, observe Paletz and Entman, "the more emboldened network correspondents are in their analysis."[39] Earlier we noted how the enthusiastic reception Soviet leader Khrushchev won from the American public favorably influenced the kind of media coverage accorded him. Likewise, as opinion turned against President Nixon during the Watergate scandal, the press delivered negative judgments upon him, "but only then—with his prestige and power in dramatic decline and his attempts at media manipulation more transparent than ever"; for it was then safe to do so.[40]

Aware that active segments of the public are mobilized around an issue, the media must take account of that agitation, even if only to devalue and minimize it—as with most protest movements. Yet even in the course of doing this, the press ends up acknowledging and publicizing the existence of popular sentiments and mass movements.

7. To add to the appearance of free and diverse discourse, the press allots a small portion of its time and space to the public itself. Radio call-in shows enable us to hear directly from listeners and provide opportunities for the brief airing of dissident viewpoints. Some shows quote from the letters of listeners and viewers, little of which deviates markedly from the standard opinion range. There are also guest opinion pieces by readers and of course the letter-to-the-editor column found in most (but not all) dailies. Such meager accommodations are designed to create the impression of an open untrammeled communication between media and public where one does not exist. Furthermore, the letters columns and call-in shows provide as much opportunity for conventional, conservative, and ill-informed views as for any other. Yet they offer openings that progressive persons have sometimes utilized with effect. Even the letters that are not printed do get read and play a small part in pressuring the press.

8. If the press's *general class* function is to help make the world safe for those who own and control news organizations, it also has a *specialized institutional* function, which is to present the public with something called "the news." The news must be packaged so as to be

(a) pleasing to press moguls and other politico-economic elites; and (b) informative and believable to the public. But these two functions are not always automatically reconcilable. The goal of the owning class, as Marx and Engels put it, is to present "a particular interest as general or the 'general interest' as ruling."[41] This indeed is what the press does, as I have tried to demonstrate throughout this book, treating a wide range of subjects from a ruling class perspective but presenting this perspective as the objective, general one, as representative of things as they really are. But the press also must give the appearance of performing a public information service. To create such an appearance, it must make substantive concessions now and then to real public concerns, risking the legitimacy of the larger system in order to better secure its own.

As we have seen, the press adheres to basic class orthodoxies, especially in regard to "democratic capitalism" and anticommunism, and it is usually eager to cooperate with the state on policy questions. Deborah Davis writes that the *Washington Post* had "special arrangements" with government officials who fed it information that gave it an advantage in predicting and interpreting policies to the public. In exchange, the *Post* gave favorable treatment to the government's position.[42] To some extent all news organizations enter into this kind of exchange, trading some of their integrity for access to sources that help them carry out their newsgathering tasks. From the media's view of things, it is better to be totally knowing than totally honest. However, there are occasions when the trade-off comes at too high a price, when government or business asks the press to swallow more than it can if it is to avoid appearing ridiculous—as when it is expected to report that we are winning in Vietnam, that U.S. forces are saving the day in Lebanon, that a "safety net" will rescue the poor from the effects of domestic spending cuts, or other such misrepresentations that grossly violate the limits of actuality. Were it to follow the government (or corporate) line on all such matters the press would cast doubt on its own credibility as a news organization and as a neutral, objective social institution. So the media go along on most stories, but not all the time and sometimes not all the way.

This "relative autonomy" is what irritates and sometimes infuriates the more conservative elements of the ruling class, whose growing sense of power leaves them increasingly unwilling to tolerate deviancies, and who complain of "liberal biases" whenever the media hint at realities that do not fit the conservative picture of the world. The press's systemic class function is to purge popular consciousness of any awareness of the disturbingly inequitable, exploitative, repressive, and violent consequences of capitalist rule at home and abroad. While it cannot perform that task thoroughly enough to satisfy all elites all the time and maintain its own credibility, it does—as I have tried to show in this book—a far better, more skillful job of it than many elites appreciate.

In addition, it is not certain that corporate, congressional, and other political elites (other than the ultraright) would be satisfied with an ultraconservative propagandistic press, devoid of all accurate information and commentary (within a limited framework) on domestic affairs and world events. A press that was even more lacking in hard news and critical analysis than it is, presumably would be as unsatisfactory to the captains of industry and state as to any informed person who wished to "stay abreast with the events of the day." An entire press presenting only ax-grinding stories and reactionary opinions in the manner of the dailies published by Rupert Murdoch and the Reverend Sun Myung Moon would satisfy few.

BETWEEN CONSPIRACY AND CULTURE

The social institutions of capitalist society are the purveyors of its cultural myths, values, and legitimating viewpoints. To the extent that news producers—from publishers to reporters—are immersed in that culture, they may not be fully aware of how they misrepresent, evade, and suppress the news. Political orthodoxy, like custom itself, is a mental sedative, while political deviancy, like cultural deviancy, is an irritant. Devoid of the supportive background assumptions of the dominant belief system, the deviant view sounds just too improbable and too controversial to be treated as news, while the orthodox view appears as an objective representation of reality itself.

From this it might be concluded that what we have in the news media is not a consciously propagated *establishment* viewpoint but a socially shared *established* viewpoint, and that when radical critics complain of elite manipulation they, in effect, really are bemoaning the unpopularity of their own views. Reporters and editors are products of the same political socialization as are media owners and political leaders; and therefore they are just reporting things as they see them—and as almost everyone else sees them (including their audiences)—without knowingly misrepresenting anything. To argue otherwise, it has been maintained, is to lapse into some kind of conspiracy theory about a consciously manipulative, diabolic elite.

Several responses are in order. First, it should be noted that there *are* conspiracies among ruling groups, things done in secrecy with the intent to sustain or extend power—as Watergate, the Pentagon Papers, the FBI's COINTELPRO campaign against the left, and the CIA's daily doings have demonstrated. Just because some people have fantasies about conspiracies does not mean every conspiracy is a fantasy. Like most other cultural institutions, the media exercise their influence through overt means. Given the nature of the institution, it would be hard to imagine *secret* mass media. But there may often also be something secret and conspiratorial, something deliberately slanted and politically motivated, about news production. Examples may be found in the unpublicized owner and advertiser dominance over news personnel and editorial content, the planted and fabricated information and suppressed stories, and the instances of government interference and manipulation.

The existence of a common pool of culturally determined (systemic, nonconspiratorial) political values cannot be denied, but where did this common pool come from? Who or what determines the determining element in the culture itself? And can we reduce an entire culture, including its actively struggling political components, to a set of accumulated habituations and practices that simply build up over time?

A closer look reveals that the unconsciously shared "established" view (as opposed to a consciously propagated elite "establishment" view) is not shared by everyone and is not in fact all that established. Major portions of the public, often majorities, do not support present levels of taxation, military spending, military interventionism, the cold war, the arms race, nuclear power, and various policies harmful to the environment, the poor, and to working people. In other words, it may be true that most media elites and political elites share common views on these subjects, but much—and sometimes most—of the public does not. What we have then is an "established *establishment* view" which is given the highest media visibility, usually to the exclusion of views held by large dissident sectors of the populace. The "dominant shared values and beliefs," that are supposedly the natural accretions and expressions of our common political culture, are not shared by all or most—certainly not at the policy level—although they surely are dominant in that they tend to preempt the field of opinion visibility.

Furthermore, there is evidence, some of it introduced in this book, that members of the working press itself do not automatically share the "universal" viewpoints of the dominant political culture but often have their stories suppressed, cut, and rewritten. Along with a harmonious blending of bias among reporter, editor, publisher, and sometimes audience, we have the deliberately coercive controls by owners, advertisers, political leaders, and the anticipatory self-censorship of their journalistic employees.

In sum, media owners—like other social groups—consciously pursue their self-interest and try to influence others in ways that are advantageous to themselves. They treat information and culture as vital instruments of class power. Even if they never put it in those words, they try to keep control of the command posts of social institutions and the flow of symbols, values, opinions, and information. In a professedly democratic society, they may seek to minimize their use of coercion, preferring a willing compliance to a forcibly extracted one. Yet when necessary they are not hesitant to occupy the visible positions of power. Regardless of what their academic and journalistic apologists say on their behalf, they have no intention of leaving public discourse and mass communication openly accessible to an unrestricted popular development. Why recognition of these unexceptional facts should brand one a "conspiracy theorist" is not clear.

Can it really be argued that elites have no power over the news organizations they own or finance? Or that if they do have power, they never use it? Or that they use it only in the belief they are fostering the common interest? Certainly all modern ruling classes justify their rule in universalist terms—and have a way of believing their own propaganda. But whether they think of themselves as patriots or plotters is not the point. No doubt, they like to see themselves as the defenders of American democracy even as they bolster their class privileges. Like everyone else, they believe in the virtue of their cause and equate the pursuit of their class interests with the pursuit of the national interest. Indeed, much of their propaganda is designed to treat these two things as coterminous.

The question is not how they see themselves but how *we* see them. That a particular class has achieved cultural hegemony over the entire society does not mean it has created a democratic culture. Nor need we struggle with the question of whether the causal factor is "class" or "culture," as if these terms were mutually exclusive; for class dominance both helps to create and is fortified by cultural hegemony.

News distortion is *both* a product of shared cultural values *and* deliberate acts of disinformation. Political beliefs do not automatically reproduce and sustain themselves. They must be (at least partly) consciously propagated. And with time, yesterday's propaganda becomes today's "shared cultural values and beliefs." Consider a specific example: the lie repeated throughout the press about the Soviet Union being unable to feed its people. Stories of the starving Russians are as old as the Russian Revolution itself (and indeed, during the years of foreign invasion and civil war immediately after the revolution, there was some truth to them). Uttered today, the assertion is a falsehood, but through unchallenged and ubiquitous repetition it becomes part of the conventional wisdom. Whether or not reporters and editors are deliberately lying when they talk of the Soviets' inability to feed themselves is less significant than that they feel free to make such statements without checking the facts. It is bad enough that they circulate such baldfaced lies; but it is even worse that they themselves usually believe them, partly because such beliefs are not a personal invention but are shared by almost all the opinion makers of the mainstream press and partly because there are rewards for orthodox belief and penalties for skepticism.

Misinformation is sometimes so widespread that the line between intentional and unintentional distortion is not always easy to discern, neither for those who transmit the untruths nor for those of us who try to detect them. The American sovietologist Harold Berman relates the following incident:

> Two years ago, an American newspaper correspondent in Moscow wrote an account of the May Day parade in which he described people singing and dancing in the streets and enjoying themselves thoroughly. His newspaper published the account, but at the same time it ran an editorial in which it portrayed an embittered Russian people forced by their hated government to demonstrate in favor of a revolution which they did not want.
>
> The correspondent, in recounting this to me, said that he thereupon wrote a letter to his editor in which he said, "I was there—I saw it—they were not bitter, they were happy, they were having a good time." The editorial writer wrote back, in effect, that they may have appeared happy, but that actually they could not have been happy, in view of the evils of the system under which they live.[43]

It is hard to say whether the editorial writer was deliberately bending things to present a picture more in keeping with the orthodox view (the view of his publisher) or was "correcting" the reporter's perceptions in order to bring them more in line with what he honestly believed beforehand to be the truth. Like everyone else, reporters and editors either sincerely share in the political ideology that makes it so easy for them to believe the news they produce, or they go along with things because they know on which side their bread is buttered. It is difficult to know at what exact psychological point an individual's self-serving rationalization turns into sincere belief; but we do know there are variations among members of the working press, at least some of whom are consciously aware of the coercive controls exercised over them in the news hierarchy—even if proponents of pluralism deny the existence of such things.

THE CONFLICT WITHIN

If the dominant culture were a mystically self-sustaining perpetual motion machine, there would be nothing left for us to do but throw up our hands and wait for the natural, gradual process of change to unfold across the centuries. But neither history nor society works that way. In fact, there is an element of struggle and indeterminacy in all our social institutions and political culture. Along with institutional stability we have popular ferment; along with elite manipulation we have widespread skepticism; along with ruling class coercion we have mass resistance.

What has been said of the media is true of the law, the university, the church, political parties, science, and the state itself. Marx noted that the state has to involve itself "both in the performance of common activities arising from the nature of all communities" and the "specific functions" that ensure ruling class domination.[44] Likewise, all social institutions of capitalist society have this dichotomous tension within them. They must sustain the few while appearing to serve the many, but to bolster that appearance, they must perform some popular functions or they will have no popular following.

This brings us to Antonio Gramsci's insight about how hegemony works to induce people to consent in their own oppression. Gramsci noted that the capitalist class achieves hegemony not only by propagating manipulative values and beliefs but by actually performing vital social functions that have diffuse benefits. Railroads and highways may enrich the magnates, but they also provide transportation for much of the public. Private hospitals are for profits not for people, but people who can afford them do get treated. The law is an instrument of class control, but it must also to some degree be concerned with public safety. The media try to invent reality but they must also sometimes admit realities. So with just about every cultural and social function: The ruling interests must act affirmatively on behalf of public interests *some* of the time. If the ruling class fails to do so, Gramsci notes, its legitimacy will decline, its cultural and national hegemony will falter, and its power will shrink back to its police and military capacity, leaving it with a more overtly repressive but more isolated and less secure rule.[45]

So the ruling class rules but not quite in the way it wants. Its socializing agencies do not work with perfect effect, free of contradictions—or else this book could not have been written or published or understood. There is just so much cover rulers can give to their injustices and just so many substantive concessions they can make. And the concessions become points of vulnerability.

To best secure their legitimacy and popular acceptance, ruling interests must maintain democratic appearances and to do that they must not only lie, distort, and try to hide their oppressions and unjust privileges, but must occasionally give in to popular demands, giving a little to keep a lot, and presenting themselves as champions of democracy in the doing. In time, the legitimating ideology becomes a two-edged sword. Bourgeois hypocrisies about "fair play" and "democracy" are more than just a ruse. Such standards sometimes put limitations on ruling-class oppression once the public takes them seriously and fights for them.

Legitimacy cuts both ways also in our social institutions. We can observe its two-edged quality most dramatically in one of the oldest of legitimating institutions: the church. Nothing is more revealing of the imperfect and contradictory nature of hegemonic control than an anticommunist, cold war pope racing frenetically about the globe trying to drag his priests away from the class struggles of the impoverished while simultaneously presenting himself as a champion of the poor. There is a danger that those who preach that God's will should be done on earth as in heaven will begin to believe it and will try—along with their congregations—to see it done. Similarly the danger with teaching people that the purpose of the law is to achieve justice is that they will expect it to do so and might even make it do so from time to time. The danger with calling the university a democratic, independent institution is that students and faculty might take the assertion seriously and demand the right to ideological diversity, self-governance, and an end to complicity with the Pentagon and with corporations that invest in South Africa. The danger with claiming we have a free and independent press is that it may feel pressured—both by the public and from within its own ranks—to act that way at inconvenient times.

In sum, the capitalist monopoly culture, like its monopoly economy, suffers—shall we say—from internal contradictions. It can invent and control just so much of reality. Its socialization is an imperfect one and sometimes self-defeating. Like any monopoly it cannot rest perfectly secure because it usually does not serve the people and is dedicated to the ultimately impossible task of trying to prevent history from happening. The life of a people creates a reality that can only be partly explained away by the dominant cultural and communicational institutions. The struggle for social justice in this and other countries ebbs and flows but is never permanently stilled by police clubs nor forever smothered by the outpouring of propaganda machines. The longing for peace and betterment, for security and equality, found in the growing consciousness of people everywhere, bursts forth at unexpected times, as multitudes struggle to claim back their land and their productive capacity, their politics and their culture, their images and their reality. The democratic forces of this and other societies have won victories in the past against tremendous odds and will win more in the future. Indeed, the future itself depends on it.

Notes

1. Deborah Davis, *Katharine the Great: Katharine Graham and the Washington Post* (New York: Harcourt Brace Jovanovich, 1979), pp. 156–57.

2. Roger Wilkins, *A Man's Life,* (New York: Simon and Schuster, 1982), p. 350.

3. William Safire's column, *New York Times,* August 16, 1984.

4. *Washington Post,* November 14, 1984.

5. Mike Zagarell, "White House Control of the Media—and the Fightback," *Daily World,* November 15, 1984.

6. Ibid.

7. Quoted in David Paletz and Robert Entman, *Media Power Politics* (New York: Free Press, 1981), p. 57.

8. Mark Hertsgaard, "How Reagan Seduced Us," *Village Voice,* September 18, 1984.

9. *New York Times,* November 14, 1983; and Simon Gerson, "What Freedom of the Press?" *Daily World,* December 8, 1983.

10. Les Brown, *Television, the Business Behind the Box* (New York: Harcourt Brace Jovanovich, 1971), p. 214.

11. Paletz and Entman, *Media Power Politics,* p. 62.

12. David Wise, *The Politics of Lying* (New York: Vintage, 1973), pp. 319–22.

13. Wilkins, *A Man's Life,* p. 340.

14. See Todd Gitlin, *The Whole World Is Watching* (Berkeley: University of California Press, 1980), p. 272.

15. *United States* v. *Caldwell* (1972); see also the *New York Times,* September 4, 1976, and November 19, 1978.

16. *New York Times,* January 17, 1976.

17. Geoffrey Rips, *The Campaign Against the Underground Press* (San Francisco: City Lights, 1981).

18. Gitlin, *The Whole World Is Watching,* p. 261.

19. *Washington Post,* February 8, 1985.

20. Quotations from documents reproduced in Rips, *The Campaign Against the Underground Press,* pp. 68–71.

21. Mark Yudof, *When Government Speaks* (Berkeley: University of California Press, 1984); J. William Fulbright, *The Pentagon Propaganda Machine* (New York: Vintage, 1971).

22. Kai Bird and Max Holland, "The Philippines: Official News," *Nation,* June 30, 1984.

23. Ralph McGehee, *Deadly Deceits: My 25 Years in the CIA* (New York: Sheridan Square Publications, 1983).

24. *New York Times,* December 25, 26, 27, 1977.

25. Vitaly Petrusenko, *A Dangerous Game, CIA and the Mass Media* (Prague: Interpress, n.d.), p. 92.

26. Carl Bernstein, "The CIA and the Media," *Rolling Stone,* October 20, 1977; Stuart Loory, "The CIA's Use of the Press: A Mighty Wurlitzer," *Columbia Journalism Review,* September/October, 1974, pp. 9–18; Davis, *Katharine the Great,* pp. 176–89.

27. *New York Times,* December 25, 26, 27, 1977.

28. David Wise and Thomas Ross, *The Invisible Government* (New York: Bantam, 1965), pp. 134–35, 267; *Columbia Journalism Review,* July/August 1976, pp. 37–38.

29. *New York Times, December 25, 26, 27, 1977.*

30. Ibid.

31. John Stockwell, *In Search of Enemies* (New York: Norton, 1978), p. 195.

32. Love wrote an account of the coup and his role in it while he was a Carnegie Press Fellow for the Council of Foreign Relations; quoted in *Counterspy,* September/October 1980.

33. *New York Times,* May 12, 1984.

34. Louis Wolf, "Accuracy in Media Rewrites the News and History," *CovertAction Information Bulletin,* Spring 1984, p. 33.

35. *New York Times,* December 3, 1967.

36. Julia Preston, "Killing Off the News in Guatemala, *Columbia Journalism Review,* January/February, 1982, p. 34; William Leogrande and Carla Anne Robbins, "Oligarchs and Officers," *Foreign Affairs,* Summer 1980, pp. 1084–1103.

37. Wilkins, *A Man's Life,* pp. 326–27.

38. Mike Zagarell, "White House Control of the Media . . ."

39. Paletz and Entman, *Media Power Politics,* p. 69.

40. Ibid.

41. Karl Marx and Frederick Engels, *The German Ideology* (New York: International Publishers, 1947), p. 41.

42. Davis, *Katharine the Great,* pp. 176–77.

43. Harold J. Berman, "The Devil and Soviet Russia," *American Scholar,* 27, Spring 1958, p. 148.

44. Karl Marx, *Capital,* vol. 3 (Moscow: Progress Publications, 1966), p. 384.

45. Antonio Gramsci, *Selections From the Prison Notebooks* (New York: International Publishers, 1971), p. 171.

Index

252 INDEX

chain of command and, 42–48
ownership and, 49, 58–59
self-censorship and, 35–39
socioeconomic background and, 39
world views and, 40–41
India, 204
Indoctrination, 20–23
Indonesia, 215–216, 223
Industries Advisory Committee, 72
Inertia, opinion, 36–37
Inflation, 12, 73
Information
homogeneity of, 30–32
sources of, 51, 68
Institute on Religion and Democracy
(IRD), 107–108
Integrity, professional, 58
Interest, conflicts of, 51–53
Interlocking directorates, 4–5, 29–
30
International Association of Machinists
and Aerospace Workers (IAM),
76, 79
Isaacs, Norman E., 233
Islam, representations of, 204–205
Issues
agenda of, 23
image vs., 14
neutralizing, 222–223
Italy, fascist, 115–116

Jackson, Jesse, 11
John Olin Foundation, 106
John Paul II, 161–166
Johnson, Nicholas, 56
Jorgensen, C. Peter, 46–47
Journalism
fragmentation of functions of, 46
pack, 36–37
responsibilities of, 207
schools of, 40, 41
Journalists
centrist-liberal critiques of, 9
conditional autonomy of, 35–39,
239–240
editorial constraints on, 37–38, 42–
43
ideological conditioning of, 6–7, 42
socioeconomic backgrounds of, 39
violence against, 235–236
world views, 40–41
Judis, John, 140

Kaiser, Robert, 205
Kalb, Marvin, 164–165, 202
Keeler, William, 214
Keld, Herman, 49
Kennedy, Edward, 98
Kennedy, John, 228
KGB, 103, 108–109, 164–165
Khrushchev, Nikita, 124–125, 238
Kilpatrick, James, 47–48
King, Edward, 98
Kirkpatrick, Jeanne, 156–157
Kirteke, Suleyman, 192
Kopkind, Andrew, 214
Koppel, Ted, 219
Korean Airlines Flight 007, downing of,
156–160

Labeling, 220–222
Labor
anticommunism and, 116–117, 119,
126
coverage of, 78–87, 114
in Soviet Union, 140
Taft-Hartley Law and, 119–120
unions, 71, 78–81, 117
See also Working class
Leadership, 29–30, 206–207
Lebanon, 208, 220–221
Ledeen, Michael, 108
Leftists, Third World, 193–195
Legitimacy, exposure and, 17
Lewis, Anthony, 176
Lewis, Flora, 103, 109, 142, 204–205
Liberal-left magazines, 92
Liebling, A.J., 27, 225
London Sunday Times, 30
London Times, 30
Los Angeles Times, 116, 133, 177, 201,
203, 220
Love, Kenneth, 233
"Loyalty boards," 121
Luce, Henry, 30, 43, 45, 233
Lying, 216–217
Lynch, Roberta, 79–80

McCarran Internal Security Act (1950),
120
McCarthy, Joseph, 45, 117, 121–124,
168–170
McCloskey, Paul, 18
McDonnell Douglas, 69
MacDougall, Malcolm, 15